IMAGES
*of America*

# FRIDAY HARBOR

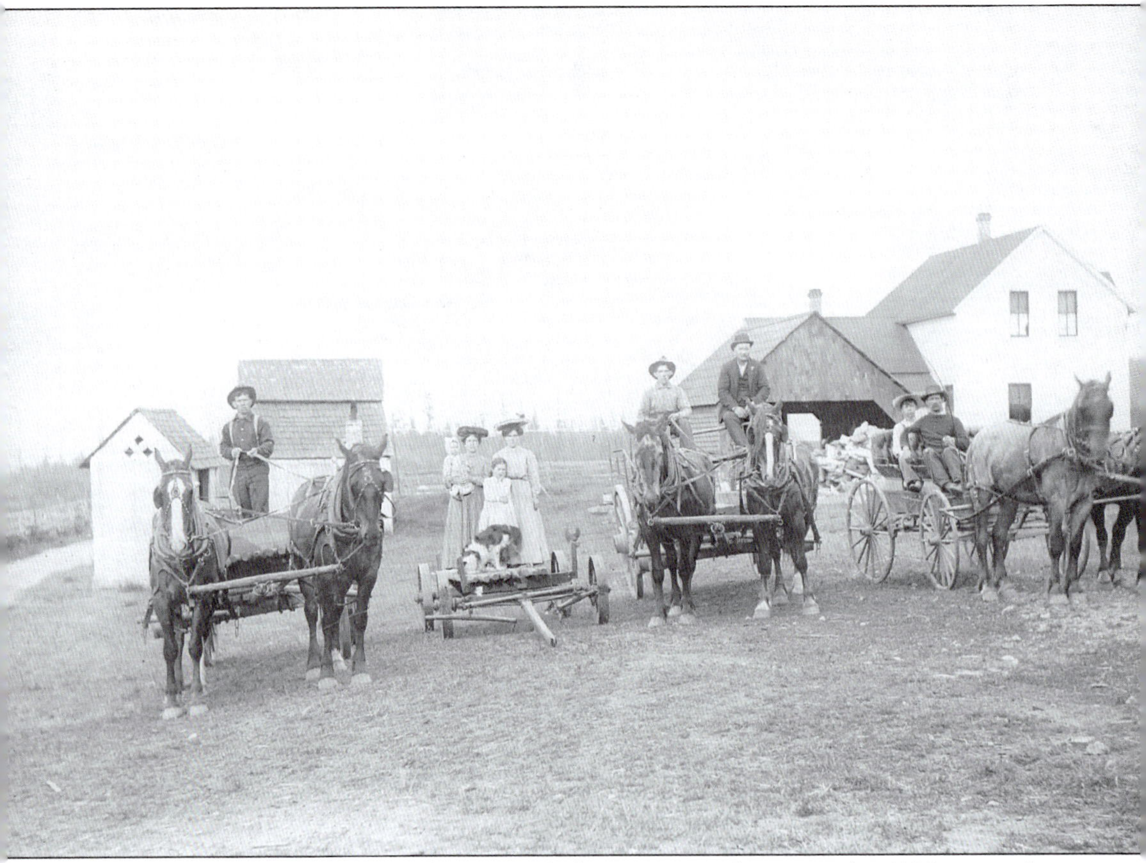

The James F. King family proudly poses with their wagons and teams in this 1905 image taken on the family farm at the foot of "King Hill," the rocky hillock that rises above the town at the head of Spring Street. King claimed his land in 1877, which grew to 445 acres by 1900—80 for crops, the balance for grazing. (San Juan Historical Society.)

**ON THE COVER:** Friday Harbor was a growing rural port when this c. 1900 image was captured from King Hill at the head of Spring Street. The Odd Fellows Hall (now the Whale Museum) is the white structure at far left, and the original cannery buildings are located beneath the smokestack at center. James King's orchard of 300 fruit trees underscores the importance of fruit in the local economy. (San Juan Historical Society.)

IMAGES
*of America*

# FRIDAY HARBOR

Mike and Julia Vouri and the
San Juan Historical Society and Museum

ARCADIA
PUBLISHING

ISBN 978-0-7385-5869-1

Published by Arcadia Publishing
Charleston, South Carolina

Printed in the United States of America

Library of Congress Catalog Card Number: 2008934524

For all general information contact Arcadia Publishing at:
Telephone 843-853-2070
Fax 843-853-0044
E-mail sales@arcadiapublishing.com

Visit us on the Internet at www.arcadiapublishing.com

*For Jim and Mary Jean Cahail*
*Thanks for the memories.*

# Contents


| | | |
|---|---|---|
| Acknowledgments | | 6 |
| Foreword | | 7 |
| Introduction | | 8 |
| 1. | A New Town | 9 |
| 2. | A Town Rises | 31 |
| 3. | A Town in Deed | 51 |
| 4. | A Town on an Inland Sea | 61 |
| 5. | A Town at Heart | 73 |
| 6. | A Town in Class | 91 |
| 7. | A Neighborly Town | 99 |
| 8. | A Town in Transition | 113 |
| Bibliography | | 127 |

# ACKNOWLEDGMENTS

Former Friday Harbor mayor Jim Cahail is really the third author of this book. The great grandson of pioneers (his dad was also mayor and his grandfather town treasurer), Jim identified most of the people and places in these photographs. He also told some great stories. Special thanks to E.A. "Ted" Middleton and Rob Roy McGregor. Their generous donations made this book possible. Thanks also to Nourdine Jensen and Roy Franklin for their photos and recollections; and to Dr. David M. Kennedy, Mary Jean Cahail, Kitty Roberts, Al Sundstrom, Peggy Sue McRae, Shaun Hubbard, Steve Hudson, Sam Buck Sr., Colin Hermans, Boyd Pratt, Jeff Jewell, Toni Nagel, Mitzi Johnson, Richard Walker, Sandy Strehlou, Kris Day Vincent, Kevin Loftus, and Kim Kennedy.

COURTESY ABBREVIATIONS
Beinecke Rare Book and Manuscript Library, Yale University–BRBML
San Juan Island National Historical Park–SAJH
University of Washington Special Collections–UWSC
Whatcom Museum of History and Art–WMHA

The San Juan Historical Society owns all images not otherwise credited. For information on purchasing prints of these images, call the society at (360) 378-3949, e-mail museum_admin@sjmuseum.org, or write P.O. Box 441, Friday Harbor, WA 98250.

# FOREWORD

The centuries-long saga of the frontier largely defined America, and frontier towns, both those that thrived and those that died, are among the most characteristically American creations. From 17th-century Hartford in the Connecticut River Valley to 18th-century Pittsburgh at the forks of the Ohio River to 19th-century Chicago, Abilene, Dodge, Denver, and San Francisco, westering pioneers planted raw settlements in often improbable places and built them into vibrant communities—or watched them wither into mute and moldy ghost towns, like Bodie, California, or Virginia City, Montana.

For much of American history, few places seemed less likely for settlement than San Juan Island. Few were as remote from the nation's heartland. (When the writer Edward Everett Hale, in his celebrated 1863 short story, "The Man without a Country," wanted to convey to his readers the exotic distance of the Mississippi Valley in the Republic's early years, he described it as "farther from us than Puget's Sound is today.") Few remained disputed territory for so long. (The San Juan archipelago was finally determined to be part of the United States only in 1872—the last addition to the now-familiar map of the lower 48 states.) And few places seemed more likely than Friday Harbor to suffer the eventual fate of desertion and death that befell so many towns in the West in particular, where boom gave way to bust with cruel regularity.

Like other frontier towns, Friday Harbor attracted a strikingly polyglot population: Coast Salish Indians; rough-hewn American and Canadian loggers, fishermen, ranchers, and drifters; and Kanakas (Hawaiians), including, conspicuously, the Hudson's Bay Company shepherd from whom the town took its name. Like other pioneers, Friday Harbor's citizens flourished during various commodity cycles—timber, salmon, limestone, apples, pears—and repeatedly faced ruin when they exhausted the resource or more efficient producers came to dominate the market.

Yet through it all, Friday Harbor had one resource that was inexhaustible and unique: the stunning beauty of its location, mantled with forest and prairie, surrounded by sea, and jacketed on the horizon by the Cascade and Olympic mountain ranges. Here is an aesthetic and spiritual frontier that will never close.

—David M. Kennedy
Donald J. McLachlan
Professor of History
Stanford University

# Introduction

It is no accident that Friday Harbor is named for a Hawaiian shepherd. Hawaiians lived and worked on the island nearly 20 years before town founder Edward Warbass erected his shack on the shoreline. They came to work for the Hudson's Bay Company (HBC), which in 1853 had established Belle Vue Sheep Farm on San Juan Island's southern end.

By 1858, the shepherd Peter Poʻalima (Friday in Hawaiian) ran an outlying station six miles north on the eastern shore and may have been there the day the British survey ship, HMS *Plumper*, steamed into the harbor. Whether he was or not, Capt. George Richards must have known who was tending the sheep because he called the harbor "Friday's Bay" on his chart. Thus, another feature was named in the San Juan Archipelago—172 islands and islets lying between Vancouver Island and the mainland of North America.

Great Britain and the United States were still trying to sort out the international water boundary running through the Strait of Georgia 12 years after the signing of the Treaty of Oregon, which had left possession of the San Juan Islands in limbo. The British insisted on the Rosario Strait, the Americans the Haro. By the summer of 1859, tempers flared and war seemed imminent after an American shot a pig belonging to the HBC. But instead of violence, the two nations agreed to jointly occupy the islands. Twelve years passed until, via arbitration, the islands became United States territory as part of Whatcom County.

When the county commissioners tried to tax their new holding, Warbass, once the army sutler on the island, exercised his influence as a former territorial legislator (and frontier wiles) in 1873 to wrest the archipelago from Whatcom and create San Juan County.

It was no surprise that the new county auditor was Warbass. As with surveyors and chartmakers before him, Warbass saw the potential of Friday's Bay as a deepwater port. It was sheltered from the severe storms that swept San Juan Village, a cluster of saloons, flophouses, and bordellos erected shortly after the army landed in 1859 on the south end of Griffin Bay. He envisioned homes, schools, and businesses on the 160 acres set aside for a county seat he called "Friday Harbor." Warbass planned to sell town lots to fund the county government, but when no buyers came, he gave up and returned to the state legislature in 1877.

The new auditor was John A. Bowman, an Orcas settler, but the town did not realize its destiny until Joseph Sweeney, also from Orcas, opened a store on the corner of Spring and Front Streets. It was not long before Bowman and Sweeney plunged into murky legal and ethical waters and bought 56 acres—the future downtown, including the waterfront—for a mere $171, deducted monthly from Bowman's auditor wages. The transaction so outraged Warbass that he vowed never to return to Friday Harbor, though years later he settled south of town at Kwan Lama.

# *One*

# A New Town

County auditor John Bowman turned heads (and further aggravated Warbass) by selling the remaining half of the county's town land to Sweeney, including most of the waterfront properties. But there was only one problem: Why would anyone spend hard cash for a town lot when, under the Homestead Act, he could claim a quarter section of land almost anywhere in the region for next to nothing?

The result was the first real estate slump on Friday's Bay. Not even Friday lived there anymore. Years passed silently until finally Bowman and Sweeney slashed prices. Waterfront lots cost $20; inland parcels went for $10. They gave away properties on the upland prairies as further incentive to come to Friday Harbor, and the results were immediate. William Douglas arrived in town, purchased a lot for $10, and opened a store with a back-room saloon, which Sweeney quickly emulated.

The stream of cash enabled Bowman to abandon the county shack in 1883 and move into a new courthouse—a two-story, wooden structure on the corner of Spring and First Streets (site of today's Coldwell Banker offices). Israel Katz, who ran stores and saloons in San Juan Town and on Argyle Avenue, next purchased the county shack and lot from Bowman and erected a two-story building, calling it the Friday Harbor Produce Exchange. It still stands on the south corner of Spring and Front Streets. Katz's investment, along with two hotels, additional stores, and a blacksmith shop soon siphoned trade from San Juan Town and spurred further urban growth in the form of a scattering of homes, a church, and a school. Upon the death of his last surviving brother, William, Katz sold his San Juan Island interests and returned to Port Townsend where he ran the family firm of Waterman and Katz until his mysterious disappearance in 1913. A vacant San Juan Town burned to the ground on July 4, 1890.

This earliest known view of Friday Harbor was probably taken *c.* 1883. The small structure on pilings, bottom left, was Joseph Sweeney's warehouse. The above is Israel Katz's "Produce Exchange." There he sold vegetables grown on land he confiscated from insolvent farmers given credit at his San Juan Town store for food and liquor. ("It is a mere matter of form," he would say on issuing a

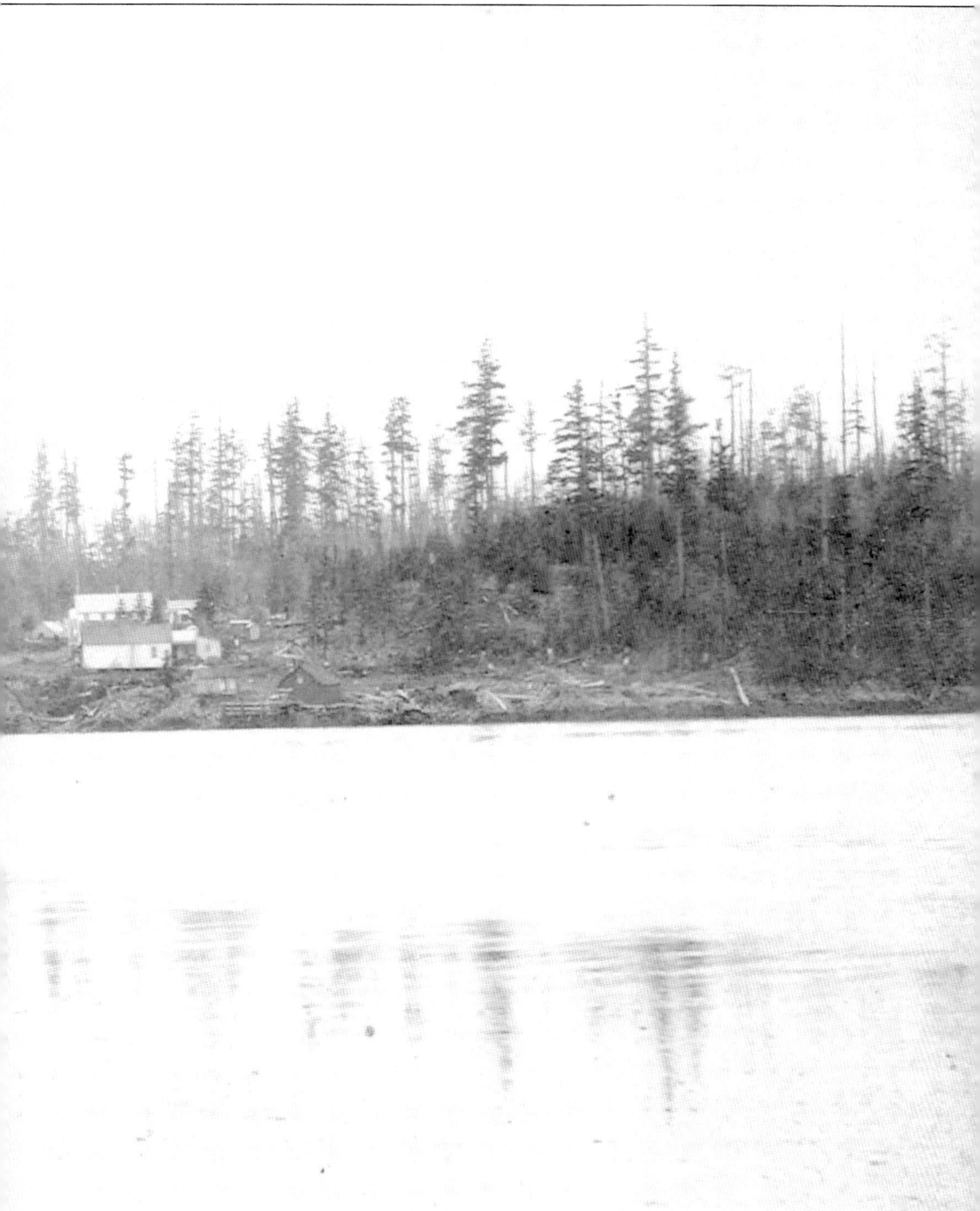

note. "Katz will never crowd you.") Next up the block is what became known as the "upper tavern" (and later a bordello), and next is the second county courthouse. At right foreground, Sweeney's store (and saloon) stands before the Douglas House hotel, owned by William Douglas.

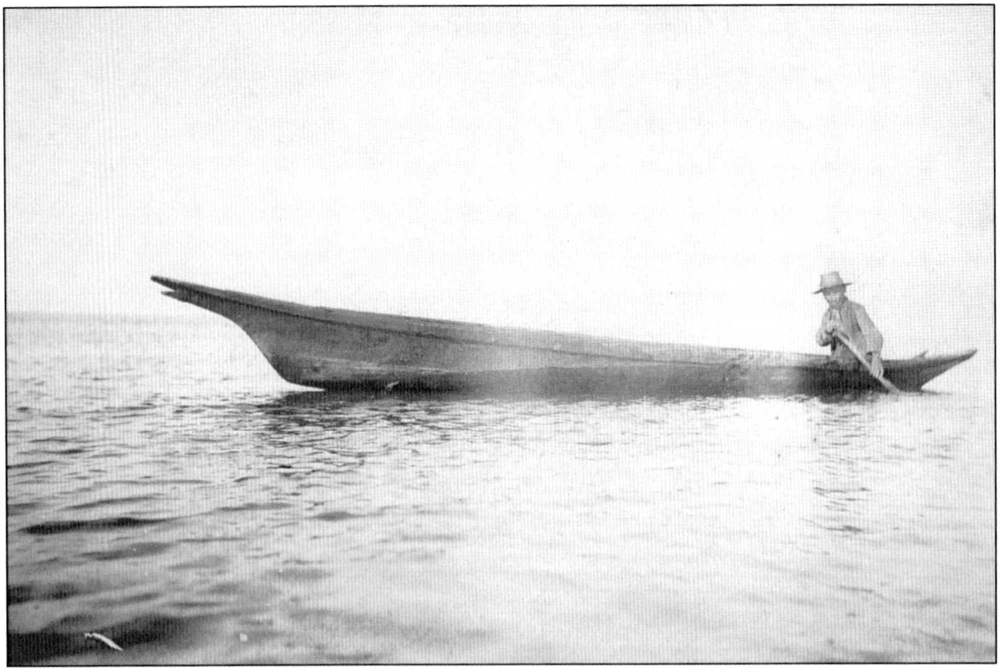

A Coast Salish man dips his paddle, probably off San Juan Island late in the 19th century. When the glacier receded about 11,000 years ago, people arrived to hunt and then cultivate the gravelly soil (glacial till) that composes the prairies on the uplands of Friday Harbor and other island locations. Later they gathered shellfish and ventured out in canoes to hook halibut and net salmon, the latter through a technique called reefnetting (shown below). Among the Northern Straits Salish groups who claim San Juan Island as an ancestral home. Over time, these native peoples developed large villages on protected shores, which thrived on San Juan Island until Europeans brought smallpox and other diseases in the late 18th century.

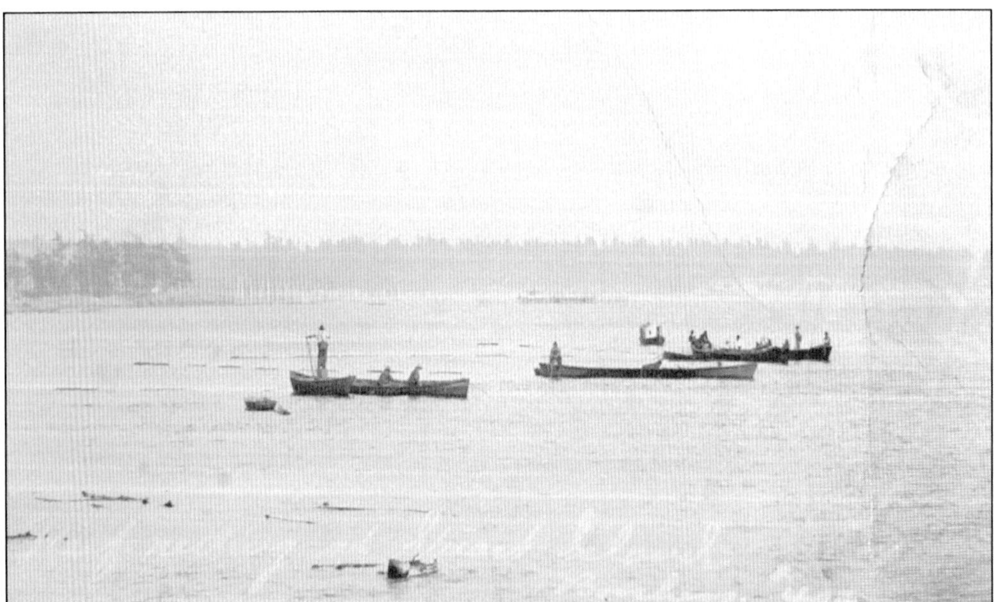

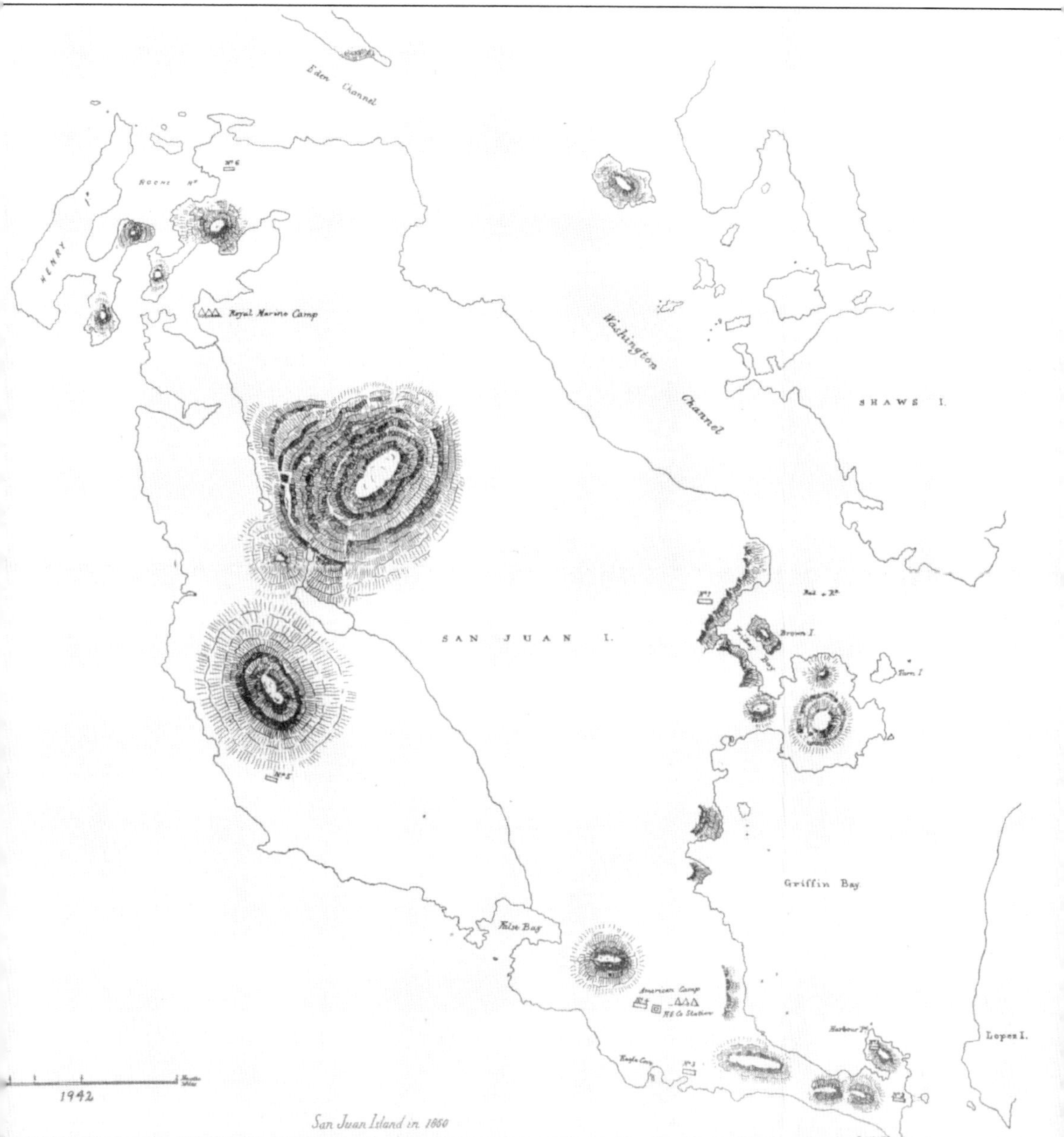


By January 1860, Capt. James Prevost of the Royal Navy submitted a list of seven island locations for a Royal Marine camp to British station commander Rear Adm. R. Lambert Baynes, each marked on a tracing of a San Juan Island map. Included was a strong recommendation for No. 7, the site of today's town of Friday Harbor. It featured, "A convenient slope of prairie land, with a running stream of fresh water within 400 yards of it; convenient of access by boats; also a safe harbour for ships of any size at all seasons of the year. I am of opinion this will be found the most eligible site for the camp. In the autumn it is used by the Hudson's Bay Company as a sheep station; at present it is unoccupied, about seven miles distant from the town, and no settlers near it." (SAJH.)

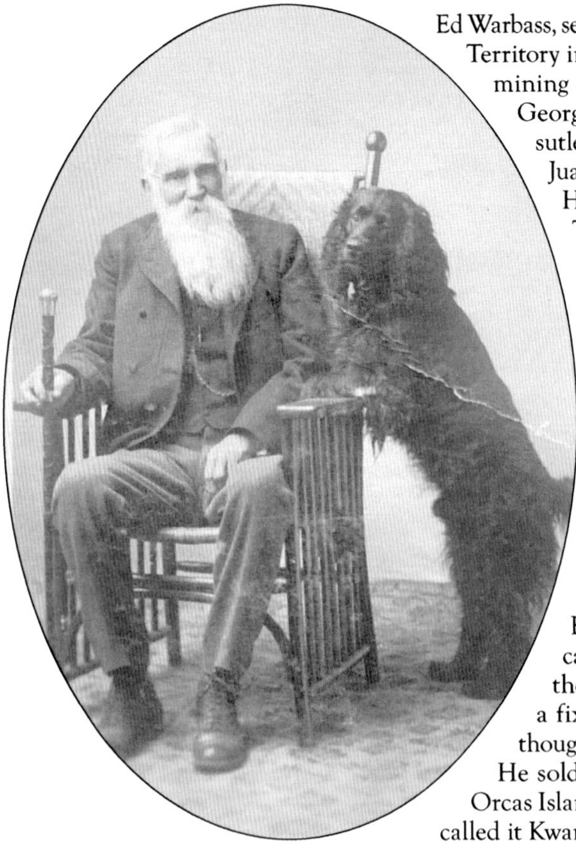

Ed Warbass, seen here with "Bob," arrived in Washington Territory in the 1850s after trying his hand at gold mining in California. He hooked up with Capt. George Pickett in 1856 and became the post sutler for Pickett at Fort Bellingham and San Juan Island during the Pig War crisis of 1859. He left the island in 1906 to mine gold on Turtleback Mountain on Orcas and died there later that year. (Peggy Sue McRae.)

Ed Warbass lived off and on in the home he called Idlewild, just south of town, through the remainder of the century. He became a fixture at Civil War veterans' gatherings, though his military pedigree remains uncertain. He sold Idlewild to Capt. Andrew Newhall of Orcas Island, who built a large, two-story home and called it Kwan Lama.

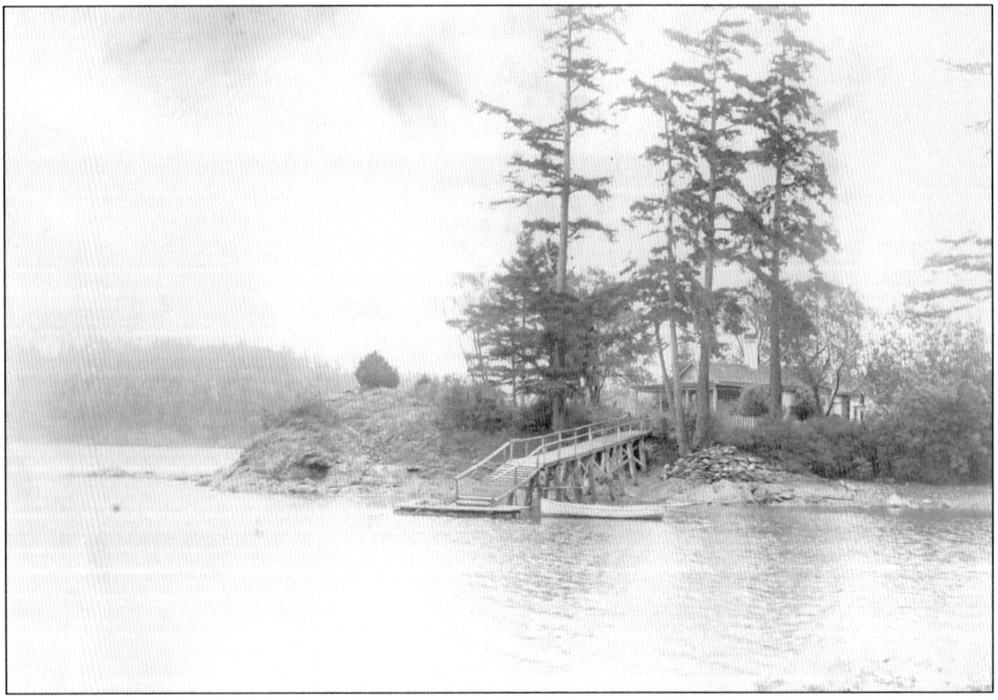

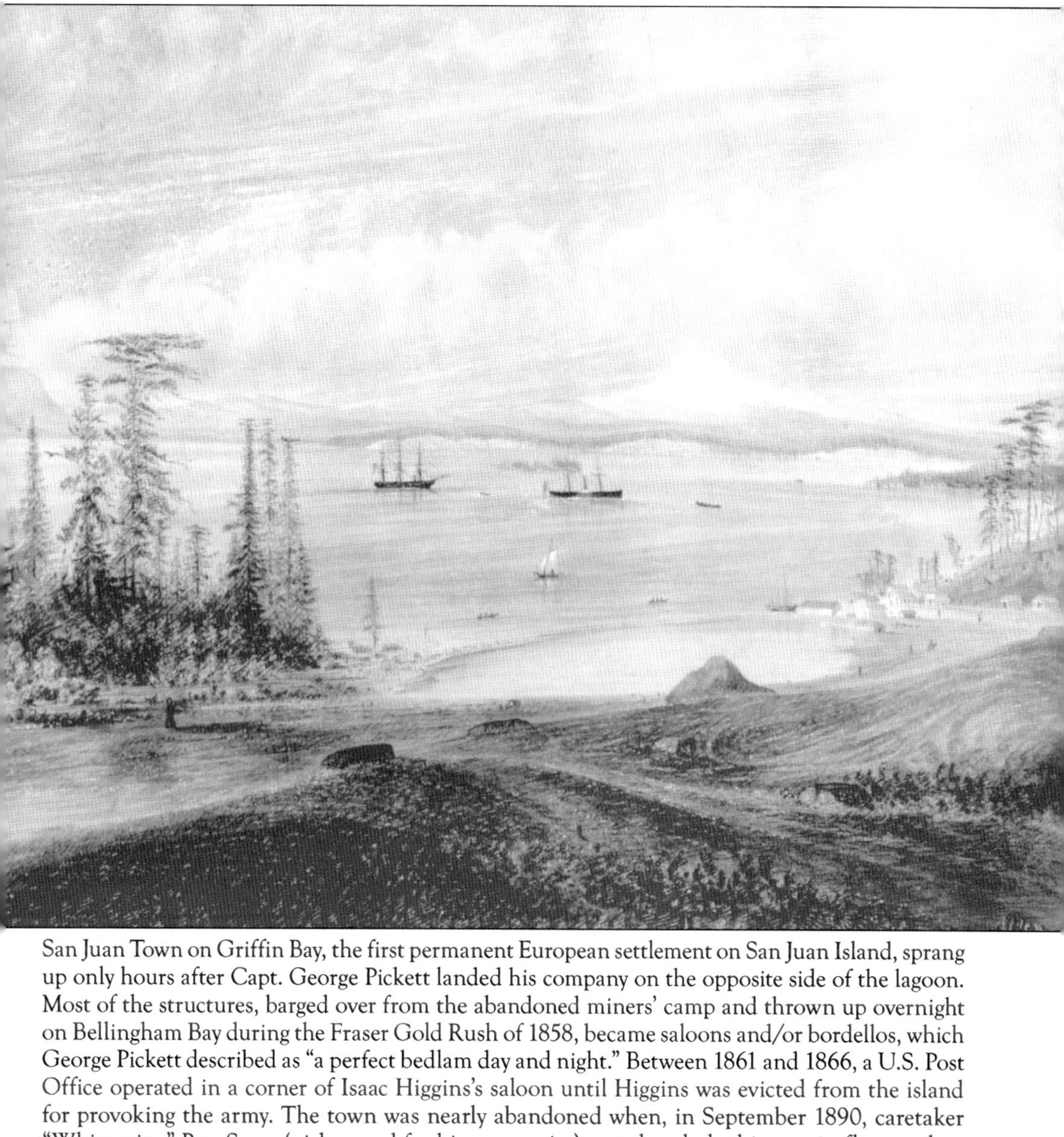

San Juan Town on Griffin Bay, the first permanent European settlement on San Juan Island, sprang up only hours after Capt. George Pickett landed his company on the opposite side of the lagoon. Most of the structures, barged over from the abandoned miners' camp and thrown up overnight on Bellingham Bay during the Fraser Gold Rush of 1858, became saloons and/or bordellos, which George Pickett described as "a perfect bedlam day and night." Between 1861 and 1866, a U.S. Post Office operated in a corner of Isaac Higgins's saloon until Higgins was evicted from the island for provoking the army. The town was nearly abandoned when, in September 1890, caretaker "Whispering" Pete Seary (nicknamed for his raspy voice) sent the whole thing up in flames when he lost control of a brush fire. (BRBML.)

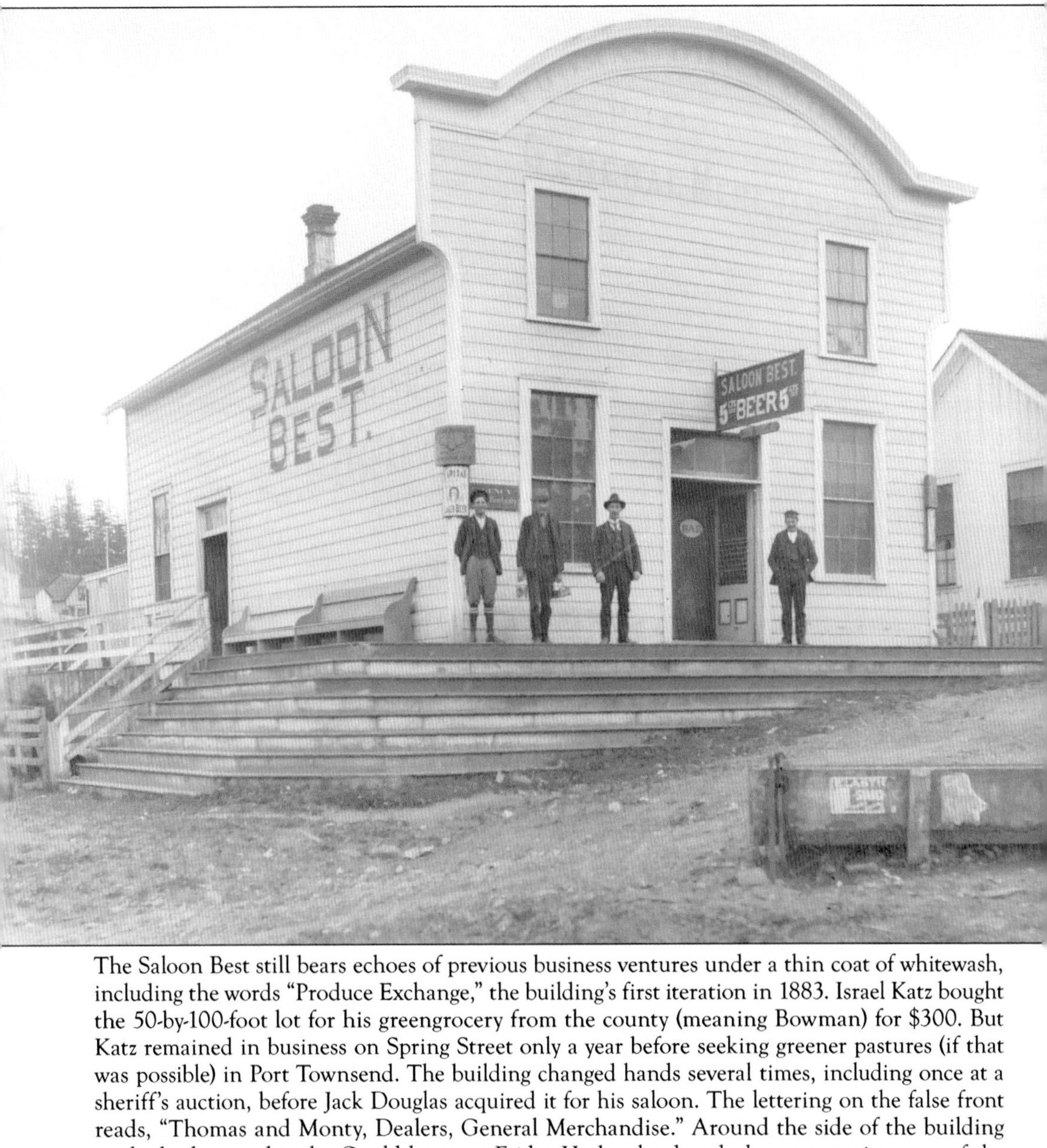


The Saloon Best still bears echoes of previous business ventures under a thin coat of whitewash, including the words "Produce Exchange," the building's first iteration in 1883. Israel Katz bought the 50-by-100-foot lot for his greengrocery from the county (meaning Bowman) for $300. But Katz remained in business on Spring Street only a year before seeking greener pastures (if that was possible) in Port Townsend. The building changed hands several times, including once at a sheriff's auction, before Jack Douglas acquired it for his saloon. The lettering on the false front reads, "Thomas and Monty, Dealers, General Merchandise." Around the side of the building in the background is the Gould house, a Friday Harbor landmark that appears in many of the photographs in this book. (UWSC.)

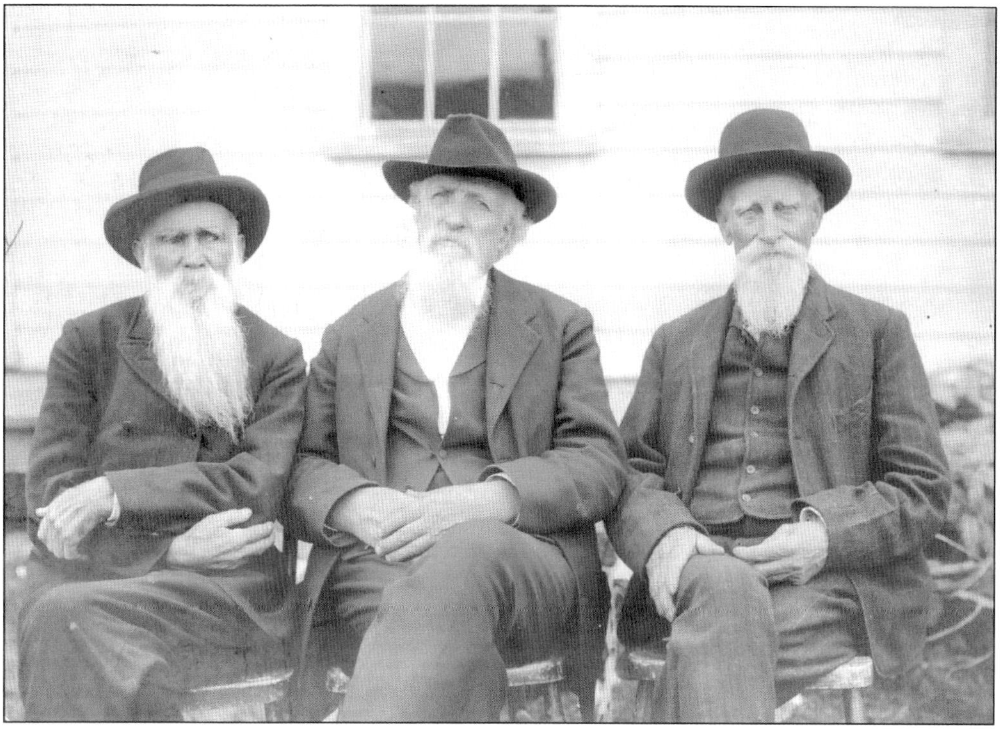

From left to right are San Juan Island pioneers Ed Warbass, 81, Charles McKay, 73, and Stephen Boyce, 77—the county's first auditor, commissioner, and sheriff, respectively. The photograph accompanied a September 9, 1906, story in the *Bellingham Herald* celebrating the roles all three men played in the region's history. Warbass died that December. (WMHA.)

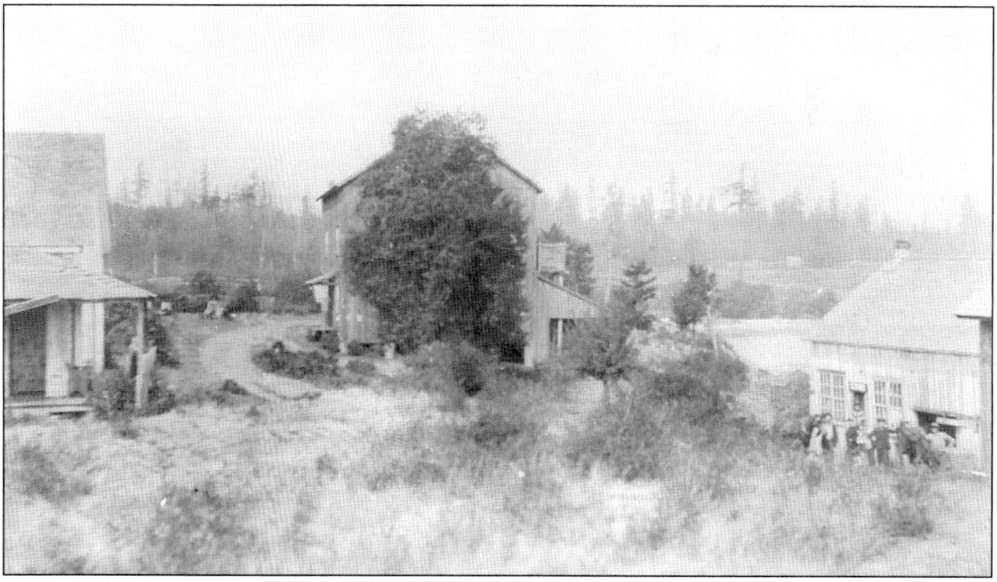

The Argyle gristmill (center), still operating when this image was taken c.1900, was one of the reasons why the Argyle Wagon Road was built in 1890. Clarence M. Tucker and J.O. Bergman built the mill in 1886 in partnership with Port Townsend businessmen. The four-foot diameter grinding stone is on view at the San Juan Historical Museum.

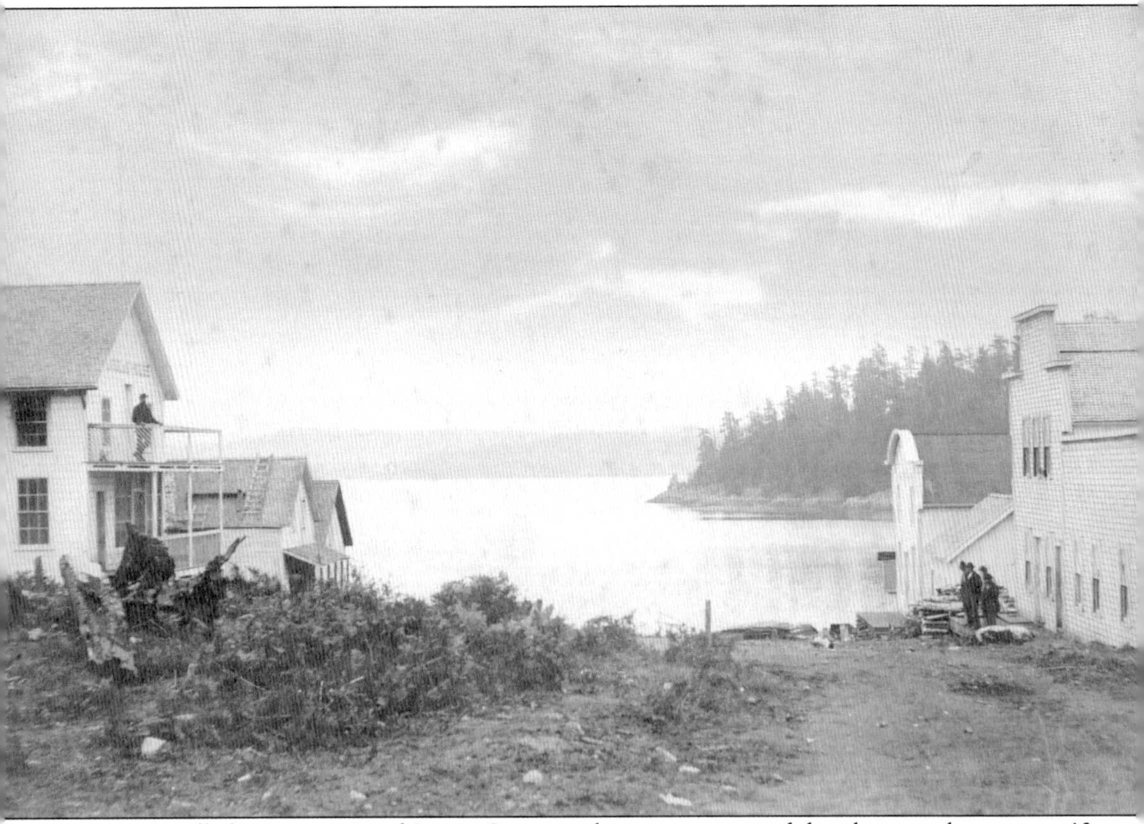

Brush still clogs a portion of Spring Street in this reverse view of the photograph on pages 10 and 11, probably taken a year or two later. The two-story structure with the man on the balcony is the Douglas House, the first hotel in town. Directly across the street is William Douglas's dry-goods store—a front for his saloon in back. In the background is Brown Island, named in 1841 by Lt. Charles Wilkes for John G. Brown, a 19th-century instrument maker. The island was offered to the town for $40,000 in the 1940s, but the city coffers were empty. It was next logged for $60,000 worth of timber, and in the 1960s, it was developed by realtors who called it "Friday on Brown Island" to attract city dwellers looking for weekend retreats.

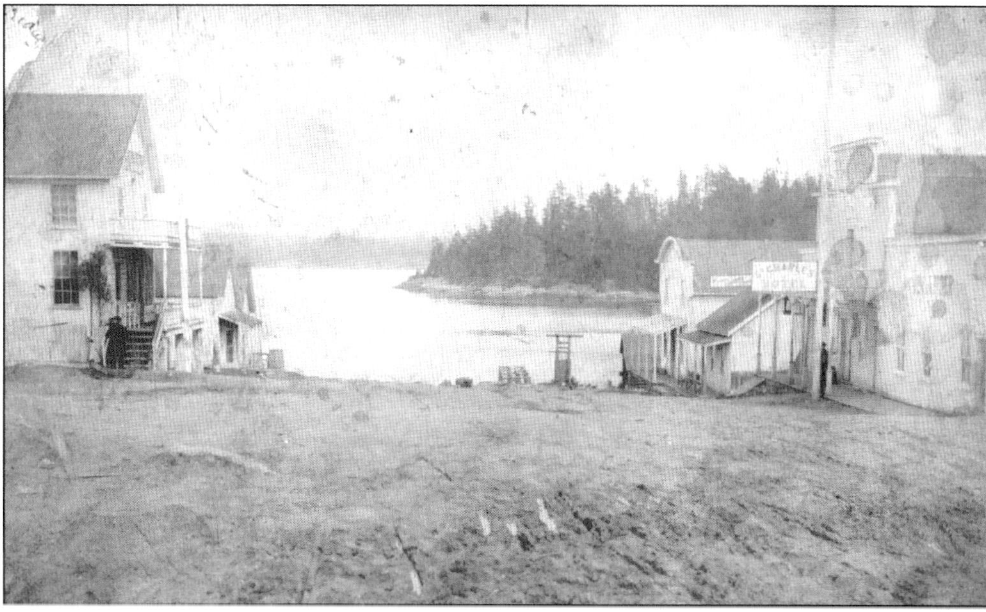

About 10 years later, the Produce Exchange became the Saloon Best, established by William Douglas's brother, Jack. William's old store and saloon was converted into the St. Charles Hotel, reputed to be a brothel, with the *Islander* newspaper established next door. Some island businessmen saw this as a perfect fit.

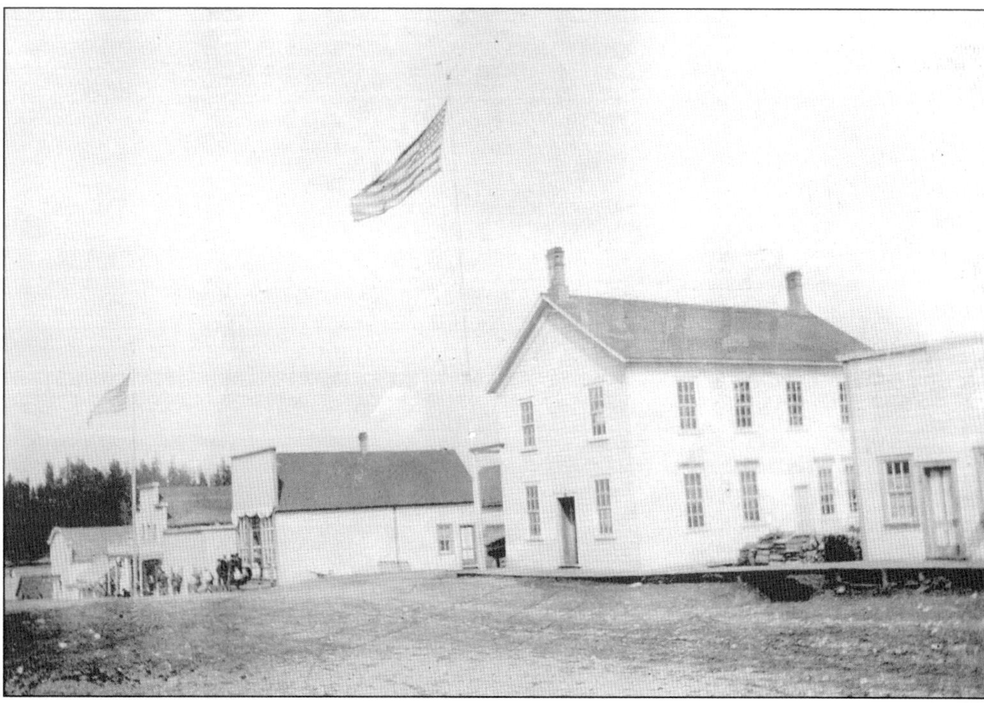

The second San Juan County Courthouse, established in 1883, signaled that Friday Harbor was a legitimate county seat and no longer a dream. A garrison flag flies from the staff in front, signifying a workday. After the new county courthouse opened in 1906, it was moved to Spring and Argyle Streets and converted into a hospital. (Jensen family.)

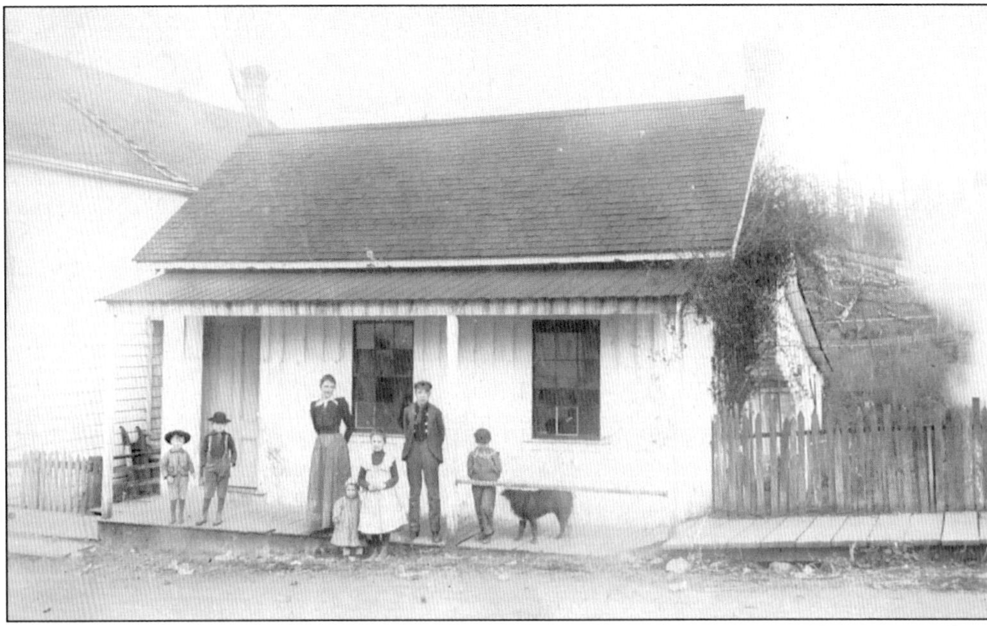

Saloon Best owner Jack Douglas moved into this house with his family after establishing his saloon in 1895. The rear of the house, like the saloon, bordered the ravine that ran down to the bay. The ravine was flushed daily at flood tide, which made it an ideal location for privies. The building was later demolished to accommodate Delmonico's Restaurant.

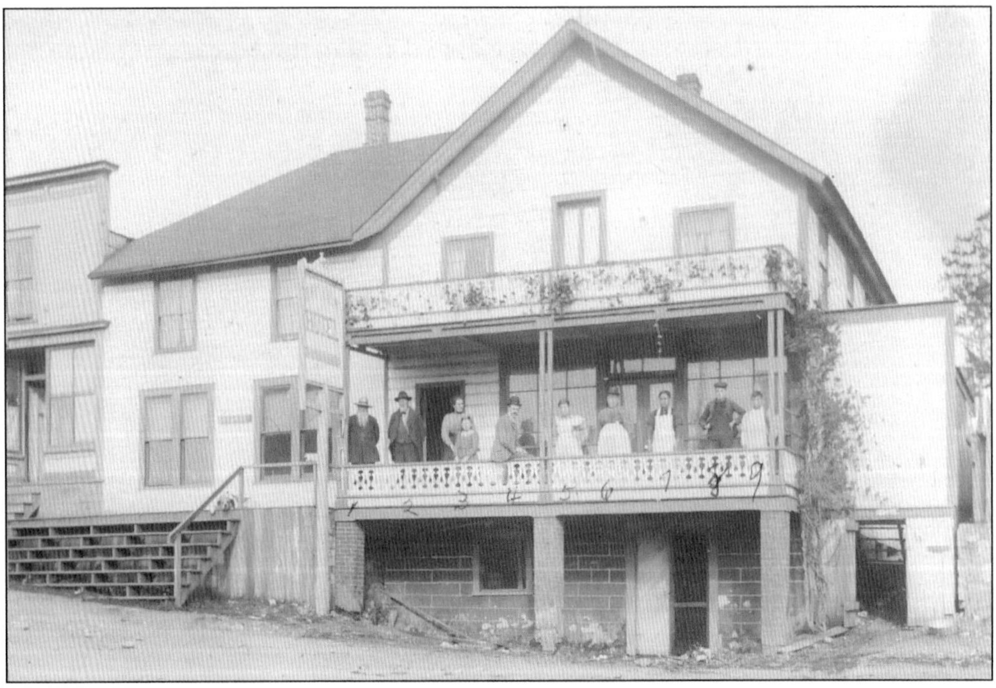

William Douglas's 1884 vintage hotel was sold in the 1890s to James Ross, who aptly renamed it the Bay View Hotel. Frank and Elizabeth Wilson (fifth and sixth from left) managed it until it was sold to Patrick Welsh, who called it the Tourists Hotel Annex. Welsh's Tourists Hotel, around the block, was the swankiest house in town.

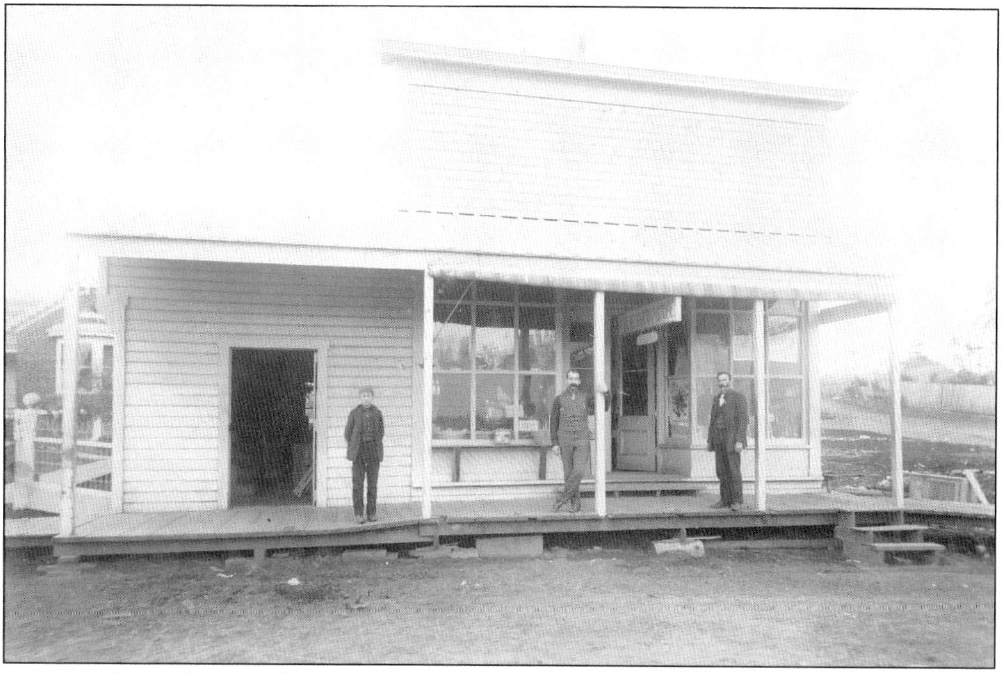

Launor B. (L. B.) Carter's Blue Front Store was located on Spring Street between First and Second Streets, about where the front door of King's Market is today. Established in 1892, a warehouse was added to the rear in 1894, expanding the store's stocking capacity. Carter announced, "Some people dance; others play the fiddle. I seldom dance and never play the fiddle, but I do sell good, clean groceries cheaper than anyone."

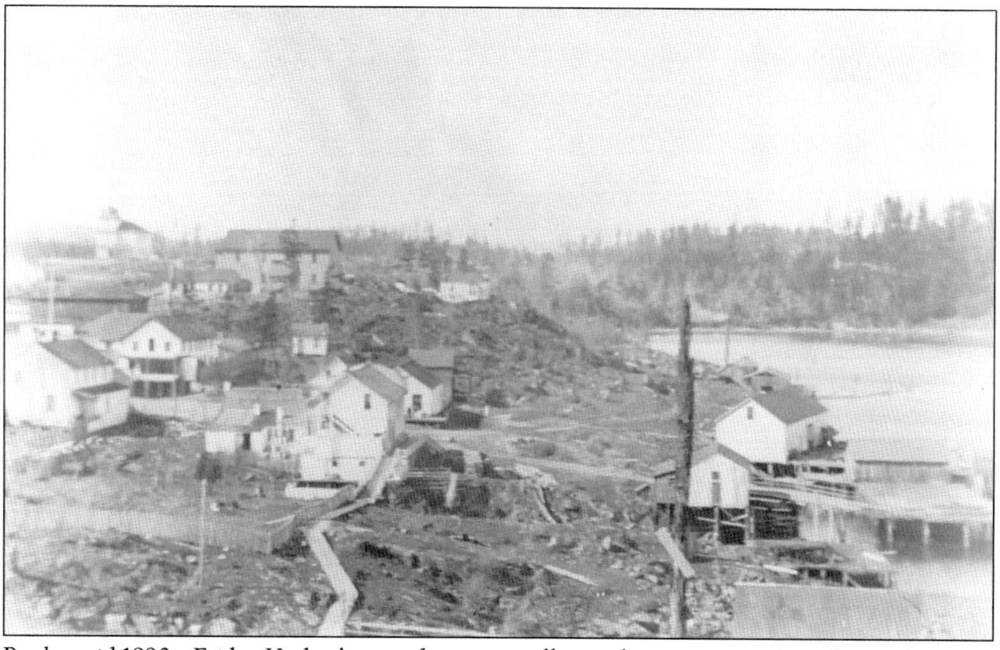

By the mid-1890s, Friday Harbor's waterfront was still a work in progress. Here the south side of Spring Street has yet to be built out, and the Douglas residence is still next to Saloon Best. The Odd Fellows Hall (center left), built in 1892, and the school, built around 1889, help date the image.

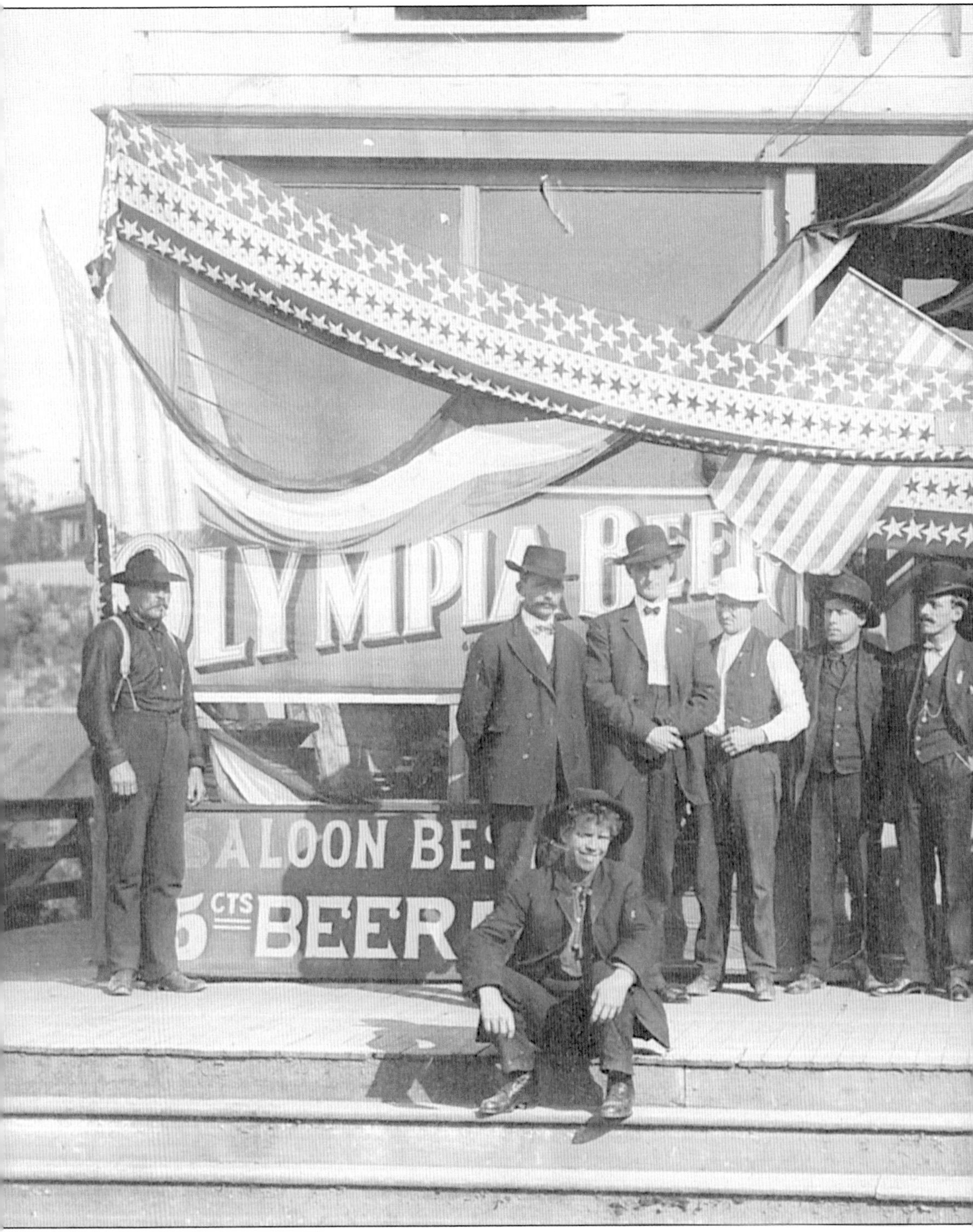


The habitués of the famous Saloon Best hang out with the bartender and owner, Jack Douglas (second from right, not counting the dog) in this *c.* 1895 view. The locals called this the "lower" tavern, and two other drinking establishments up the hill were referred to as "middle" and "upper." The smiling, curly-haired fellow seated on the step with his hat tipped back is Harry Wilkes. When he

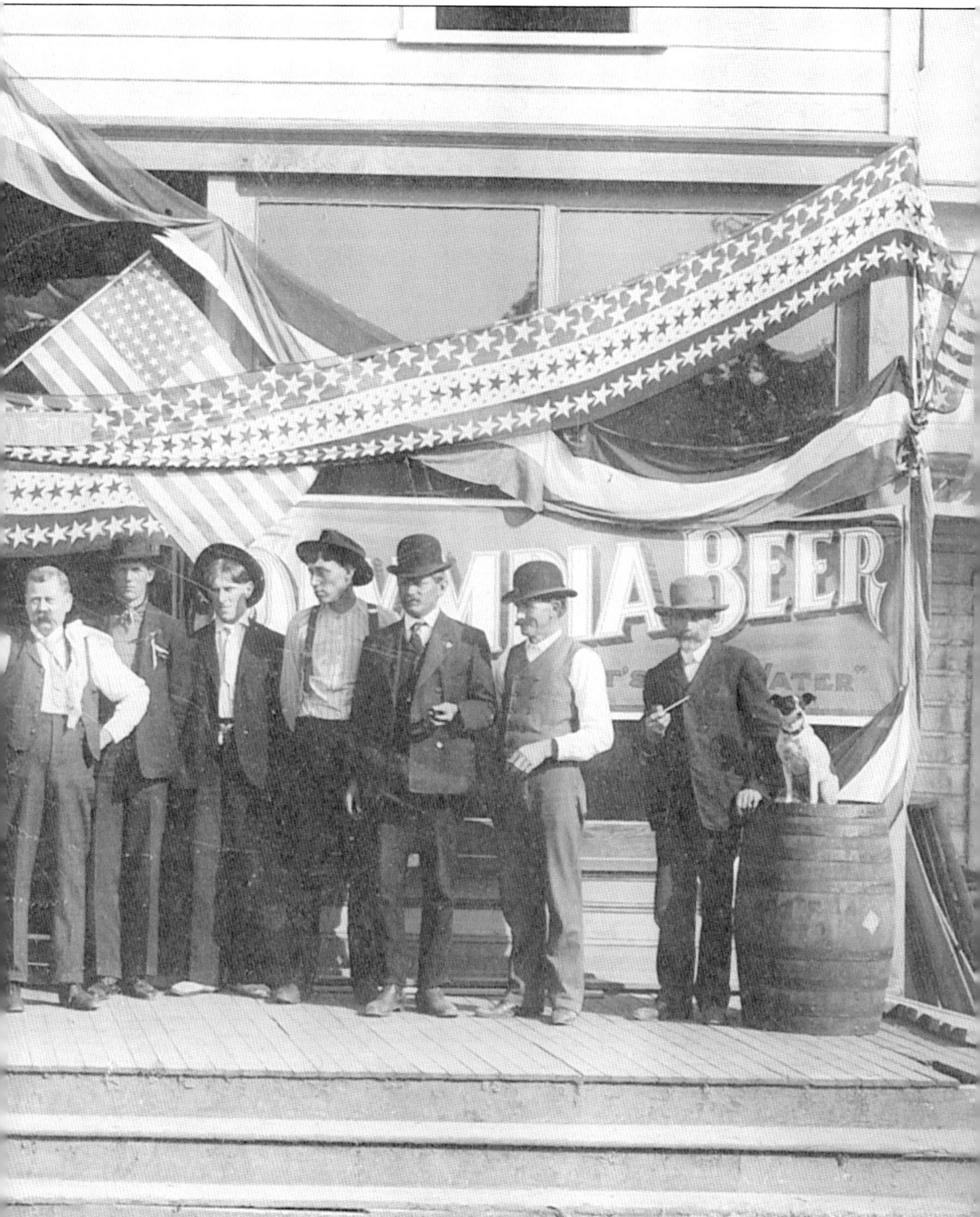

was not at Saloon Best, Wilkes wore out a succession of drills dynamiting for building contractors and the lime works. He was so skilled that he is still remembered for blasting rock out of one basement and never cracking the plaster. Saloon Best was closed in 1910 when the town council voted three to one to ban liquor sales within town limits. Douglas was the lone dissenting vote.

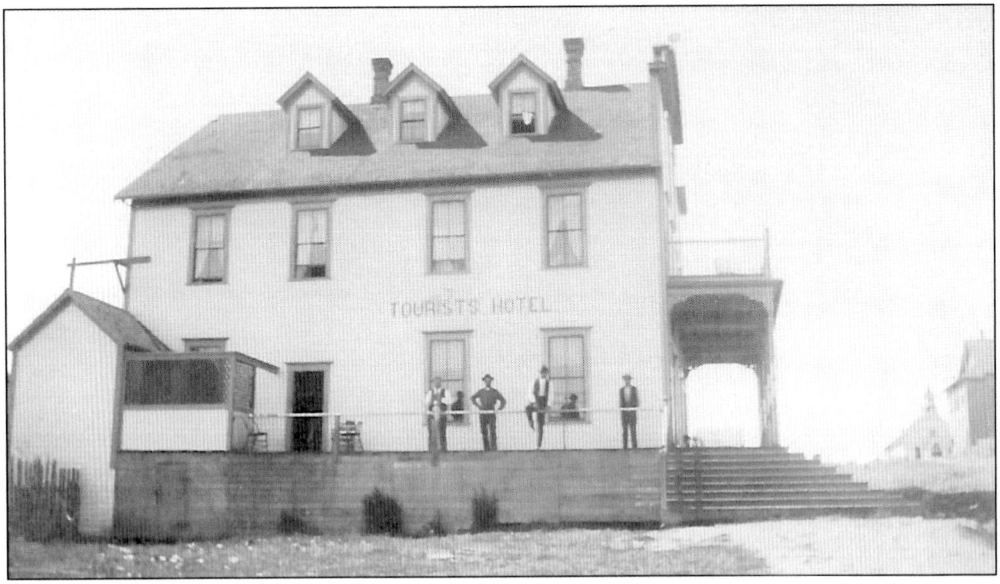


Founded in 1891 by Patrick Welch, the Tourists Hotel represented the height of luxury, with water piped to all floors, a restaurant, bar, and pool hall, and an additional reception room for the ladies. The hotel attracted a wide range of guests from traveling salesmen, to people from other islands, to a dentist who arrived periodically to drill away in the lobby with anesthetic likely provided by the saloon. Welch bought out his only competition, the Bay View Hotel on Spring Street, and turned it into the Tourists Hotel Annex. After Welch died in 1900, the hotel was leased, sold, and sold again many times over. It is still a hotel today. The Odd Fellows Hall and Methodist church (now the Whale Museum and Grange Hall) are seen up First Street. (Jensen family and UWSC.)

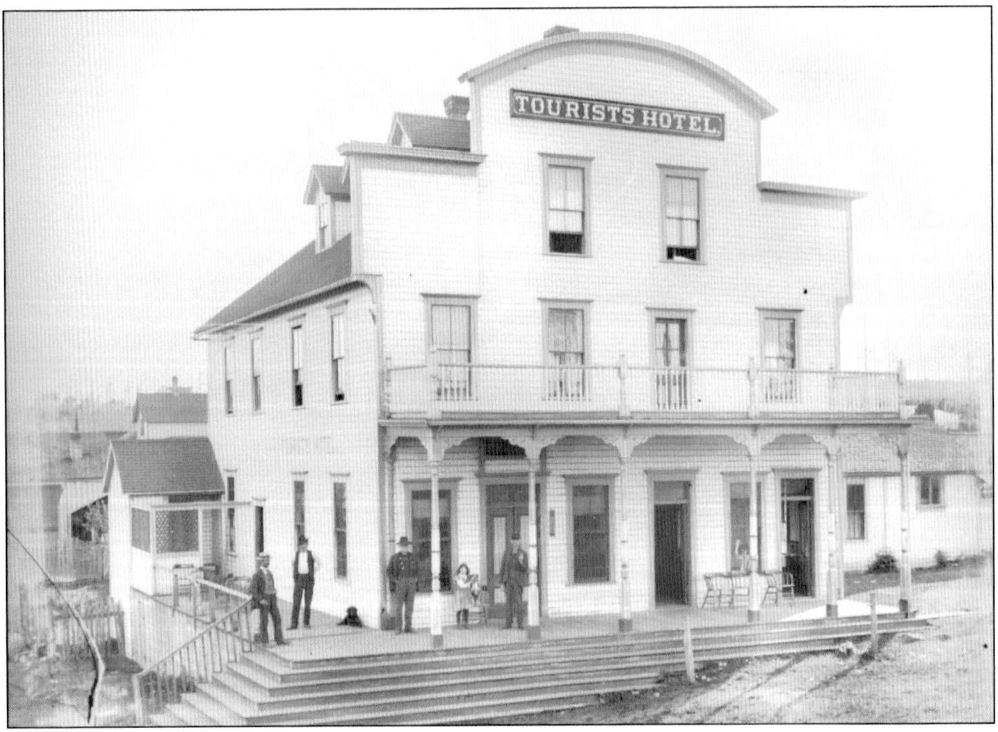

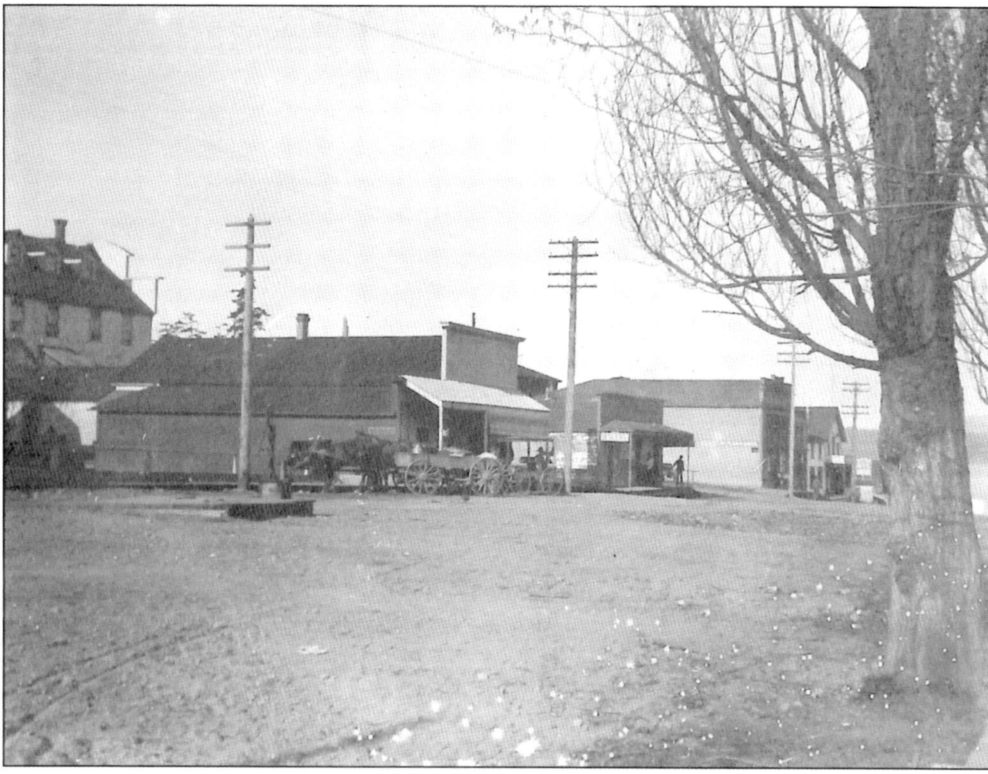

Wagons roll right up to the door of L. B. Carter's Blue Front Store on Spring Street to load merchandise. The Tourists Hotel, at left, rises on the hill that ascends from the block. Note the town pump in the foreground, from which Spring Street drew its name.

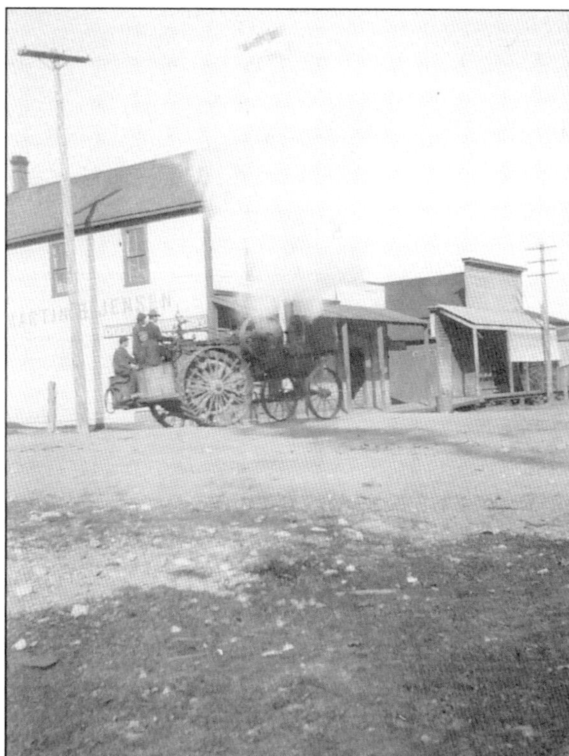

A steam tractor turns the corner at Second and Spring Streets around 1900. By then, the Martin and Jensen dry-goods store, built two years earlier, anchored the corner lot. Carter had moved the Blue Front to make way for his two-story department store. The old store was converted into a barbershop and laundry, with bathtubs in back where men scrubbed up for Saturday night.

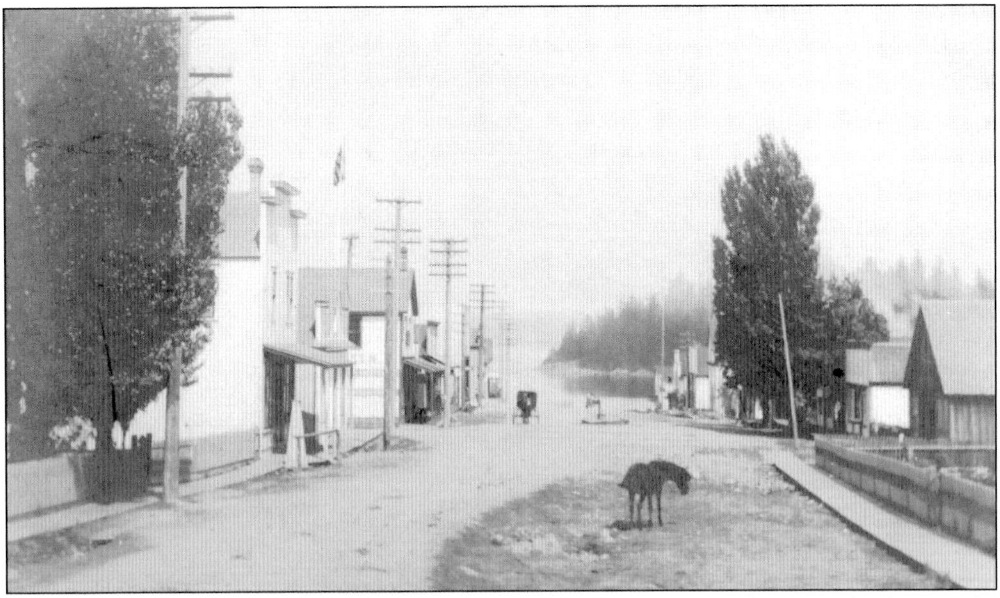

Another c. 1900 view of Spring Street shows the pump, business blocks, and Brown Island across the harbor in the background. According to a former mayor, Jim Cahail, the carriage clattering down the street and the lone nag in the foreground prove that Friday Harbor was never a one-horse town.

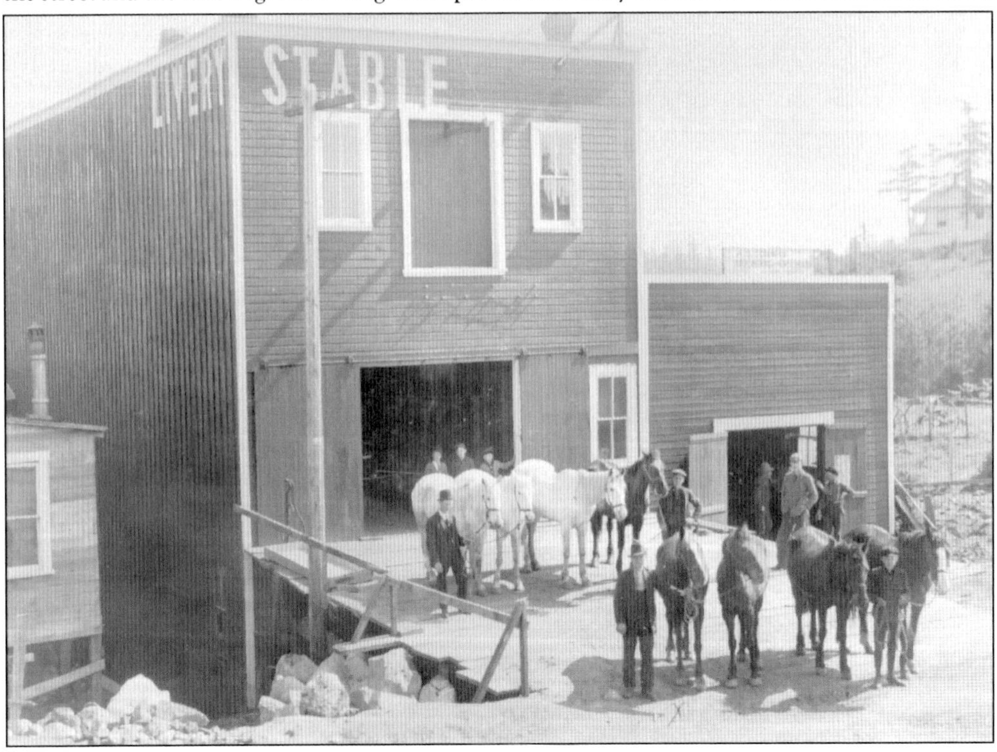


Warren Dightman's Livery Stable on First Street was one of several businesses that boarded, shod, and provided other services for a town still reliant upon horsepower at the beginning of the 20th century. The appearance of the Gould house on the hill at upper right dates the photograph at post-1893.

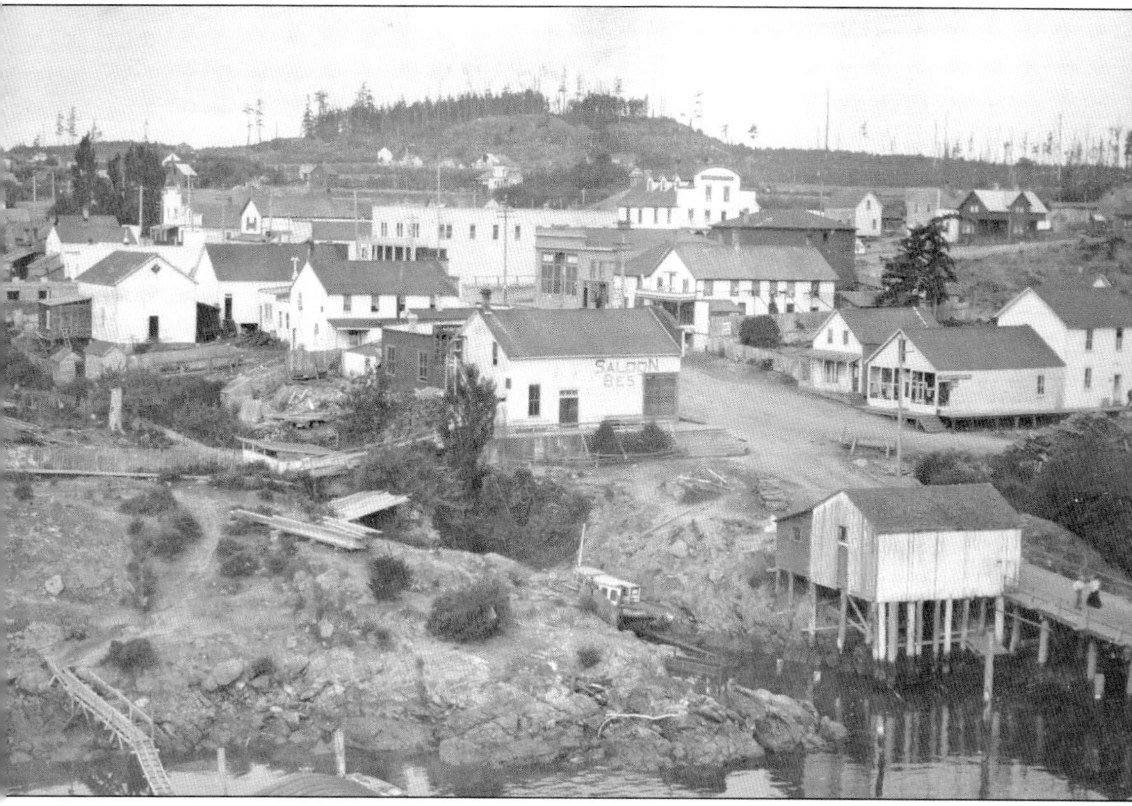


This *c.* 1900–1906 panorama taken from the cannery roof offers a remarkable view of the ravine—known to some as "Friday Creek"—that ran from just beyond First Street to the harbor. At high tide the bay would fill the ravine, enabling Saloon Best owner Jack Douglas to tie up his boat, the *Dolly D* (shown here high and dry in the ravine), almost directly under his business. Some suspected that Douglas's stock of fine, imported liquors might have arrived aboard the *Dolly D* after midnight, minus customs duties. After all, smuggling was a strong tradition on the island, going back to the joint military occupation. The blocky new Ross Building (upper center, just below the Tourists Hotel) had a hardware store downstairs and the Maple House Hotel on the second floor. The San Juan Historical Museum (then the King home) is the large white house at the base of King Hill in the far background.

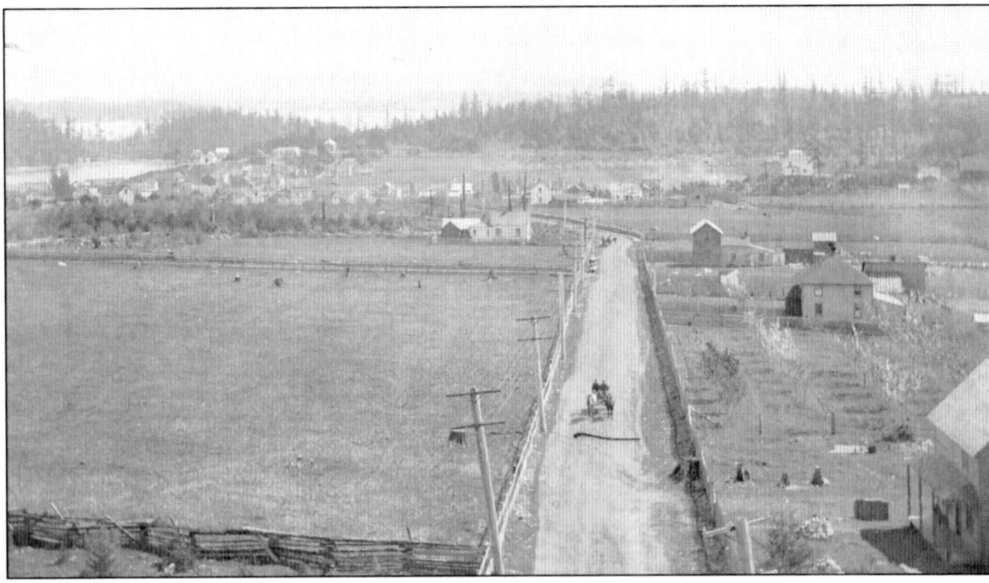

Spring Street was still a rural road winding out of Friday Harbor in this *c.* 1900–1907 view from King Hill. The smaller two-story house, third from foreground, still stands. Argyle Avenue is defined by the line of homes running center right along the old wagon road to the town of Argyle.

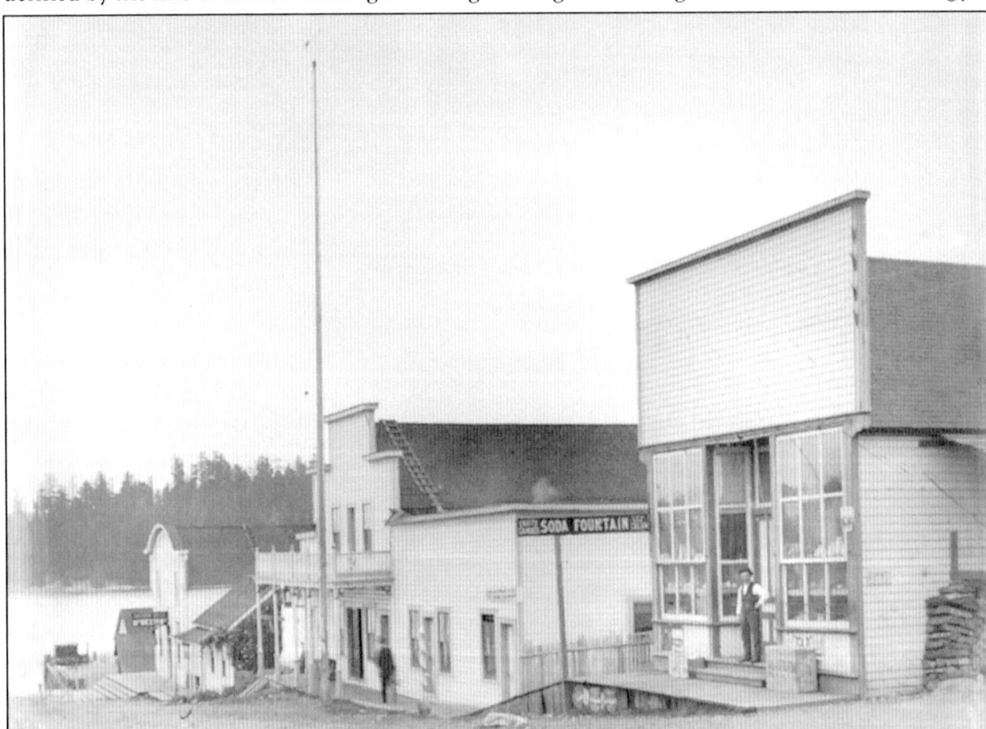


This street scene was probably taken around the same time as the photo above. Saloon Best is at the street's end, and a warehouse sits on the dock beyond. The "middle saloon" is next up the street from the residence (the "upper saloon" was the bar in the Tourists Hotel), then the barbershop, soda fountain, and dry goods store.

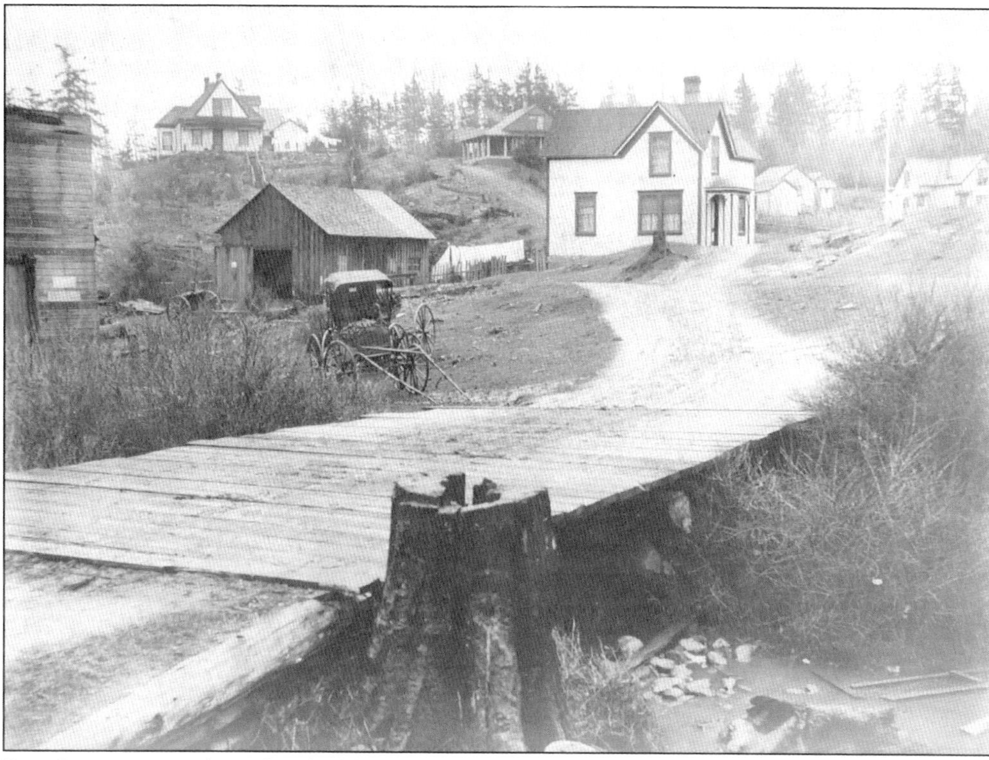

First Street crosses the tail end of the ravine, via wood planks laid on logs, on its way to becoming Harrison Street up the hill in 1906. That year Charles McKay fell off this bridge on his way home (the house, right center) on a dark night. The 73-year-old pioneer blacksmith claimed he was disabled and sued the county for $5,000. He settled for $750.

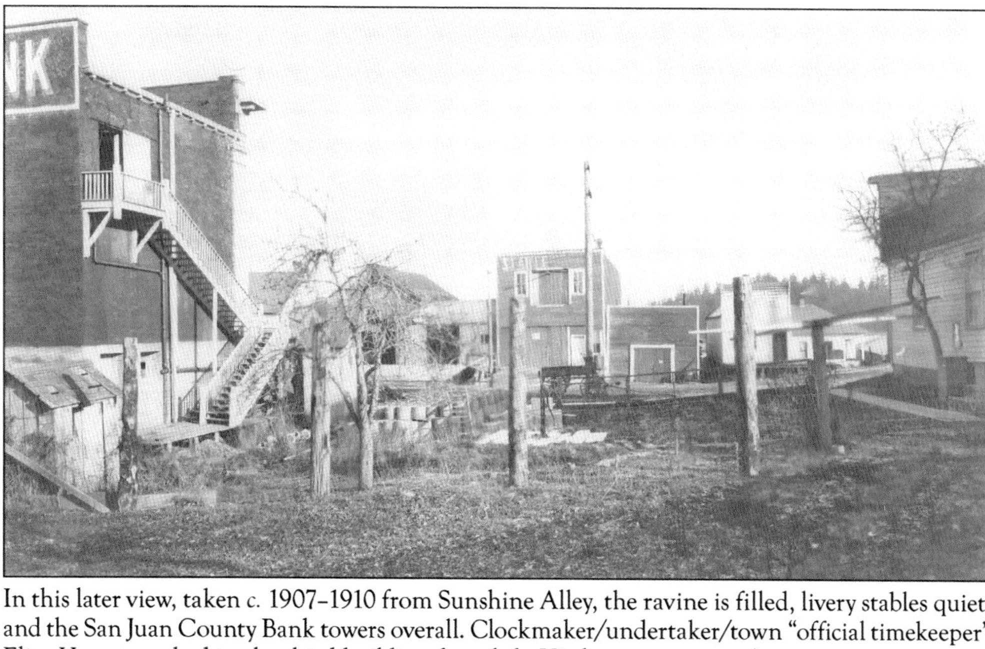


In this later view, taken *c.* 1907–1910 from Sunshine Alley, the ravine is filled, livery stables quiet, and the San Juan County Bank towers overall. Clockmaker/undertaker/town "official timekeeper" Elias Harpst worked in the third building from left. His house was next door.

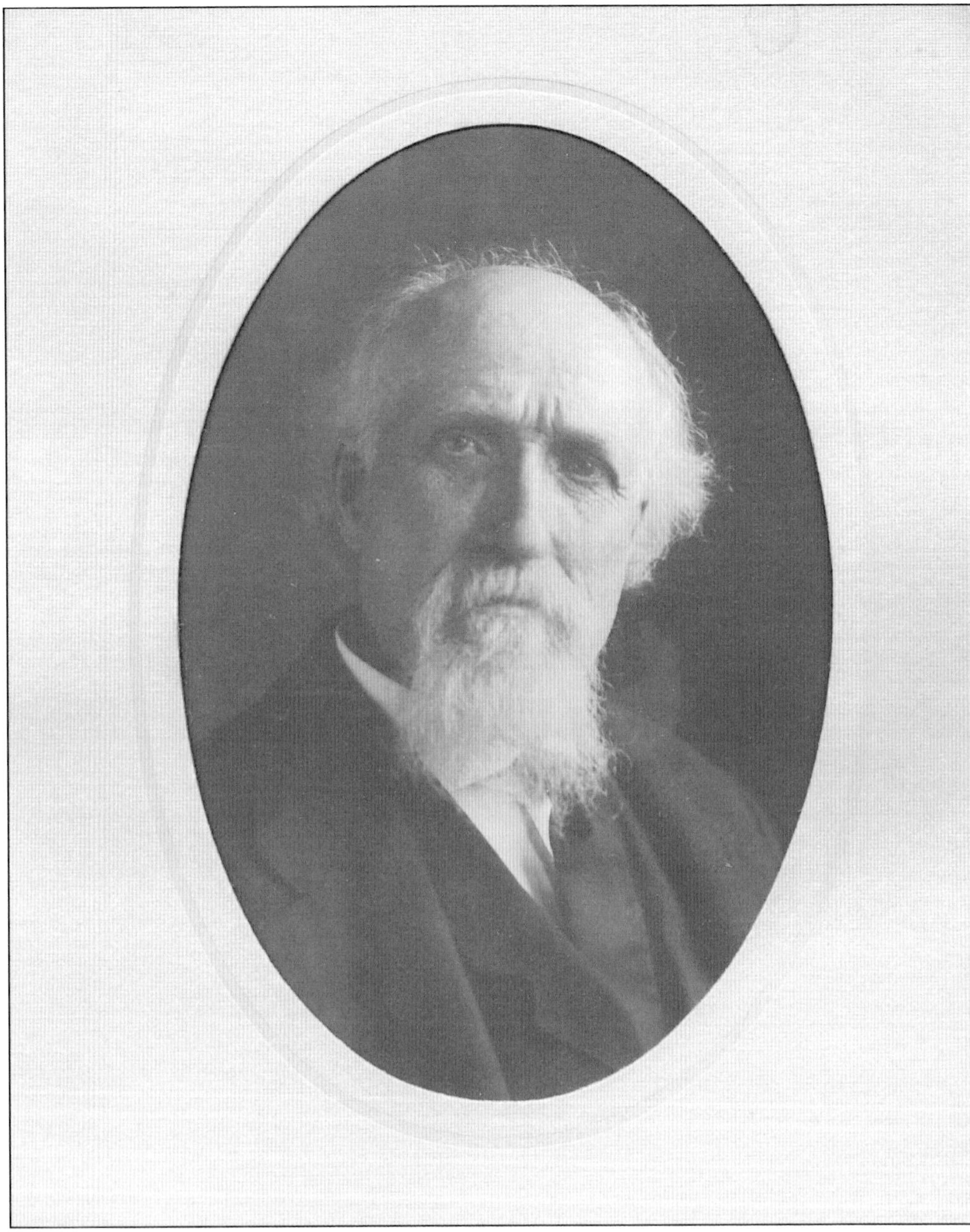

Nova Scotia native Charles McKay died at 86, or 90 years, two months, and 11 days, depending on the census year and conflicting newspaper accounts. McKay lived long enough to watch San Juan Island develop from a frontier wilderness with a scattering of Indigenous and European settlements to a vibrant agricultural /industrial community. He arrived in June 1859 after trials in the gold fields of California and British Columbia, and was just in time to participate in the Pig War crisis. McKay was a member of the first county board of commissioners and also represented the new county in the state legislature. Unfortunately, when he died in 1918, the *Bellingham Herald* staff took potluck in choosing for his obituary one of the white-bearded gentlemen in the photo on page 17. Instead of McKay, they chose his lifelong friend Ed Warbass, who died in 1906.

# *Two*

# A Town Rises

By the early 1890s, an economic synergy was developing in Friday Harbor. As one business spawned another and competition heated, the most resourceful rose to the top in the increasingly familiar pattern of American capitalism.

Friday Harbor was becoming typical of the small port towns on Washington's rural coast, sustained mainly by farming, fishing, some logging, and commercial enterprises such as groceries, dry goods, and blacksmithing. Cash money also flowed in the form of pay stubs from the burgeoning lime industry in place at Roche Harbor, Lime Kiln Point, and elsewhere on the island.

But the big money did not arrive until 1894 when the Island Packing Company began operations on the site of today's Cannery Landing. During that first summer, more than 18,000 cases of sockeye salmon were packed. "It was like a bolt of thunder into a silent little community and before 20 days had passed there wasn't a man, woman or child who wanted to work that didn't have a job," recalled Capt. William P. Thornton. By the beginning of the 20th century, a lumber and shake mill was added to the mix, and agriculture boomed. In addition to dairy and cereal crops, the San Juan Islands became the fruit-growing capital of the Pacific Northwest. Apples, pears, peaches, strawberries, and apricots were grown throughout the island, including in most of the backyards in town. In 1907 alone, 72,000 boxes of apples, at 80¢ each, were shipped from Friday Harbor to points south such as the Pike Place Market in Seattle. Pears ranked second with 12,000 boxes at $1.25 each.

With prosperity came infrastructure. Docks were built to accommodate the growing freight and passenger trade. Telephone service between Friday Harbor and Roche Harbor started in 1901, and in January 1907, the first electric arc lamp, the *Friday Harbor Journal* wrote, "shed its welcome effulgence" at the intersection of Spring and First Streets between the old courthouse (yet to be moved) and Churchill Corner. The newspaper went on to predict, "The event will go down in history as an advanced step toward better conditions!"

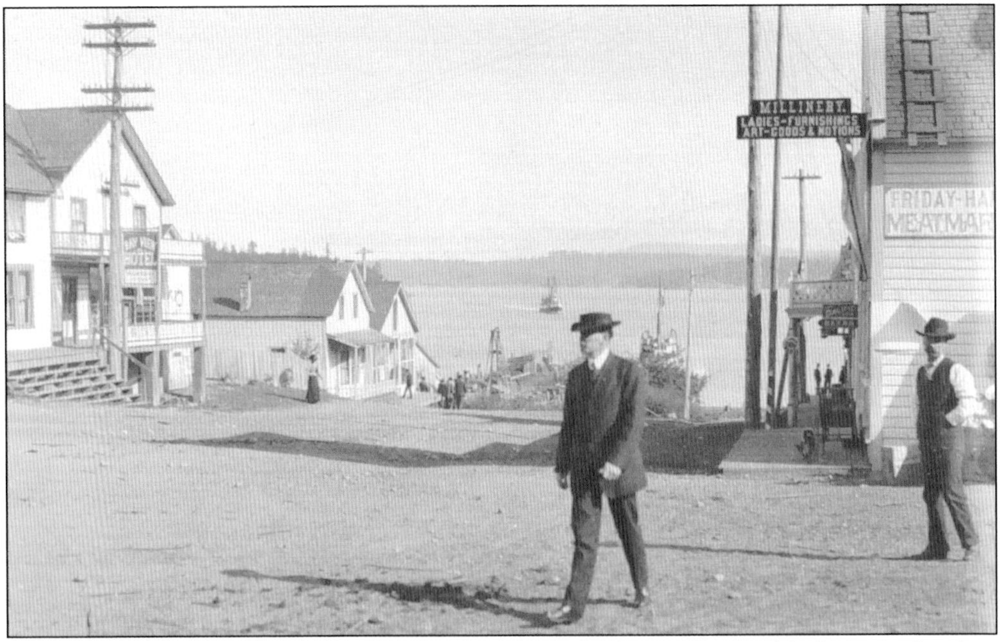


San Juan County Bank cashier Gene Gould crosses First and Spring Streets like he owns the place around 1900. And in a way, he did. His father, J. A. Gould, cofounded the bank in 1893, was sole shareholder by 1901, and handed it to his son in 1907. At 29, Gene was the youngest bank president in the nation. He would also become the town's first mayor.

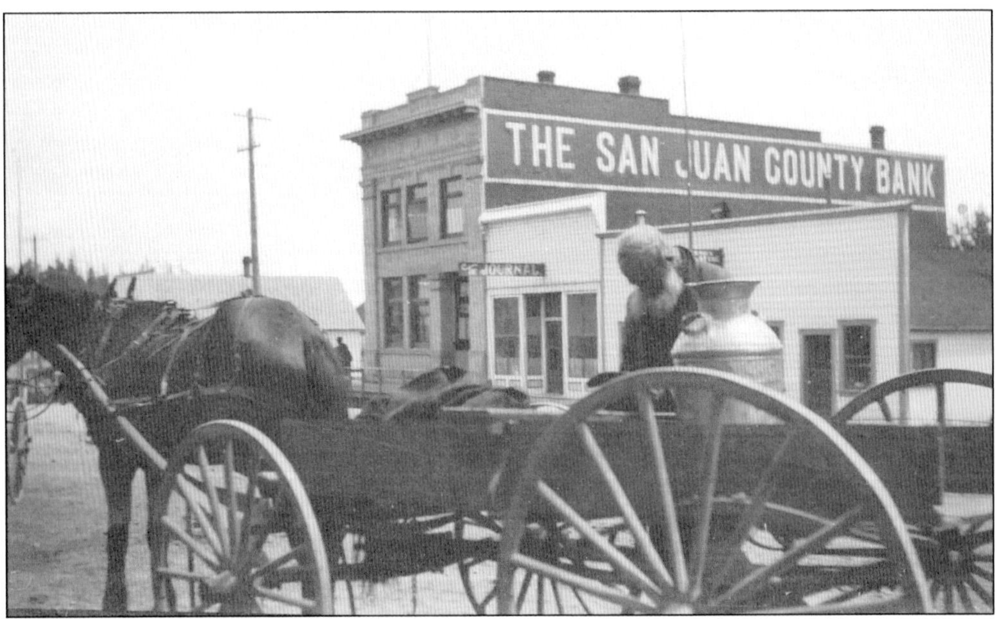


A dairyman delivers an order on Spring Street around 1907. The San Juan County Bank stands on the site of the second county courthouse (see page 19). Other businesses in the photograph include the *Friday Harbor Journal* and the Puckingham Meat Market.

A. C. Brown launched the first sawmill in Friday Harbor in 1894, and, being a Seventh Day Adventist, blew his steam whistle every Sunday at noon to disrupt the Methodists in the church atop the bluff above (right). This 1906 view from Point Caution captures a new lumber mill in action. Begun in 1904 by the Jensen brothers and James Groll, the mill also generated electricity for the town and served as a shipyard.

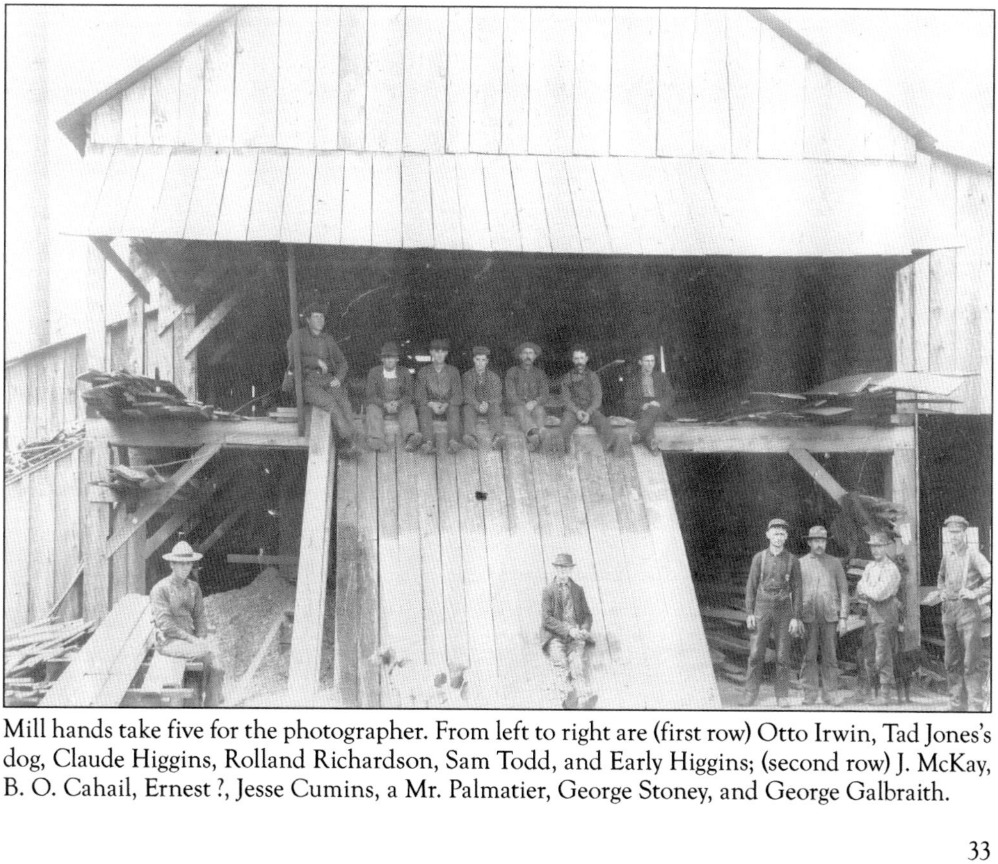

Mill hands take five for the photographer. From left to right are (first row) Otto Irwin, Tad Jones's dog, Claude Higgins, Rolland Richardson, Sam Todd, and Early Higgins; (second row) J. McKay, B. O. Cahail, Ernest ?, Jesse Cumins, a Mr. Palmatier, George Stoney, and George Galbraith.

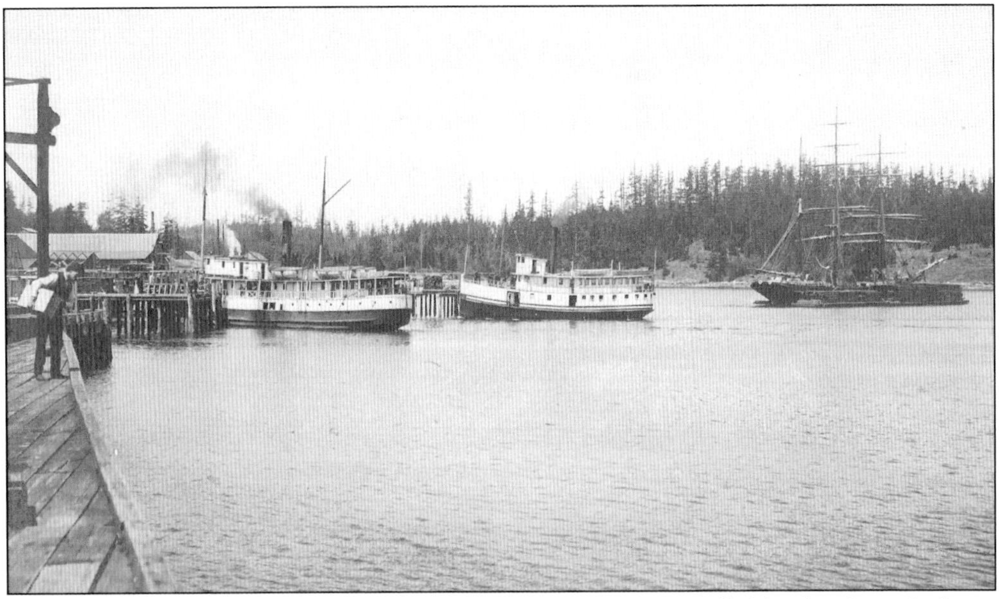

The waterfront is abuzz as a square-rigged ship takes on a cargo of milled lumber from the barge *Hester*, which has been dispatched from the mill dock around 1906. By then, a system of docks was located between the lumber mill and the cannery dock, where the above photograph was taken.

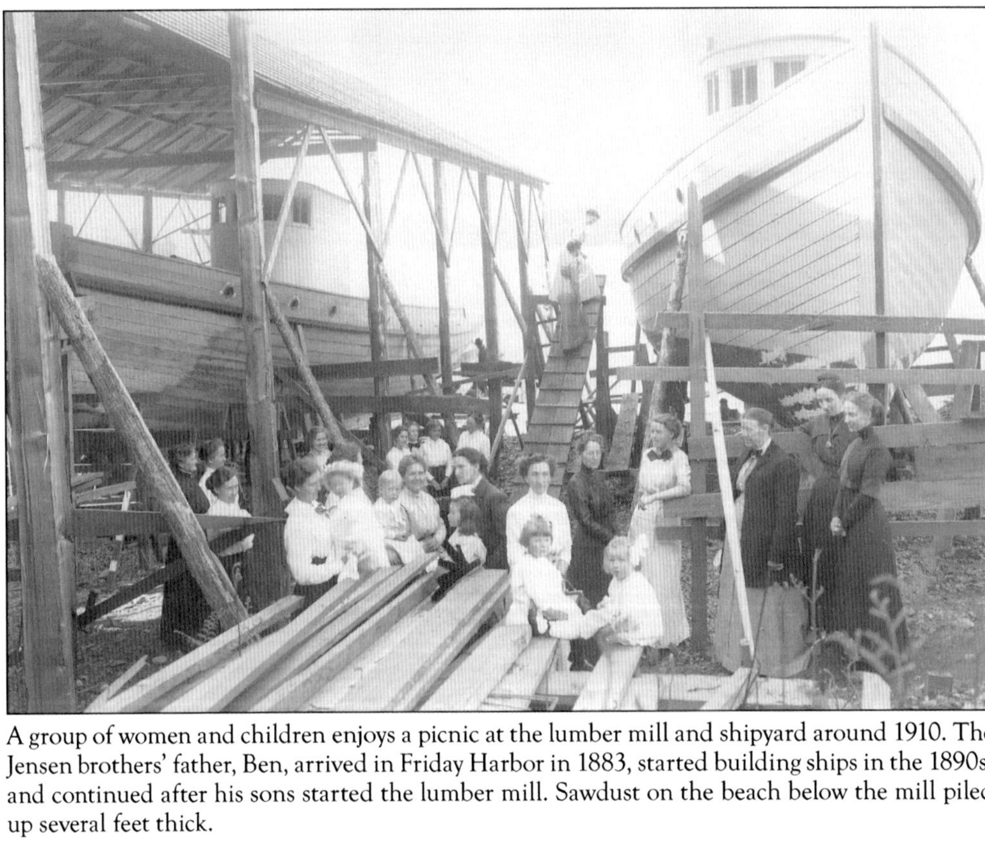

A group of women and children enjoys a picnic at the lumber mill and shipyard around 1910. The Jensen brothers' father, Ben, arrived in Friday Harbor in 1883, started building ships in the 1890s, and continued after his sons started the lumber mill. Sawdust on the beach below the mill piled up several feet thick.

Albert, Frank, Joe, and Pete Jensen (clockwise from the top left) launched a sawmill about where the marina and Jack Fairweather Park are today. Albert had worked as a steam engineer and as a teacher in a one-room schoolhouse on Shaw Island. He left the mill in 1910 to start the Albert Jensen and Son Shipyard.

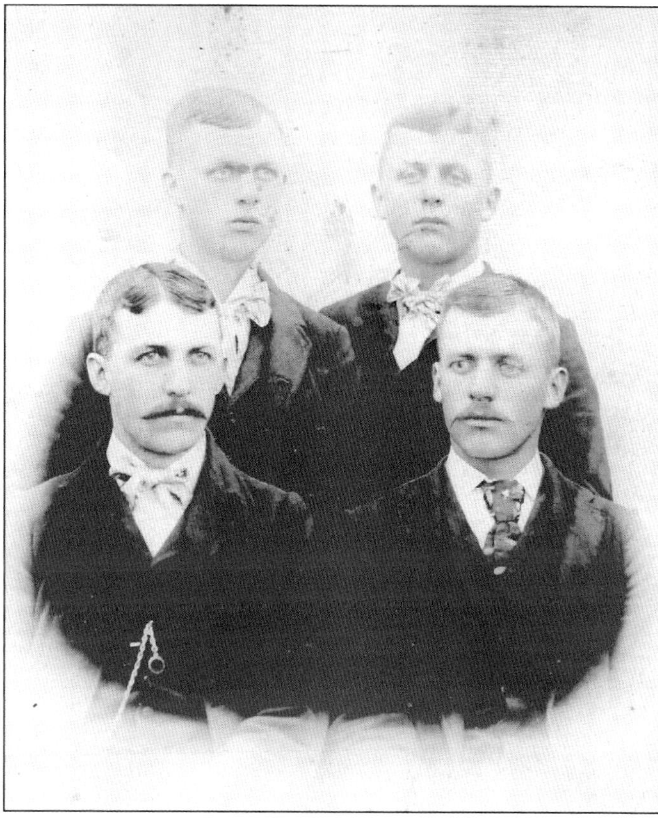

This additional view of the lumber mill and dock was taken from where the Port of Friday Harbor offices are today. On October 18, 1906, the *Friday Harbor Journal* recorded that the newspaper had placed its order for electricity generated by the mill and was "at the head of the list." The mill burned to the ground in 1911.

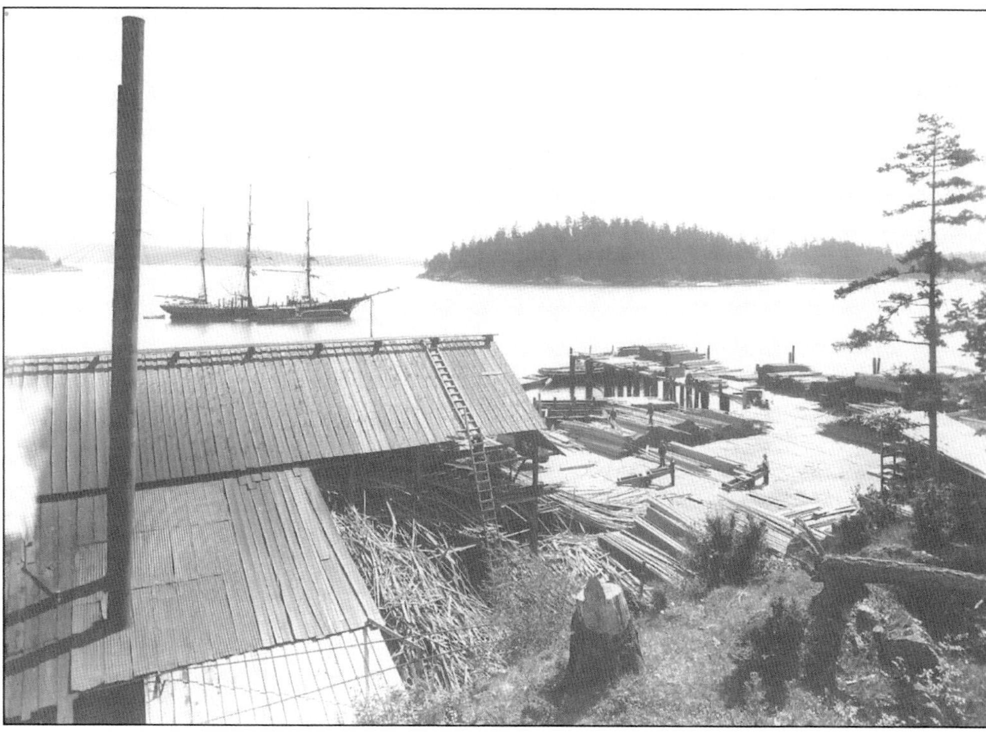

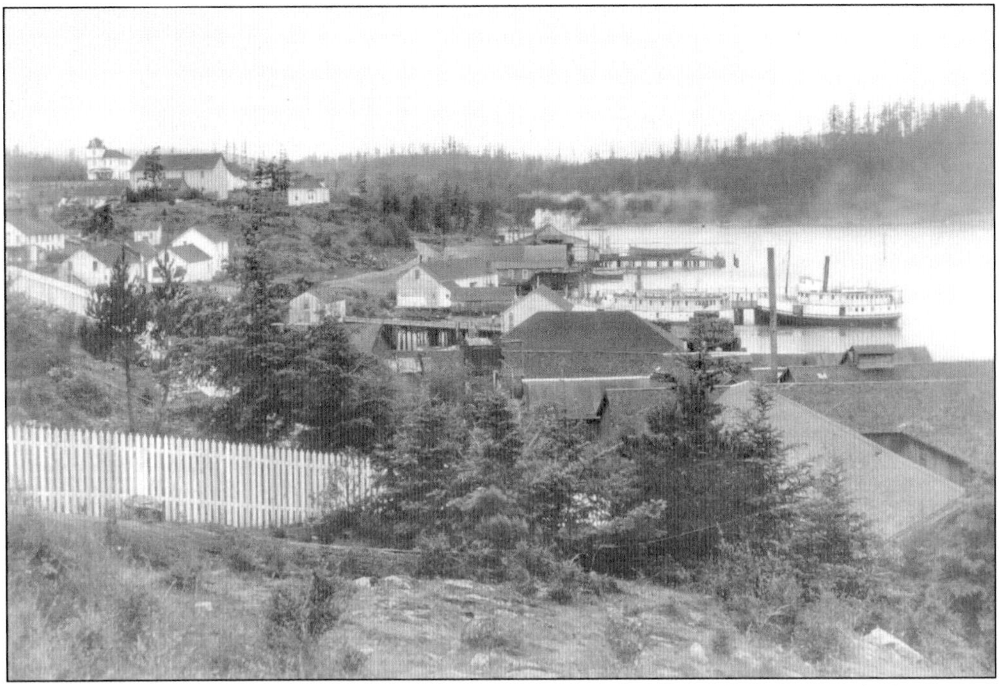

To judge how rapidly the waterfront developed in 10 years, compare this image with the one on page 21, taken from the same vantage point. A road that would become Front Street has been cut around the bluff, the lumber mill is in full swing, new docks are in place, and the cannery has become a massive complex.

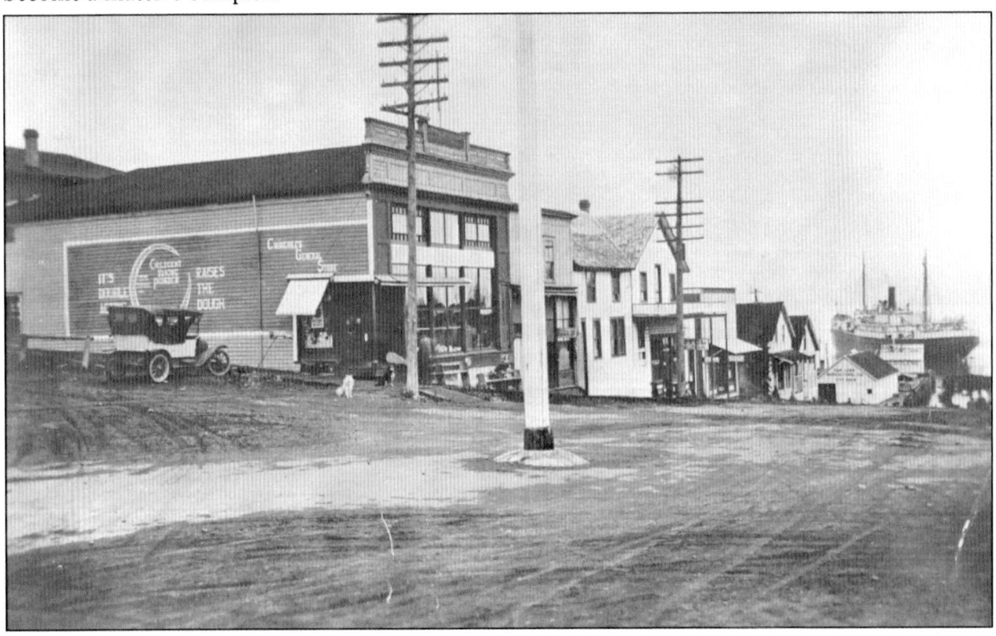


A tramp steamer rides at anchor at the foot of Spring Street in 1917. This image is dated post 1917 because of the flagpole in the intersection. Churchill's General Store, later Herb's tavern, occupied this corner from 1892 until consumed by fire in April 2022 along with the historic former Douglas House.

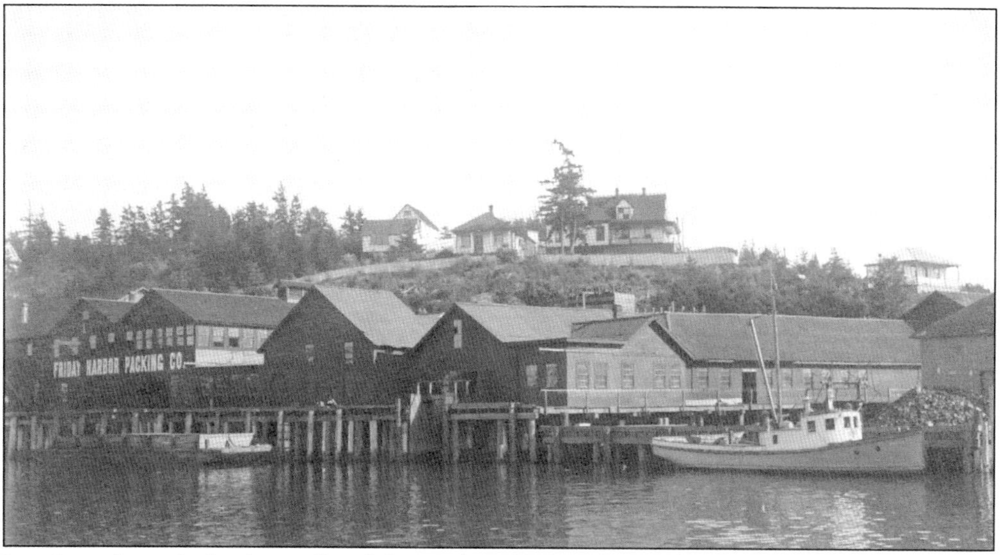


Just down from the lumber mill and shipyard, and below the Gould house was the Friday Harbor Packing Company. It was owned by the mammoth Pacific American Fisheries (PAF), which bought out the Island Packing Company in 1899. PAF also owned most of the fish traps surrounding the island.

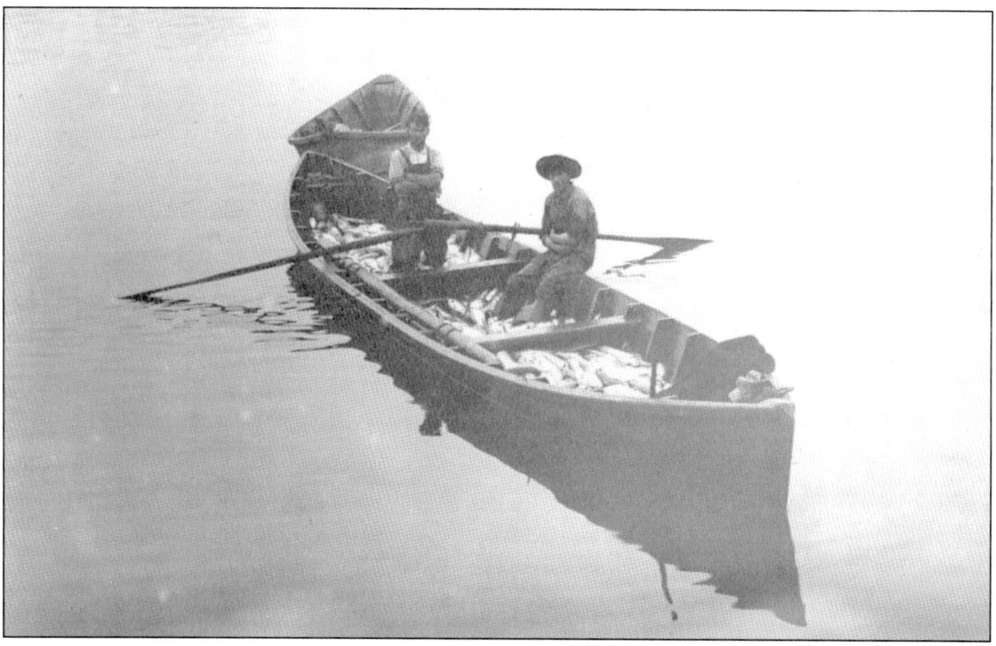

Native reefnetters, who lured salmon into their nets long before the time of fish traps, tenders, scows, and canneries, still caught and sold fish to buyers during the fish-trap era. In this image, the lead boat is full of fish (note the rail where the net was affixed), and the rear vessel carries the net.

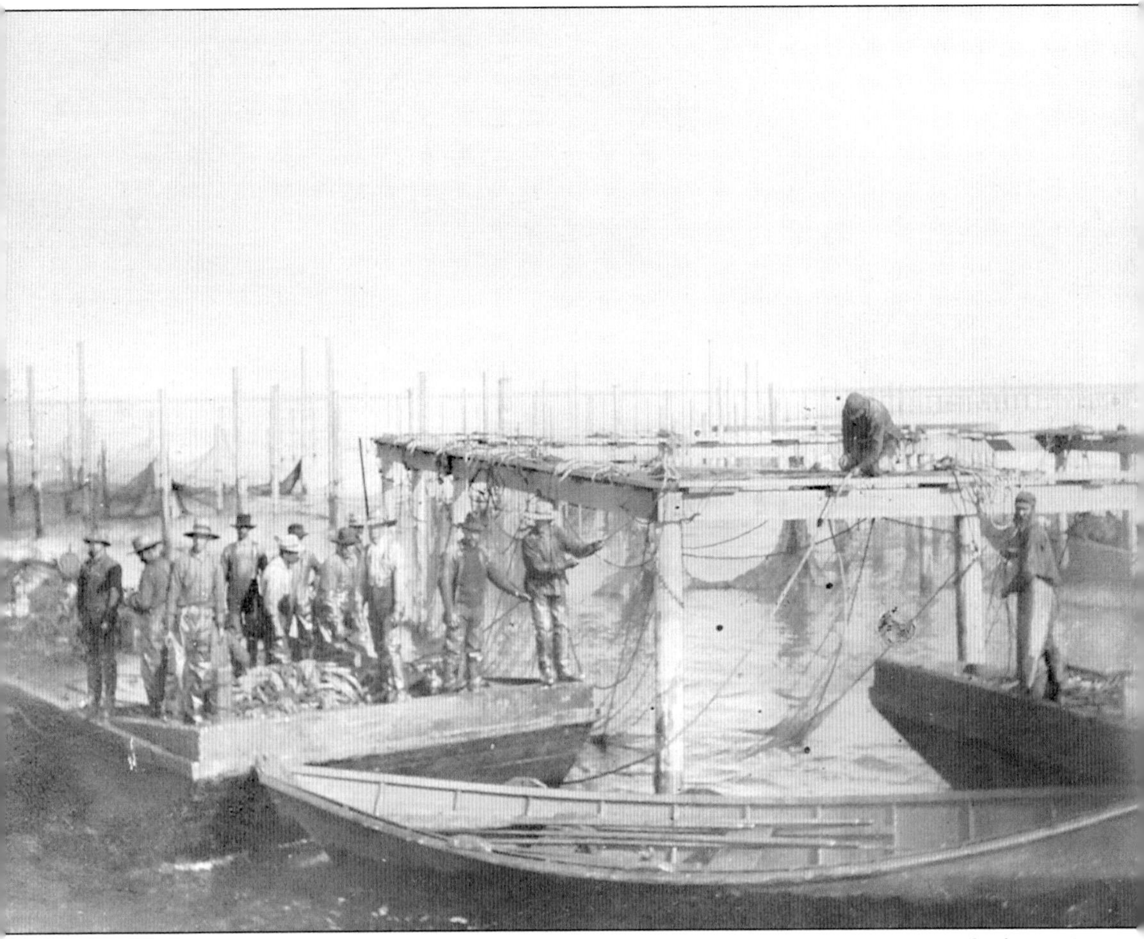

A fish trap crew off South Beach finesses a net in preparation for trapping a run of salmon. In principle, the fish-trap technique was similar to reefnetting, corralling sockeye that gathered in eddies closer to shore that before could only be caught with seine or gill nets. Migrating fish encountered the 400-yard leads and then swam along them into the "hearts," a series of inverted Vs that forced the fish into the "pot" or corral and then into the spiller. A net was raised to capture the fish, which were then "brailed" from the net (much as one squeegees water from a window surface) into a waiting scow that hauled them off to the cannery. Fish traps were essential to the Friday Harbor economy from 1893 until they were outlawed by the state in 1934.

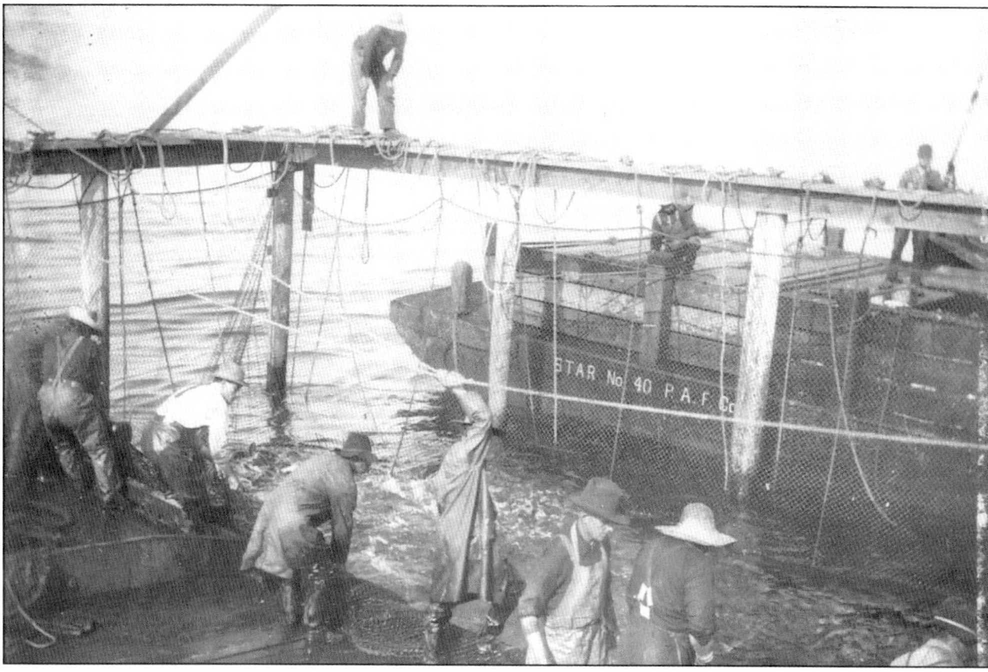


Workers raise a net full of sockeye salmon off South Beach before brailing them into the adjoining scow. A PAF tender provided the power for this operation. In 1900, one such trap caught 7,000 fish in one day, although the cannery in Friday Harbor counted about 1,500 fish less—a common discrepancy.

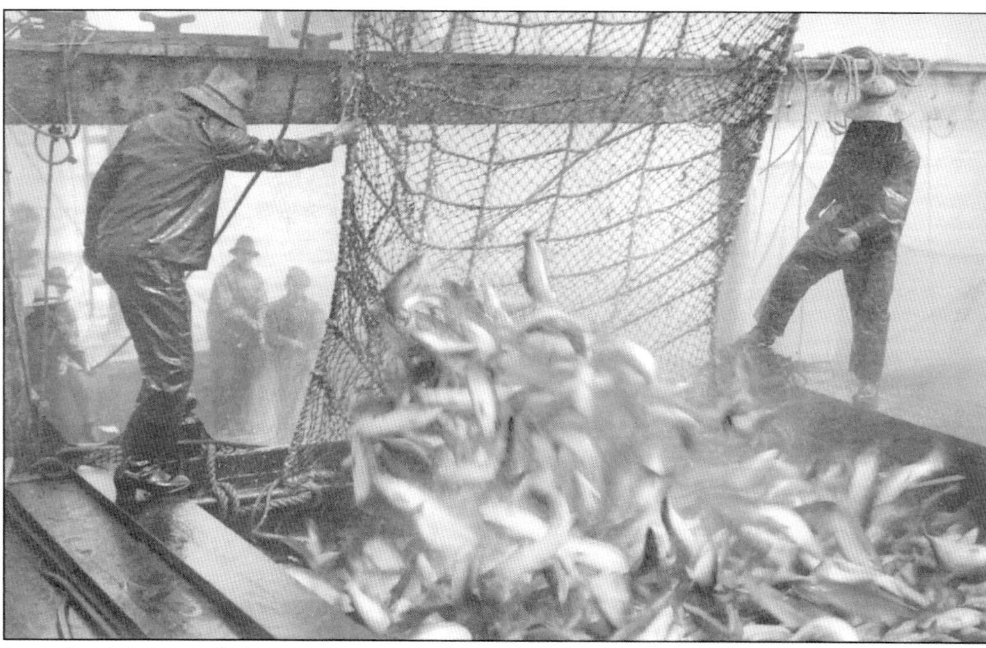

Here the fish are spilled into a scow, completing the task begun above. (Large scows could hold up to 12,000 fish.) By 1899, twelve such traps were located off South Beach alone. Nearly all traps located in the Northern Straits and Puget Sound region were owned by corporations such as PAF.

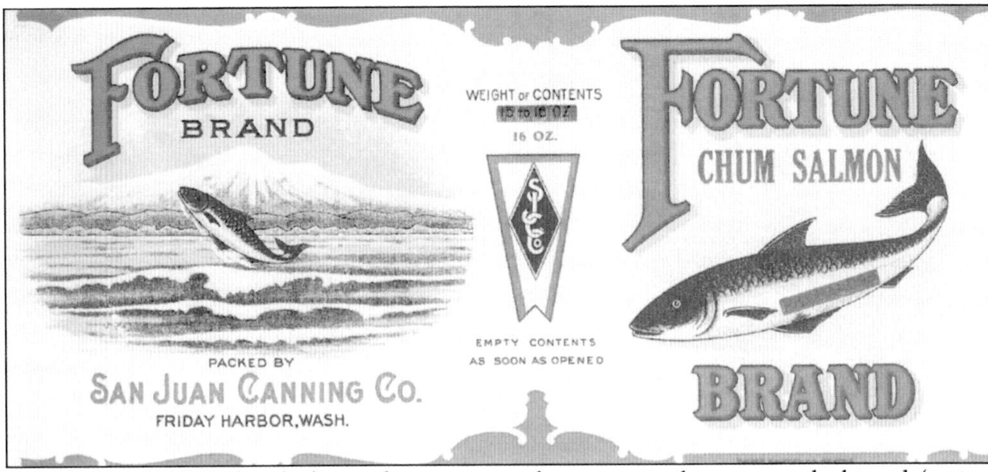


Salmon was graded and packed according to species, beginning in the spring with chinook (spring, king, tyee, and quinnat), followed by sockeye (red, blueback, or quinault) in July and August, pink or humpback in August and September, coho (medium red and silversides) in October, and finally chum (calico, keta, or dog salmon) in November. The label above represents the Fortune brand, packed around 1930 at the Friday Harbor cannery.

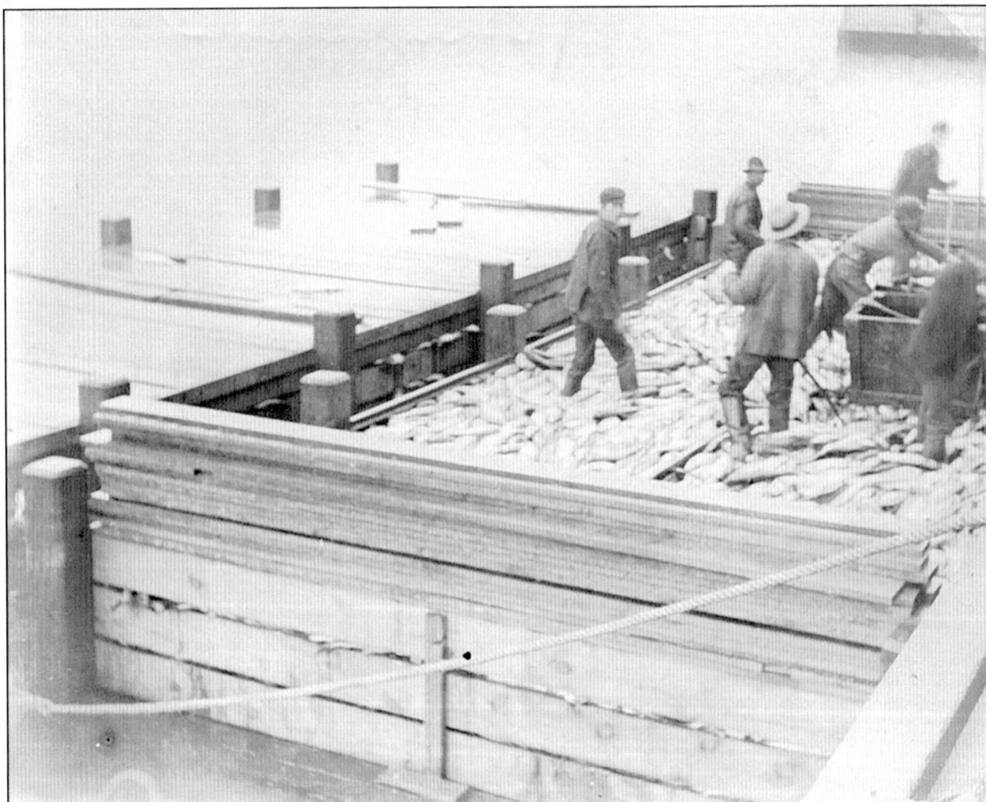

Cannery workers wade through a scow full of fish, preparing to pitch them into a chute leading to the plant floor. Early on, many of the workers were from Japan, the Philippine Islands or China. The 1900 U. S. Census listed nearly 50 Chinese in San Juan County. Some may have been smuggled into the country following the Chinese Exclusion Act of 1882.

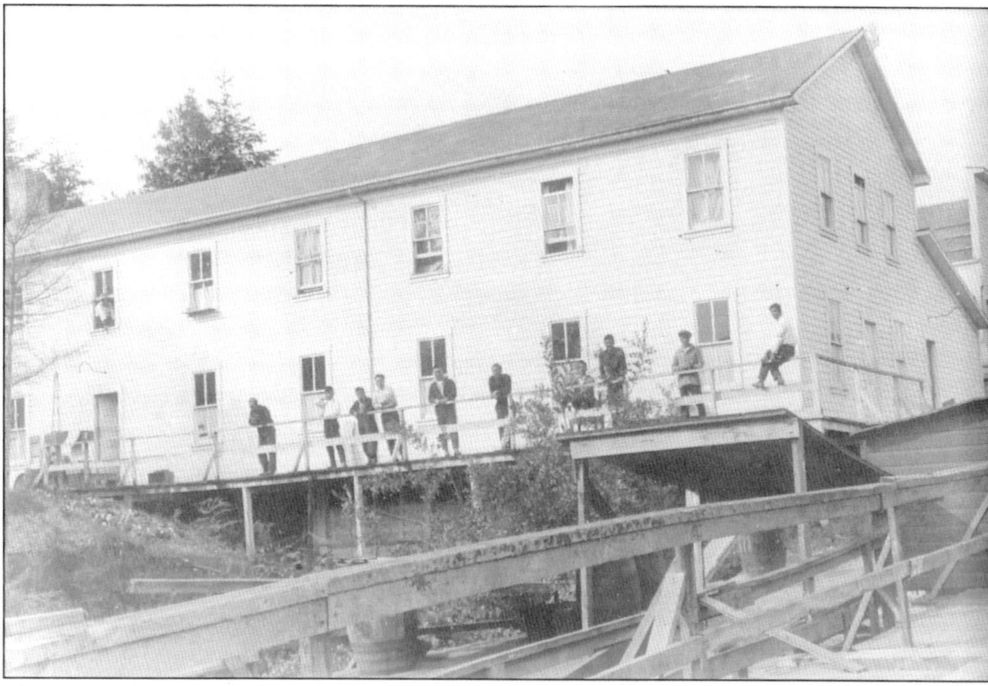

The cannery's employee dormitory, located on the site of today's main ferry line area, was labeled the "China House" on the cannery's plant diagram, but locals also knew it as the "Jap House," despite the small numbers of Japanese. The false-front building just up the hill is Carl King's slaughterhouse, which was built in 1914 as a creamery.

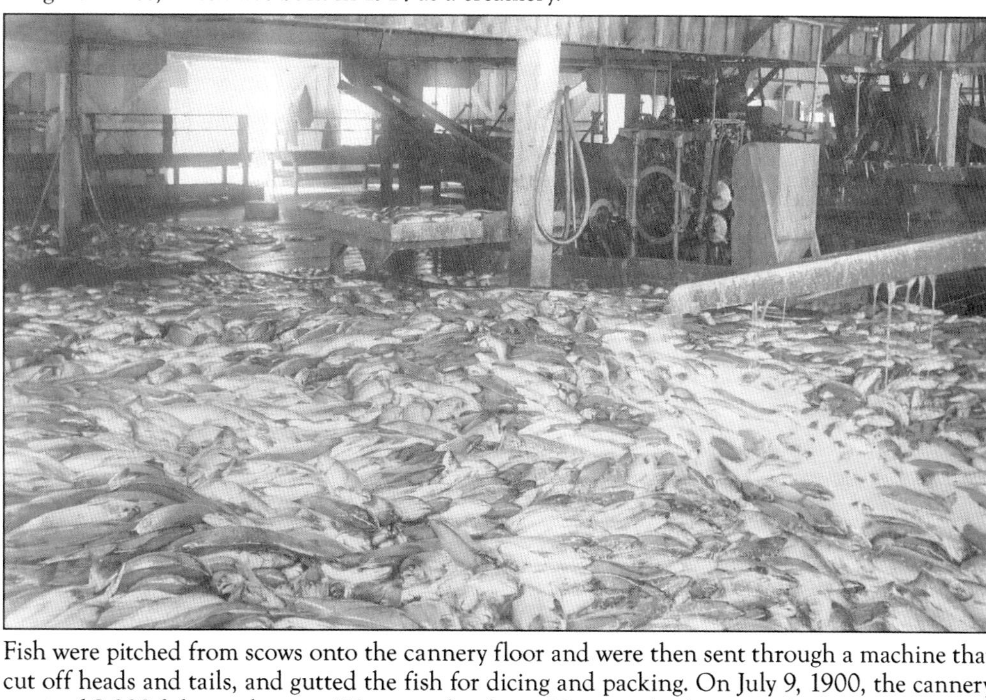

Fish were pitched from scows onto the cannery floor and were then sent through a machine that cut off heads and tails, and gutted the fish for dicing and packing. On July 9, 1900, the cannery received 2,000 fish, resulting in 178 cases of sockeye, 35 cases of red spring salmon, and 8 cases of white spring salmon. A few days later, the catch was 5,790 sockeye and 540 spring salmon.

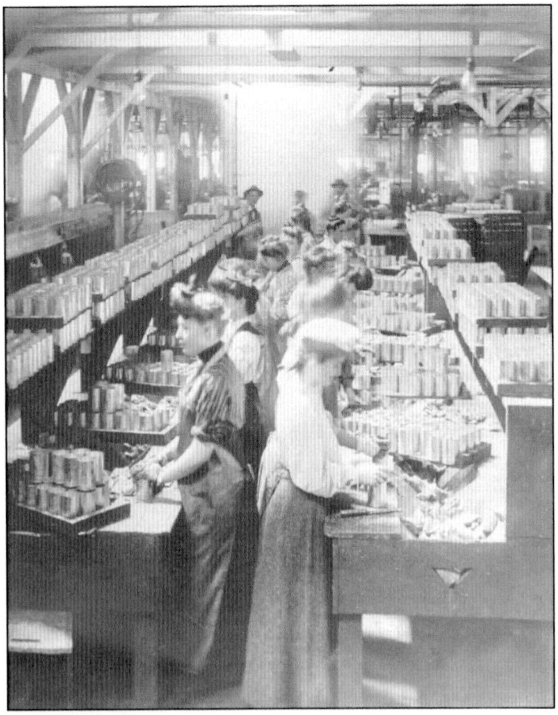

Men and women worked round-the-clock shifts on the line in the cannery each summer. The floors were damp, the work bays drafty, and the noise relentless. But the money was good. Here workers pack diced salmon into cans that were then sent into the cooker before being labeled and shipped. By 1912, the Friday Harbor Packing Company ranked fifth of 19 canneries in the greater Puget Sound/Northern Straits region.

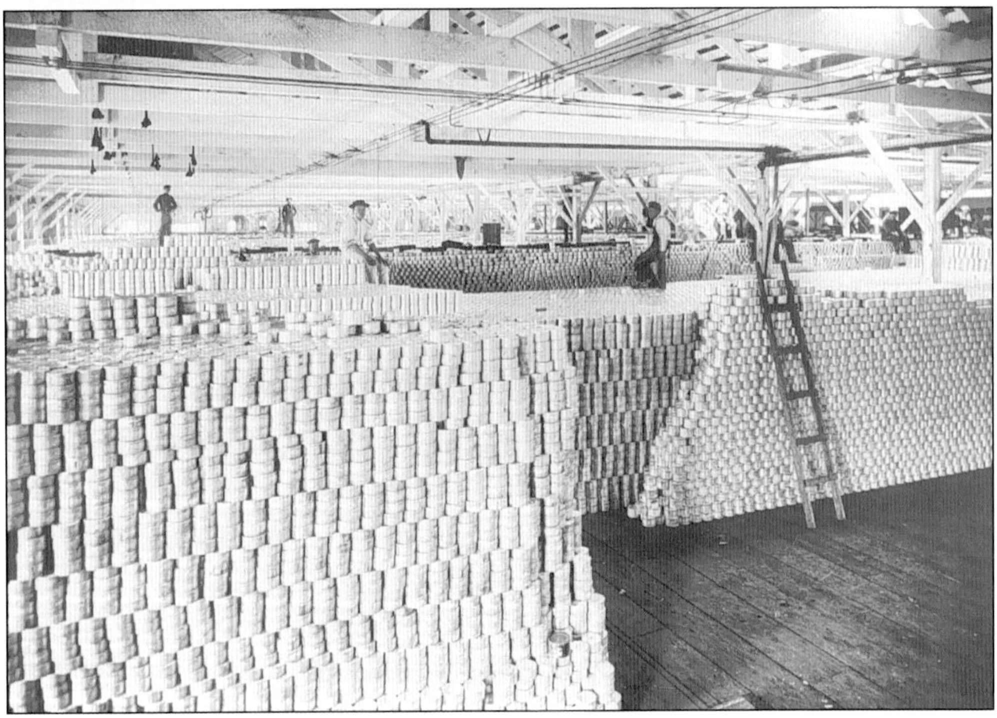

Freshly packed cans of salmon await shipment to the far corners of the country at the Friday Harbor Packing Company. Business was so good—in 1909, more than 40,000 fish were processed in one day alone—that the cannery was rebuilt and enlarged in 1912 at a cost of $100,000. One employee claims that by the 1940s, more than 100,000 fish filled the cannery floor.

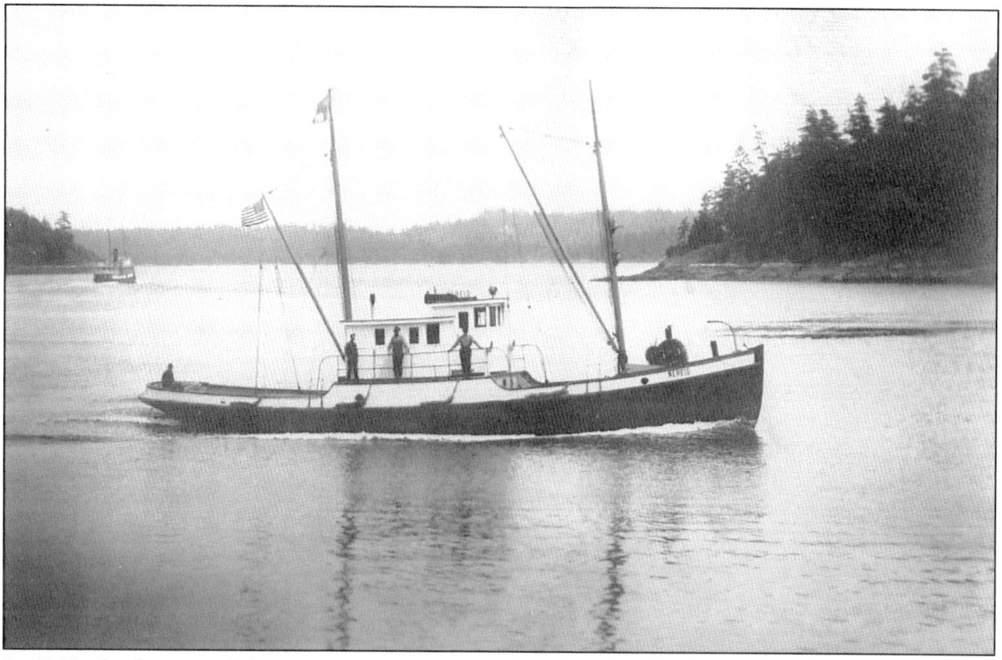

In 1911, the first vessel down the ways at Albert Jensen & Sons Shipyard in Shipyard Cove was the *Nereid*. The vessel was almost immediately sold to the Friday Harbor Packing Company as a buyer and tender. For years, the *Nereid* motored to Neah Bay, took on fish, and returned to the cannery. She was also rigged for sail. Here, *c.* 1912–1920, the crew pauses in front of the wheelhouse.

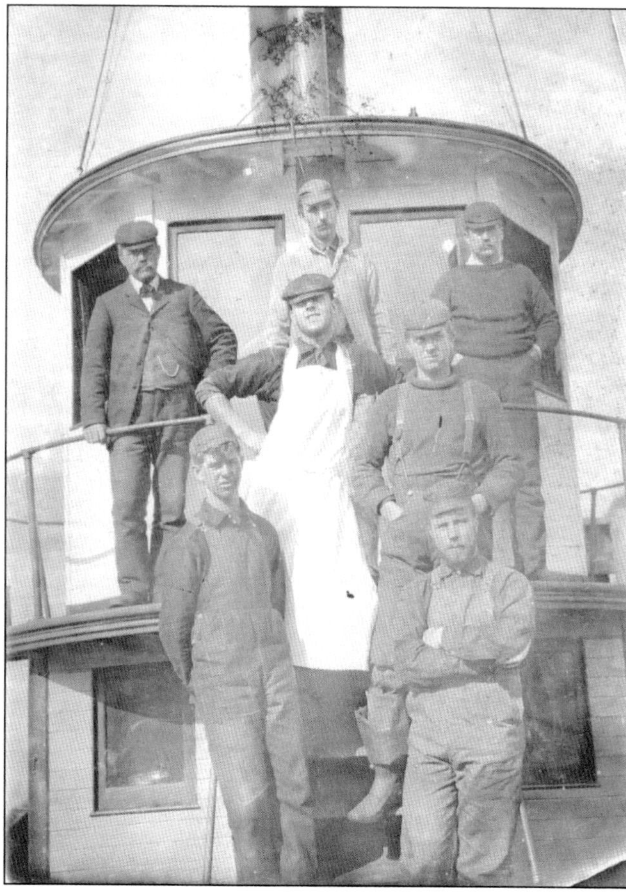

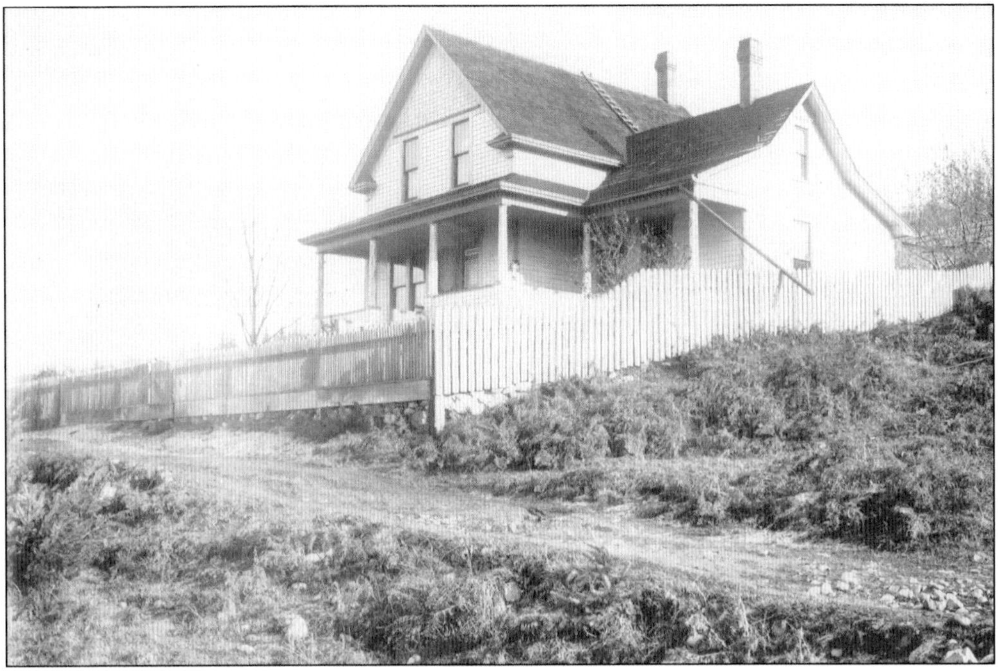

The cannery's success resulted in a fine new house being built in 1905 on Front Street (still a primitive track) for the plant superintendent at the time, William Schultz. From 1945, it was known as the "Jeffers House" for the cannery owner, George Jeffers. Sold to a developer in 1978, it is currently an espresso bar.

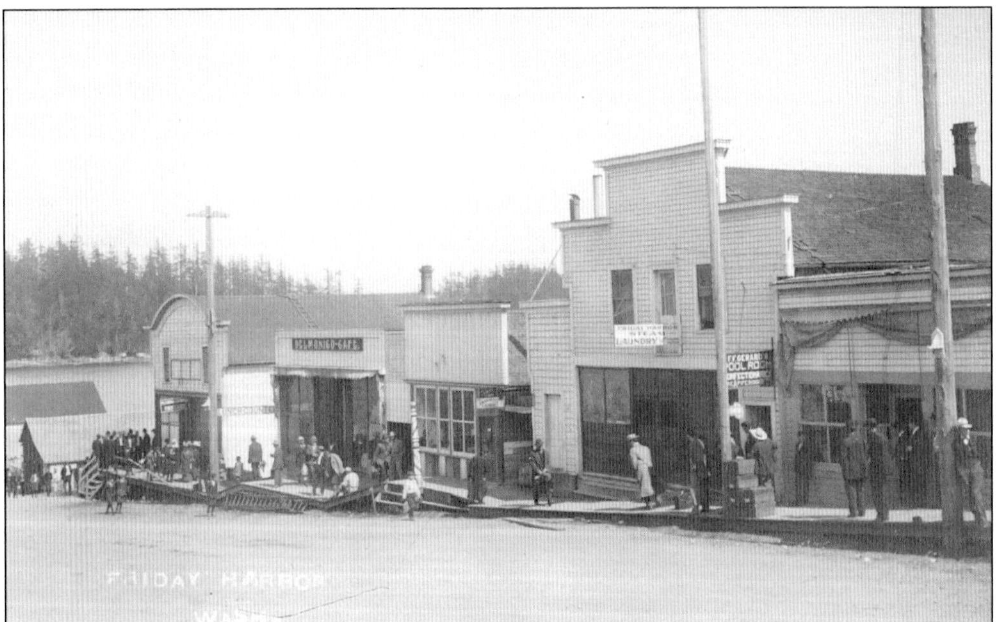


Lower Spring Street has taken on a decidedly more cosmopolitan look (compare with the same view on page 28) in this post-1910 image, probably taken after a ship arrived. With the banishment of alcohol from town limits, Saloon Best was replaced by a grocery store, but one could still play pool and suck on a jawbreaker at F. F. Gerard and Company, four doors up the street.

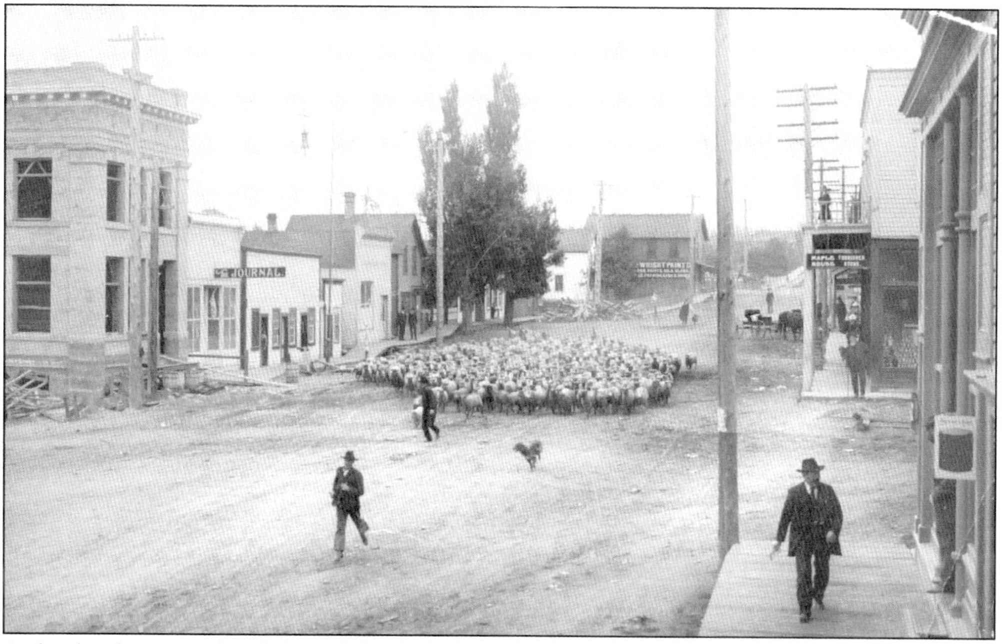


A shepherd sprints ahead toward the docks with a flock hot on his heels, the dogs circling and nipping, while another shepherd leads the bell sheep by a tether. The San Juan County Bank under construction (the original is located at center left) and the electric arc light above the intersection indicate the town was rapidly changing by 1907.

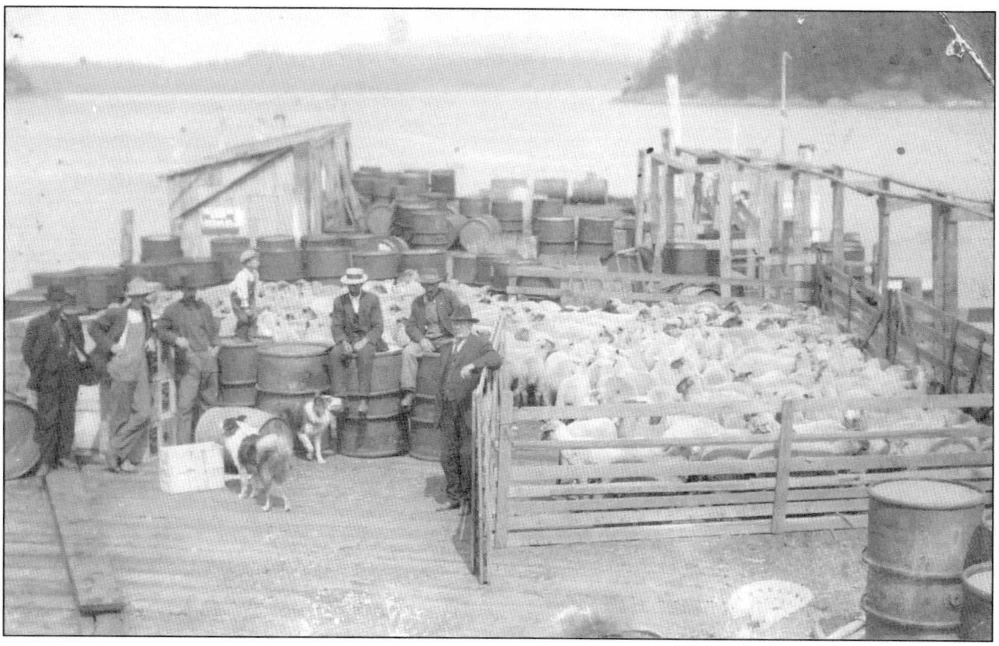

Shepherds and dogs now have the flock penned on the "city float" awaiting shipment to Speiden Island for grazing. Note the boy standing atop the 55-gallon drum at center left. Despite all the trappings of a growing town, Brown Island and Shaw Island beyond were still virgin wilderness.

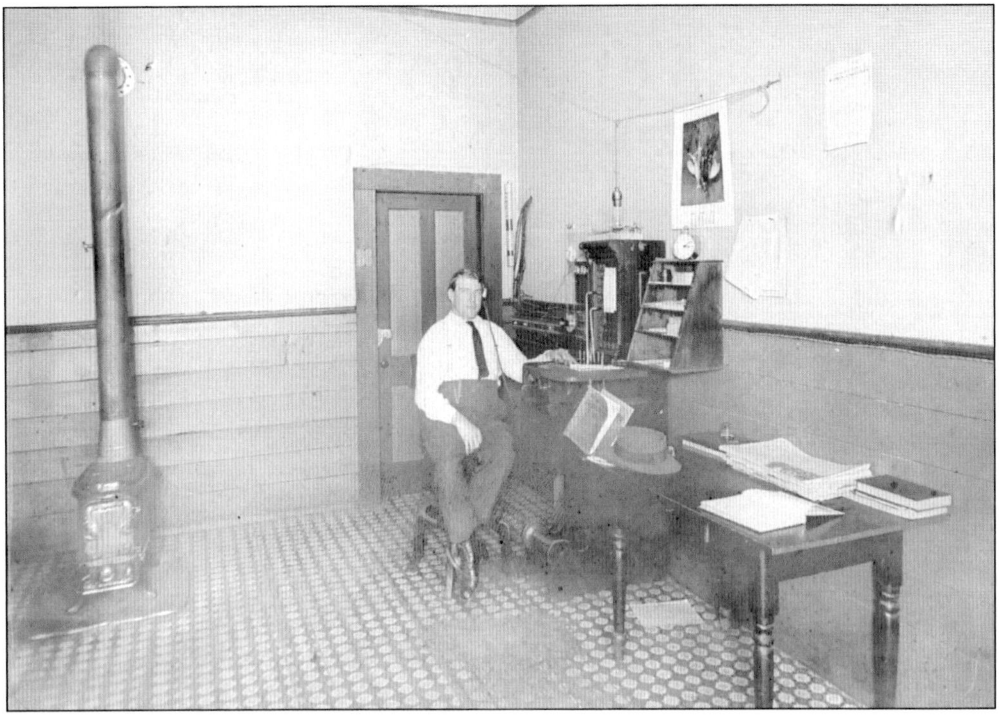

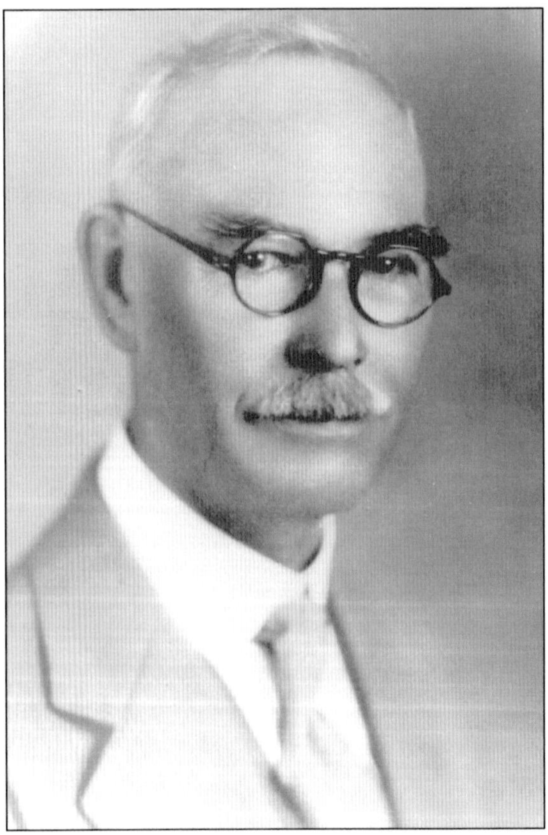

Harry McMillan (above) was the first operator for the San Juan Island telephone system, which was underwritten and installed in 1901 by Dr. Victor Capron (left), twice Friday Harbor mayor and the physician for the Roche Harbor Lime and Cement Company. Telephones became a necessity because roads were not always passable between Roche Harbor and Friday Harbor. Dr. Capron took a correspondence course, built the system, and enrolled his first eight customers in 1901. By 1909, twenty-five miles of line connected the island, with 33 subscribers paying $2.50 apiece per month for the service. The first central switchboard was in Sweeney's Mercantile Company until it was moved to the Bay View Hotel in 1911. Some who could not afford the tariff paid in kind with salmon.

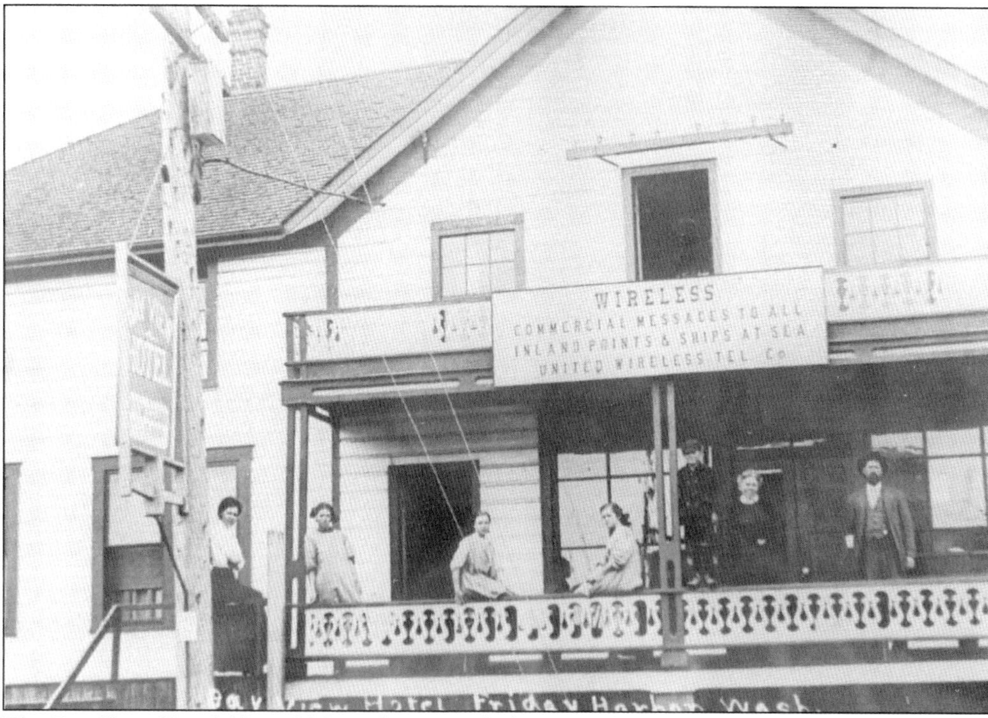


The Bay View Hotel (the Old Douglas House) also served as a wireless office and housed the telephone switchboard. The building achieved notoriety for its backroom saloon and illegal gambling activities that in 1907 drew headlines around the state and prompted a clampdown by the sheriff. Friday Harbor had yet to expunge its frontier character.

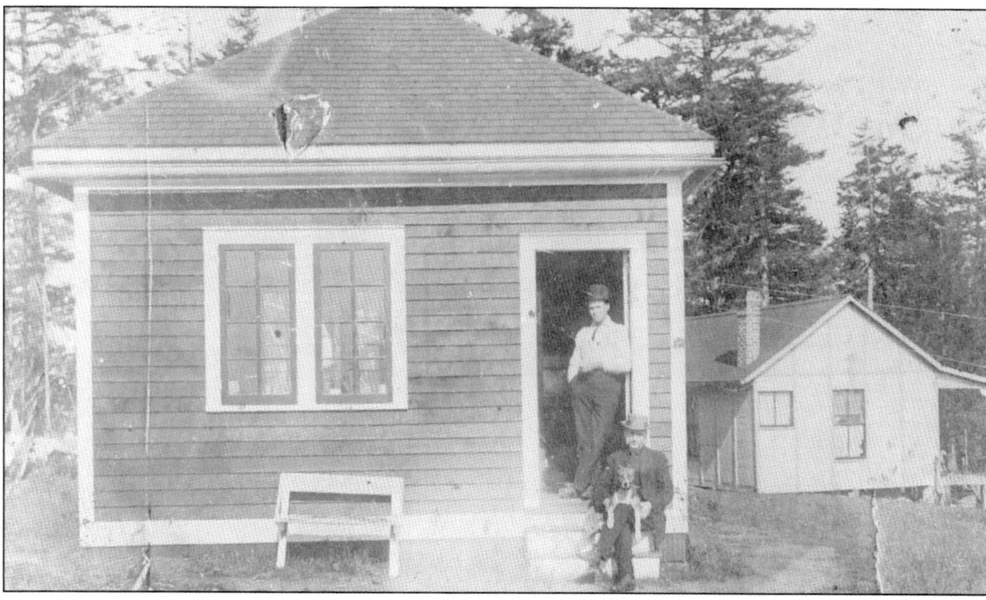

Friday Harbor citizens were excited when in 1909 the federal government announced that a new radio direction-finding station, once positioned on the site of the new courthouse, was to be erected on 320-foot Bald Hill. Alec Buchanan, A. Nicholson, and yet another Friday Harbor dog are shown in the doorway of the station on Griffin Bay.

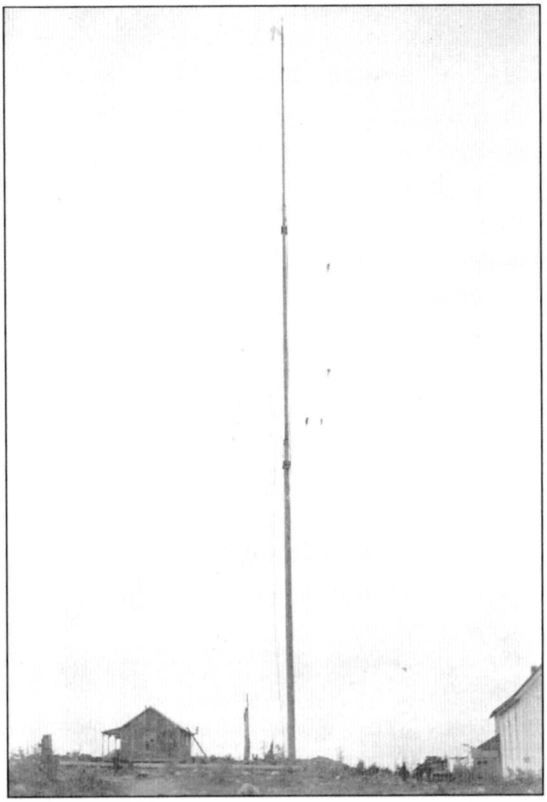

The first antenna of San Juan's wireless station, located on the site of today's courthouse, measured about 200 feet and could pick up clear signals from ships at sea and Alaska. When high winds snapped off 80 feet in 1904, the government was compelled not only to rebuild, but also to improve the antenna's range. The new apparatus on Bald Hill was more than 237 feet high, enabling operators to receive signals from as far off as the Hawaiian Islands. When the station became obsolete, it was torn down and the property sold, but not to graze sheep or build a palatial house with a splendid view (see page 49).

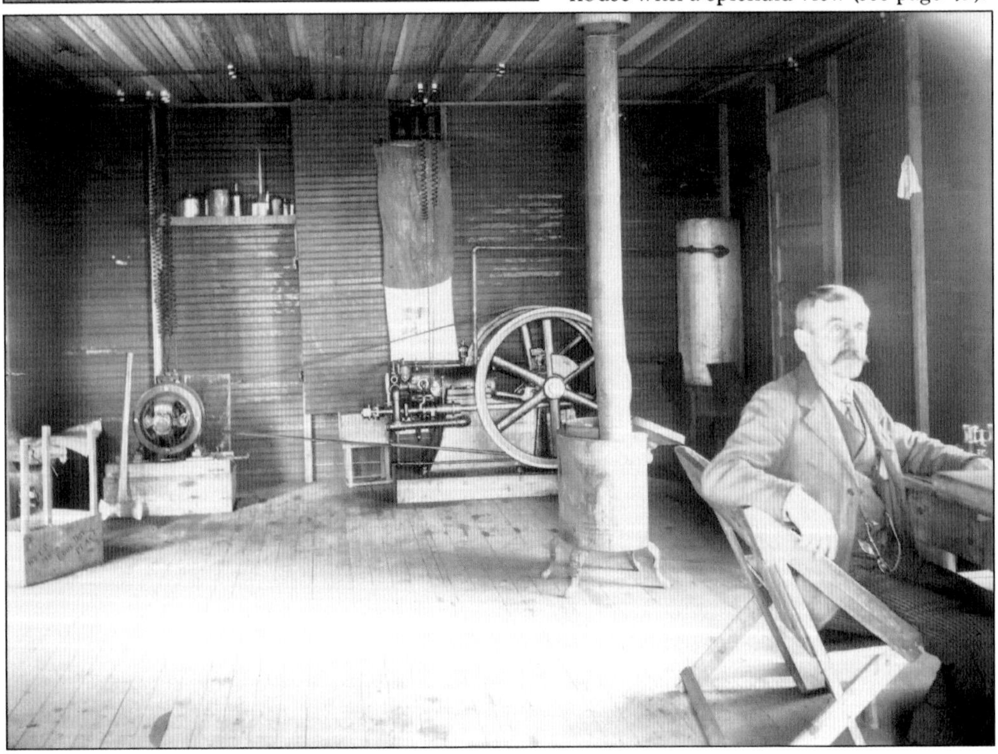

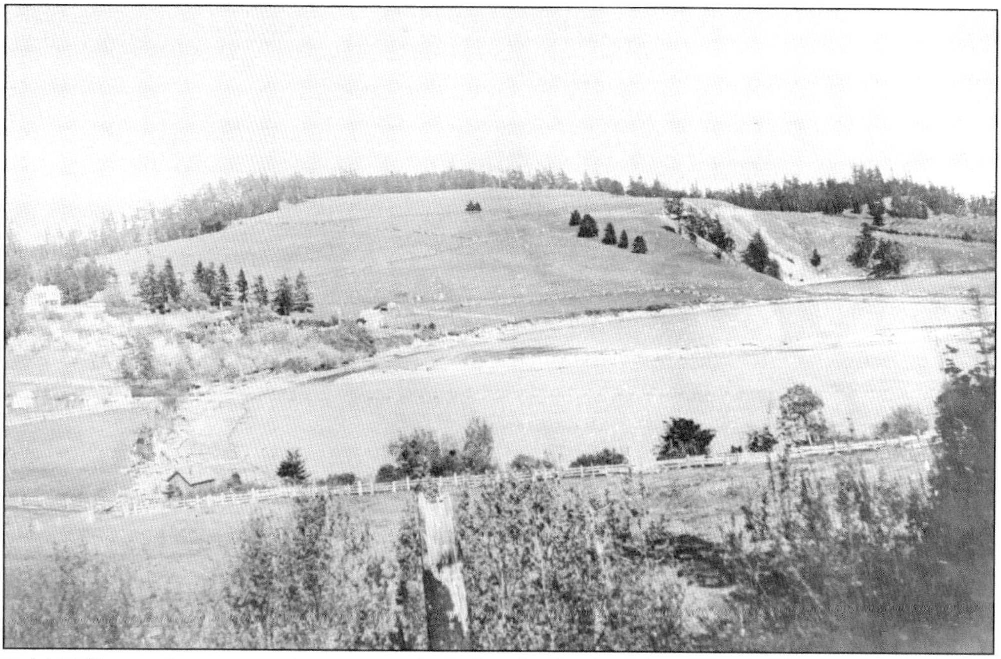

Bald Hill was almost entirely composed of glacial till, ideal for excavating and manufacturing gravel. This scenic image of Jackson Beach on Griffin Bay, c. 1900, dramatically illustrates just how completely quarrymen from the late 1950s reduced the once gently sloping hillock into today's barren Pear Point gravel pit. Because much of the gravel was shipped to Canada, locals quipped the British were reclaiming the island, one barge at a time.

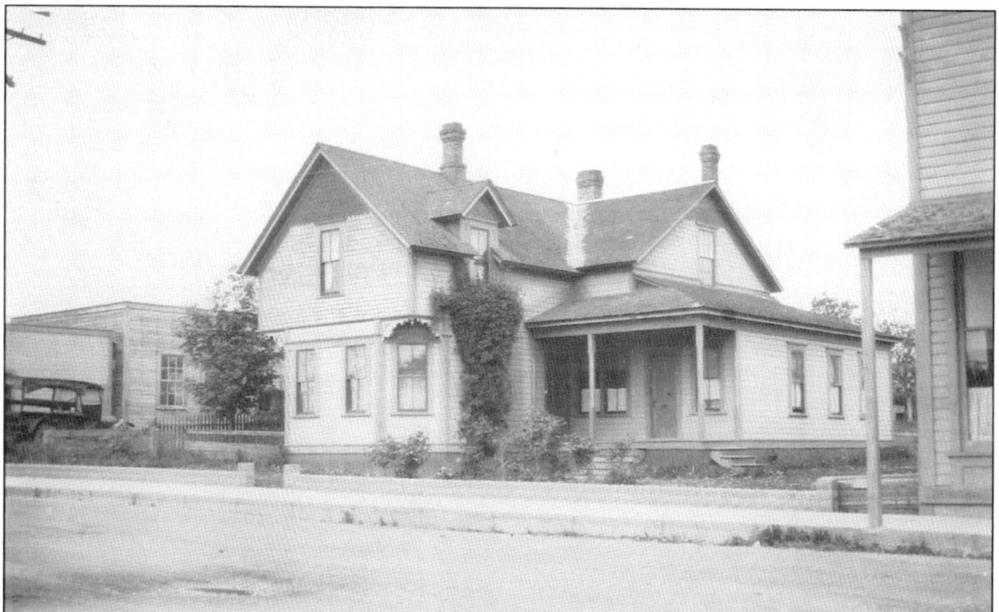

Dr. George S. Wright's c. 1890s home was, and still is, a landmark on Spring Street. A graduate of Yale Medical School, Wright came to the island in 1892. The house's next resident was undertaker Harry King, who converted the front parlor into the mortuary viewing room. The house was moved up the street from next door to the drugstore.

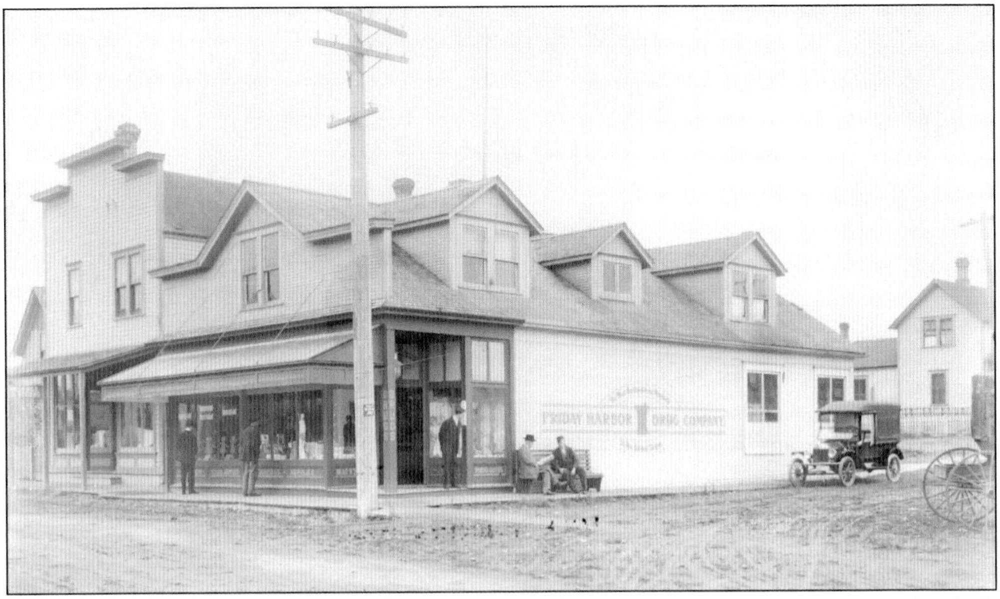


The original Friday Harbor Drug Company began in 1896 as the two-story portion of today's store. Dr. George Wright purchased the store in 1902 and hired his cousin, Leon Little, to run it. In 1912, the business was moved into the vintage 1892 one-story building at Spring and Second Streets. The two-story building continued its long life, first as a post office and then a library on the ground floor. The upstairs housed the San Juan Commercial Club and then the American Legion meeting hall and bar, which featured several slot machines. On returning home from World War I, Little, in partnership with Albert Nash, bought the pharmacy from Wright.

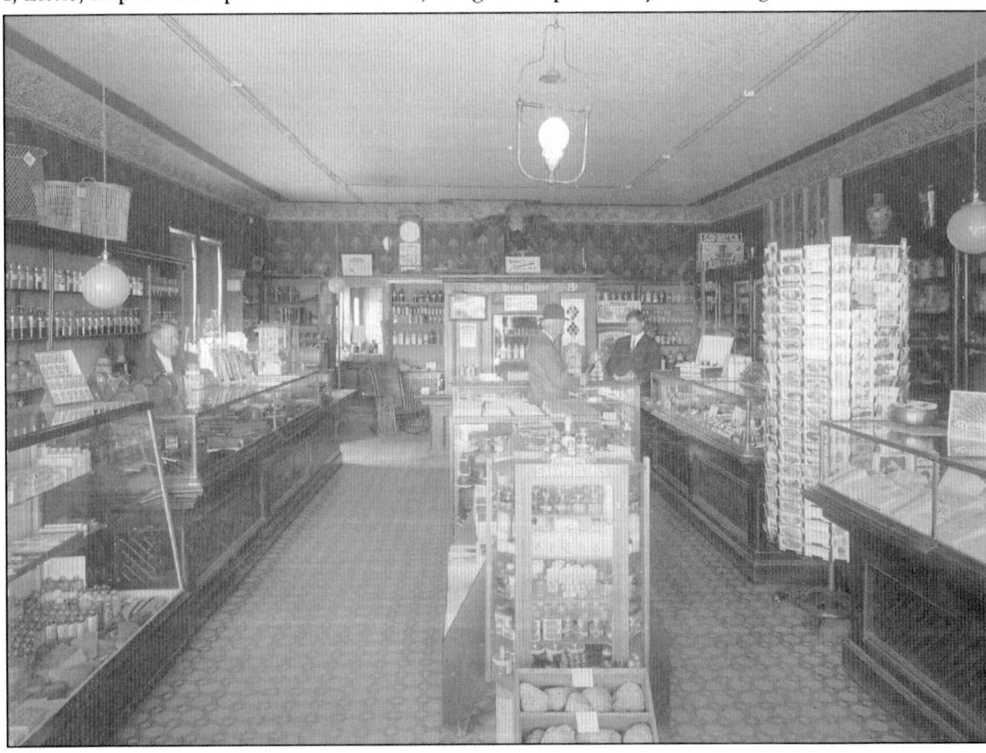

# *Three*

# A Town in Deed

By 1907, Friday Harbor's development was threatened by rising insurance costs stemming from no police or fire protection. Moreover, the town was still drawing water from private wells and a rapidly polluted spring under its namesake street, and sewage was handled by privy and cesspool.

The solution, said the *Friday Harbor Journal* in 1906, was incorporation, which would bring local control, law and order, fire protection, "100 conveniences," and increased civic pride. Community leader L. B. Carter agreed, saying, "We must incorporate and build here the prettiest city on the island sea . . . even if our taxes are a little higher."

Two years later, a "Convention of Incorporation" was held on January 12, 1909, and attended by 53 of the town's 400 residents. This was despite rumblings from the Anti-Saloon League, who railed against Saloon Best owner Jack Douglas for being on the convention steering committee. But three weeks later, incorporation was validated in a general election—70 for, 55 against.

It was no accident that those elected to the first council were prominent businessmen who also served on the steering committee. They included John Douglas, "prominent liquor dealer;" L. B. Carter, merchant; Norman E. Churchill, merchant; Sam Bugge, creamery owner; and Dr. C. L. McKinns, dentist. Bank president Gene Gould was elected mayor and bank vice president Clarence M. Tucker treasurer. But if Douglas and his fellow saloon keepers were cocky about the future of their industry, their hopes were soon dashed by the stomp of big government. In late February, the council passed an ordinance regulating sales of intoxicating liquors and socked saloons $700 per year for licenses. This amounted to double taxation, as they were already paying county fees. To add further insult, saloons were also directed to post $1,000 bonds, limit operating hours from 6:00 a.m. to 11:00 p.m., and close on Sunday. The landlords cried foul, but the public was more alarmed by a polluted well that triggered an outbreak of typhoid fever. The town stepped in, and it seemed that incorporation had come in the nick of time.

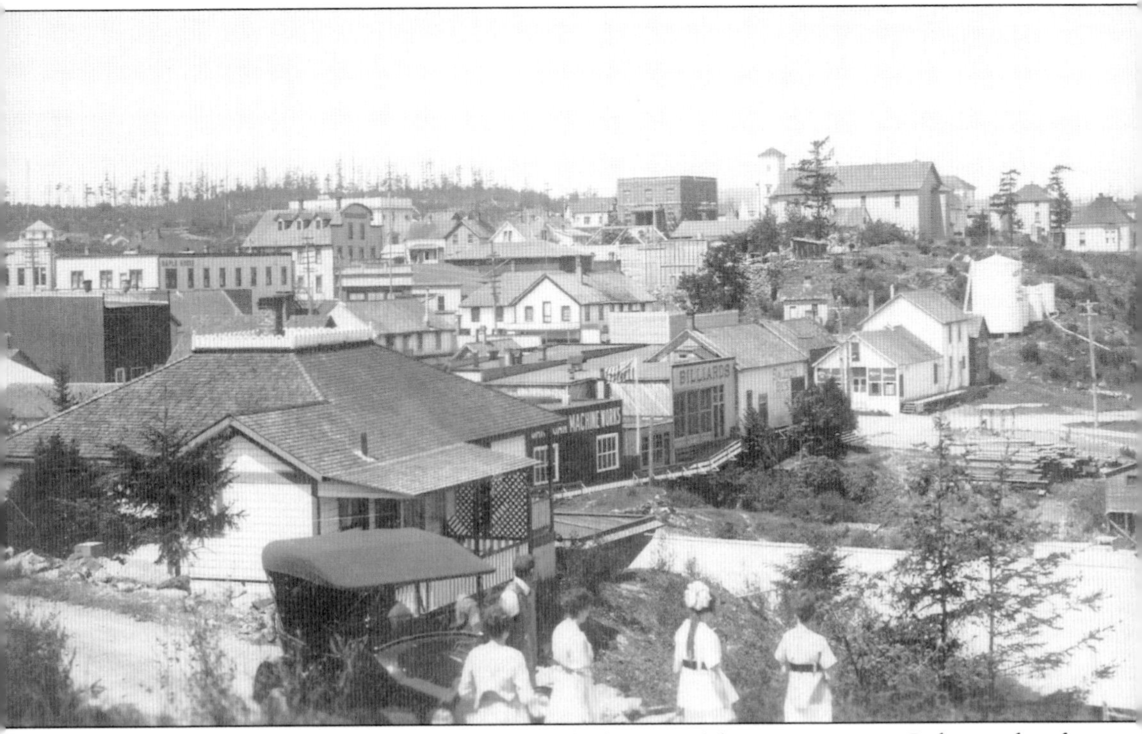

An automobile stops along Warbass Way to afford a view of the growing town. Only months after incorporation (the Saloon Best is still in business), Friday Harbor was booming. A number of successful businesses sprinkled the town, including L. B. Carter's new brick department store next to the Ross Building on Spring Street between First and Second Streets. Crowning the hills above the businesses are the county courthouse, the Masonic and Odd Fellows lodges, and the town's consolidated school and water tower. When the town council in 1912 approved a gravity-fed water system originating at Trout Lake, a real estate boom ensued until property owners along the route balked, stalling any expansion. But with the cannery requiring 15,000 gallons of water a day to operate in the summer months (it had reopened in 1909 after several years closure for lack of water), the property owners soon changed their tune. The system was completed and on line by 1913.

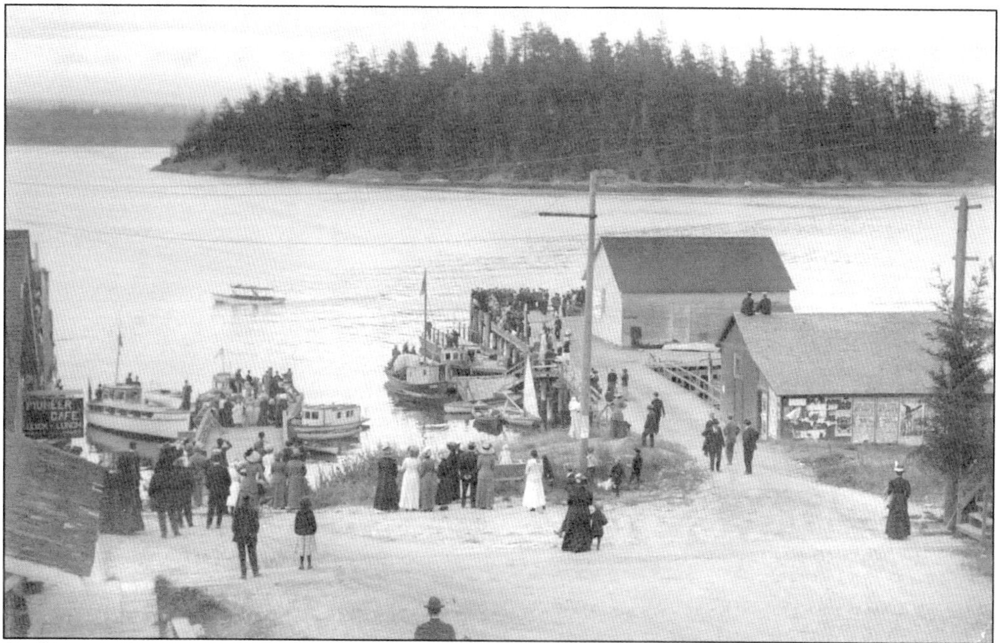


In this c. 1906 view, Spring Street slopes into the bay prior to the creation of the rock bulkhead. Passengers boarding the smaller launches used the ramp to access what was to become known, in several guises over the years, as the "city float." Joseph Sweeney's old warehouse, bottom right, is the only structure, save for the bulkhead, still standing.

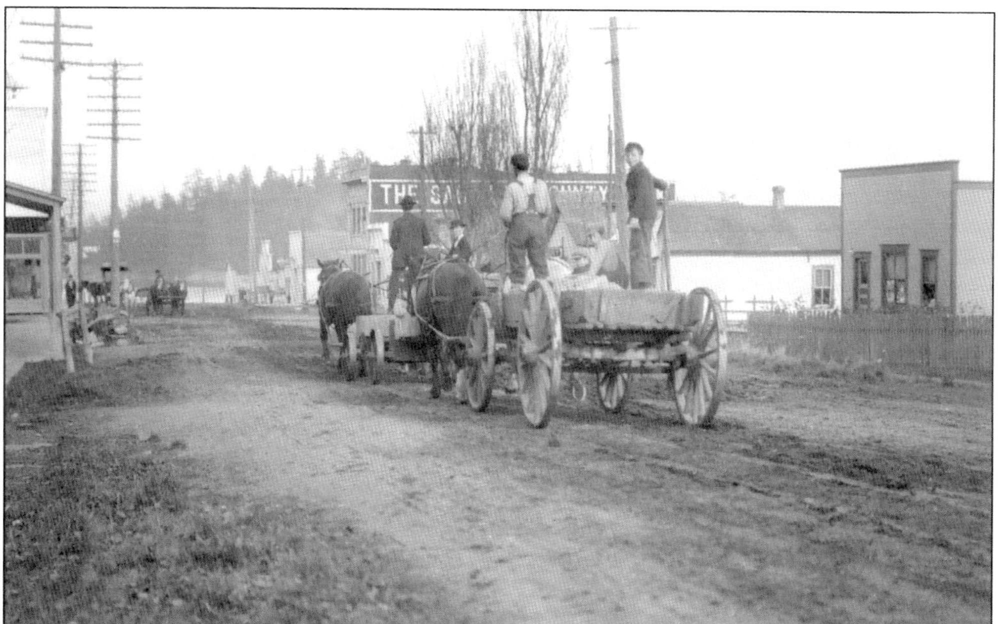

As any Friday Harbor gardener will attest, rocks are one of the island's richest natural resources. Here two wagon teams haul loads down Spring Street to the waterfront. Shortly after incorporation, the council voted to build a retaining wall and public dock, and to plank the frontage road.

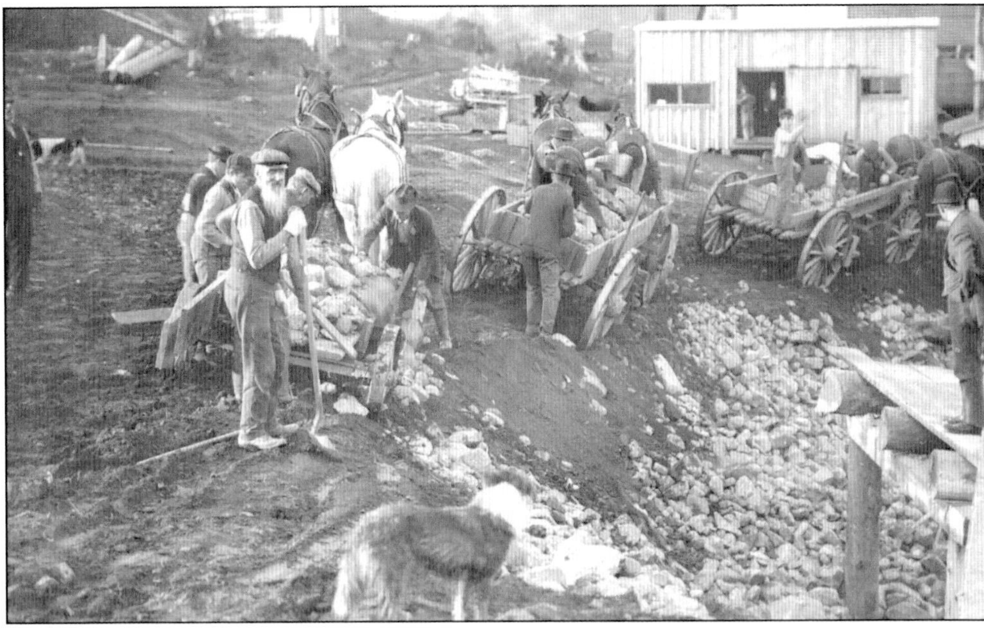

Volunteers manhandle boulders out of the wagon beds and tumble them to the waterline from Front Street's dirt track. The man with the white beard may be Charles McKay, whose blacksmith shop was just around the block. At far right, a man "supervises" from the dock while two dogs kibitz. Friday Harbor always has been a dog town.

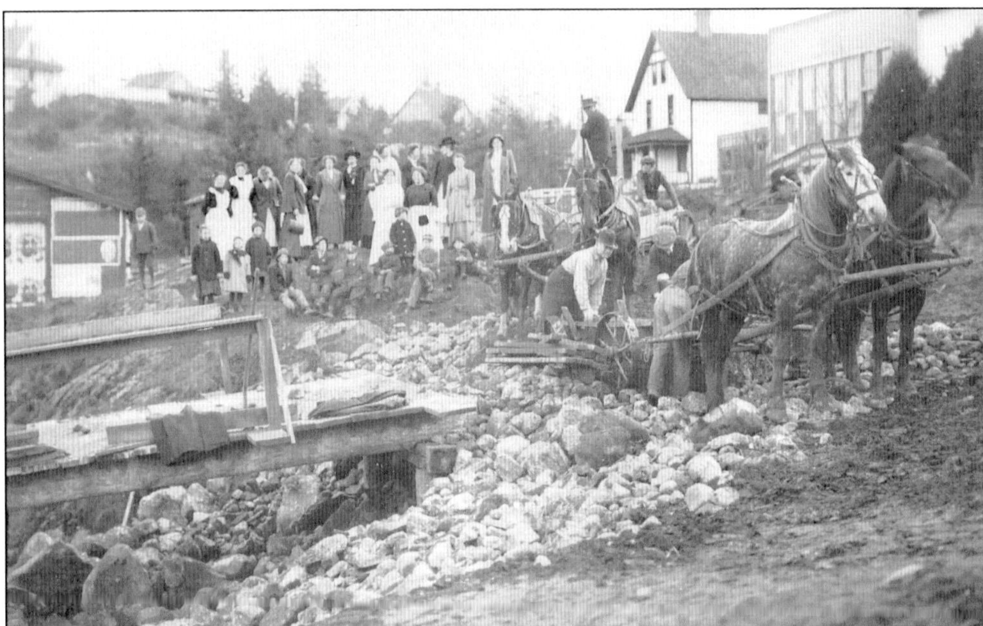

Dray horses wait patiently as rocks are added to the pile, which by now has enclosed the front of the pier piles. The cannery manager's house and the poolroom of the Saloon Best face Front Street, and Sweeney's 1870s vintage warehouse endured, though plastered with posters.

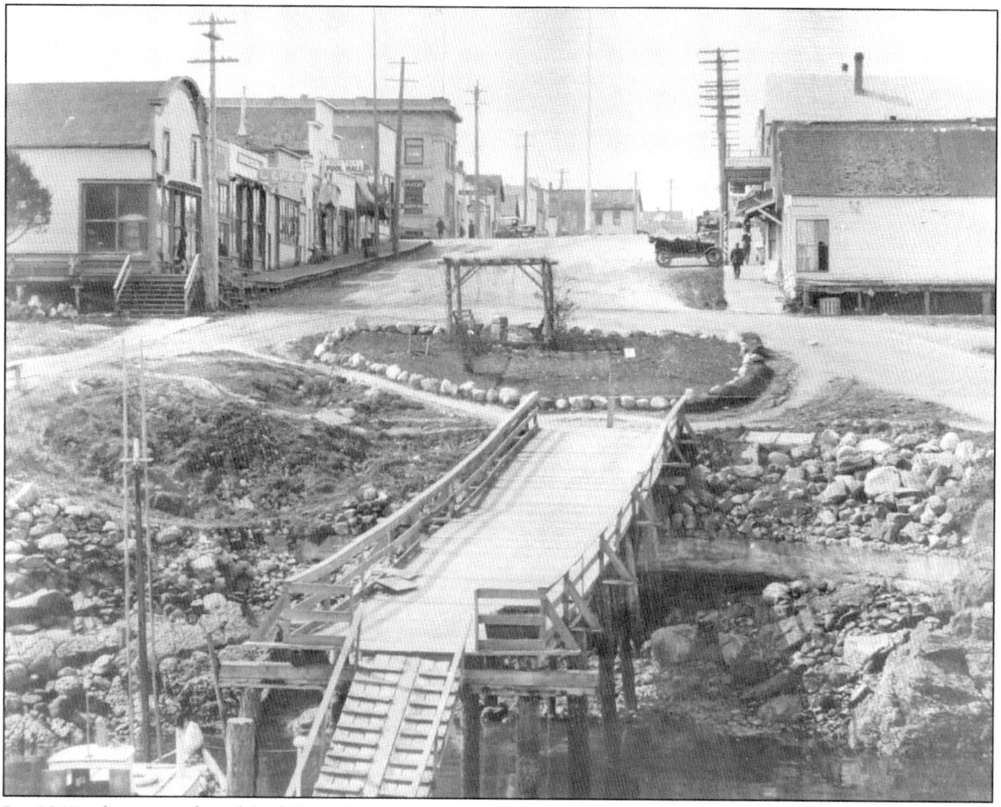

In 1917, the completed bulkhead was a tiny, tidy park encircled by stones, presumably surplus from the riprap operation. An arbor was erected in hopes of a shady rest at some future date. The flagpole in the intersection of First and Spring Streets was erected as a show of patriotism on the U.S. entry into World War I but was removed after one too many Model Ts wrapped around it.

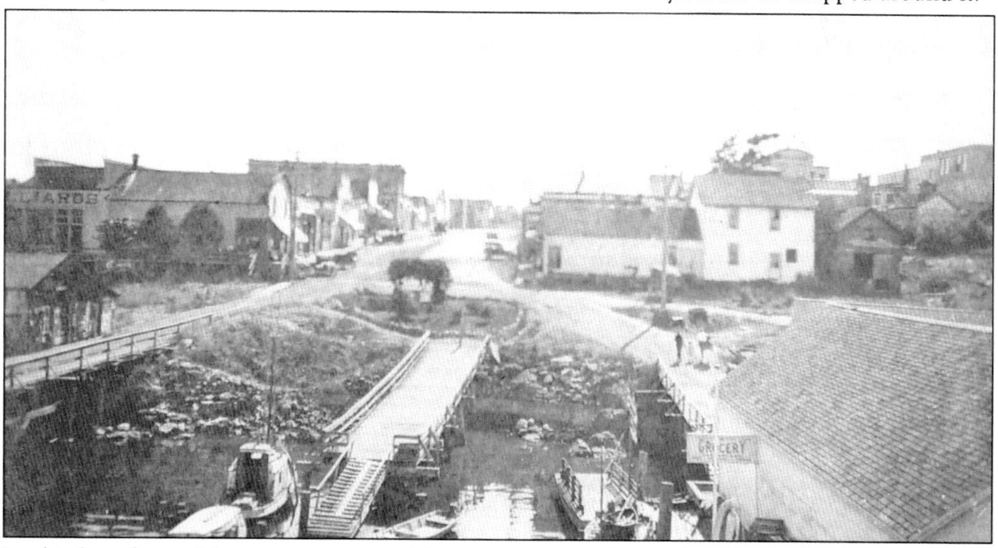

In this broader and later perspective of the same view as above, the arbor is leafing out, but no monument has been erected. The McKenzie dock at right was the main commercial wharf, although steamers could also tie up at the cannery landing.

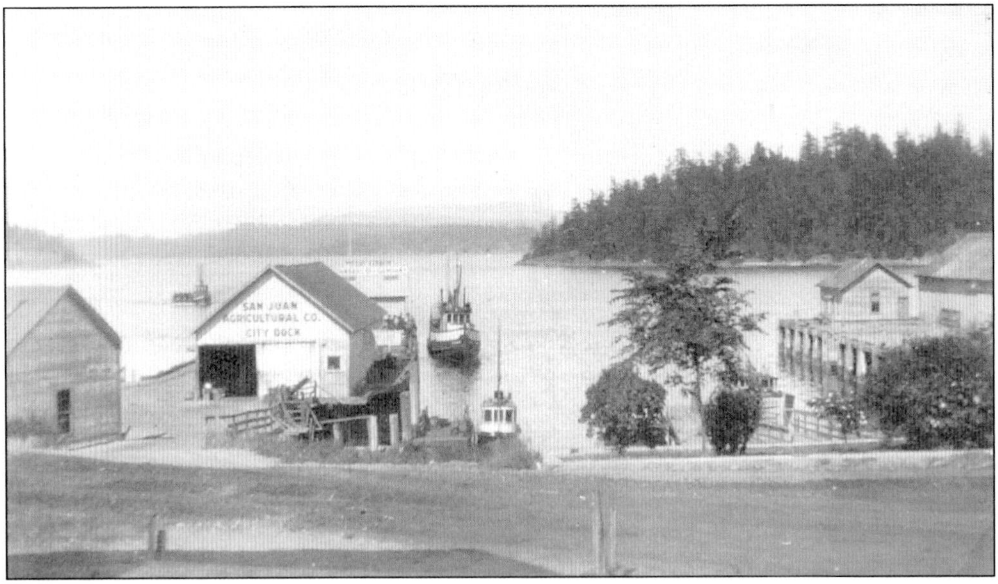


Several more years have passed, and the shrubbery in the park has matured, providing the setting for what will become Memorial Park. McKenzie's warehouse is still at left, and Carter's dock is beginning to show wear at far right. The McKenzie dock served as the town's ferry dock from the mid-1920s until the new one was installed in 1968.

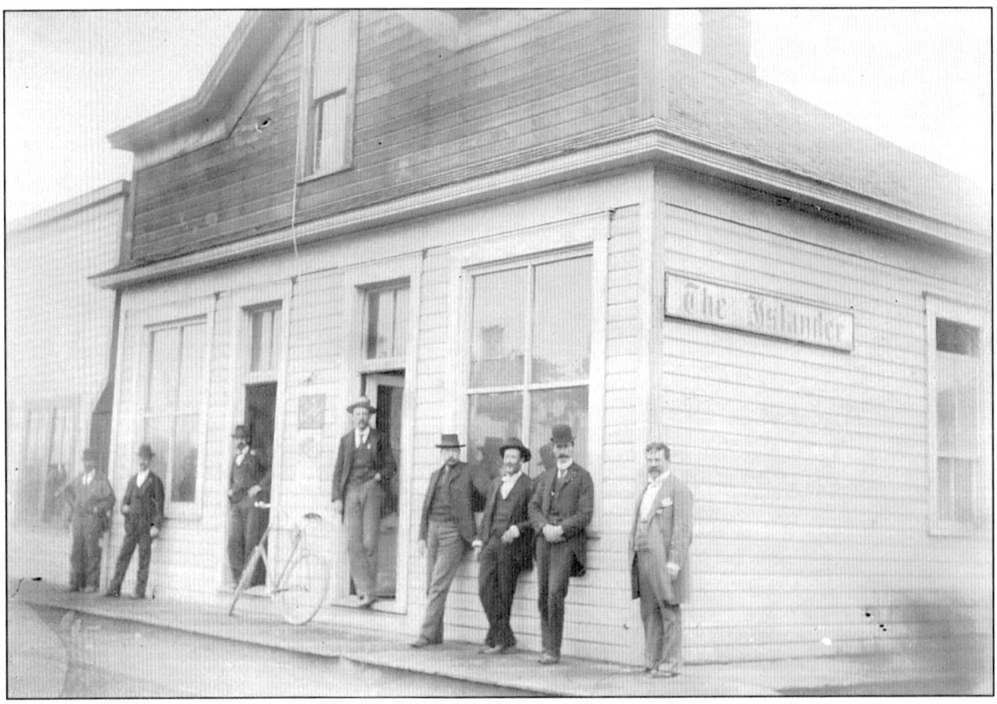


The *Islander* was Friday Harbor's first newspaper, but businessmen embraced the more liberal *Friday Harbor Journal* when it was established in 1907. When incorporation seemed assured, the *Islander* recommended Pickett (for Gen. George E.) as the town's new name. The *Journal* promoted Corbell, the maiden name of Pickett's widow, LaSalle. Other proposals were Alderbrook, Bonneyview, and Warbass.

*Friday Harbor Journal* editor and publisher Virgil Frits locks up after a long day at the linotype machine. The newspaper was founded in 1906 by Oscar G. Wall and Gus A. Ludwig, the latter a journeyman printer. In 1907, the two hired Frits, who at 24 became the printer/editor. Frits owned the newspaper until he retired 51 years later, and he was known for the cold cigar that perennially dangled from his lip.

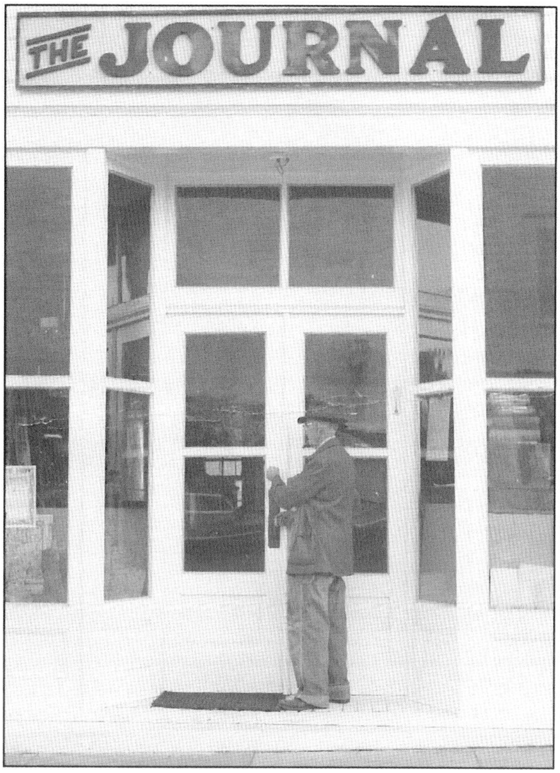


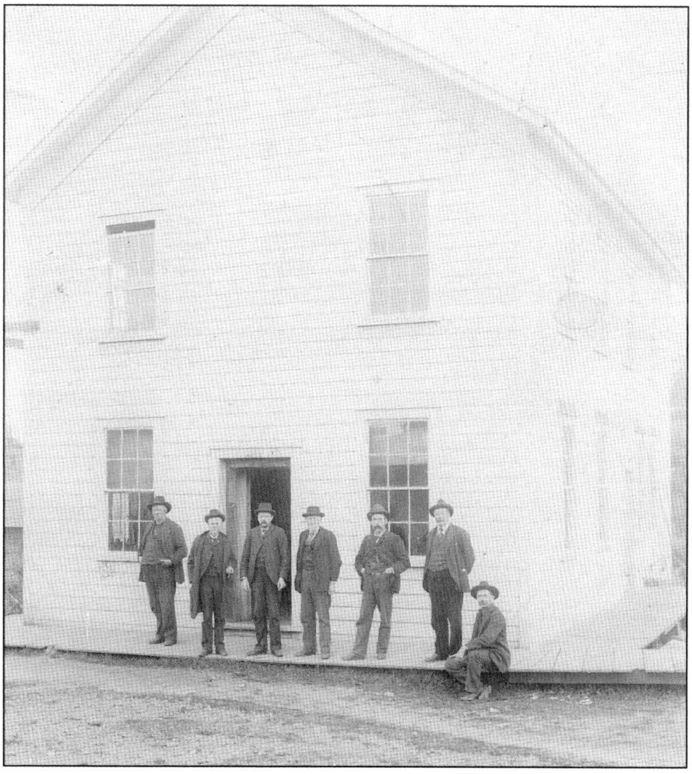

San Juan County officials line up in front of the second courthouse around 1900. In 1907, the *Friday Harbor Journal* wrote: "Let us have a local government and emerge from the state of chaos present conditions have entailed. The commissioners have given us the best such a system would permit, but the system is inimical to the best interests of Friday Harbor." It would be two years before the "yoke" was broken.

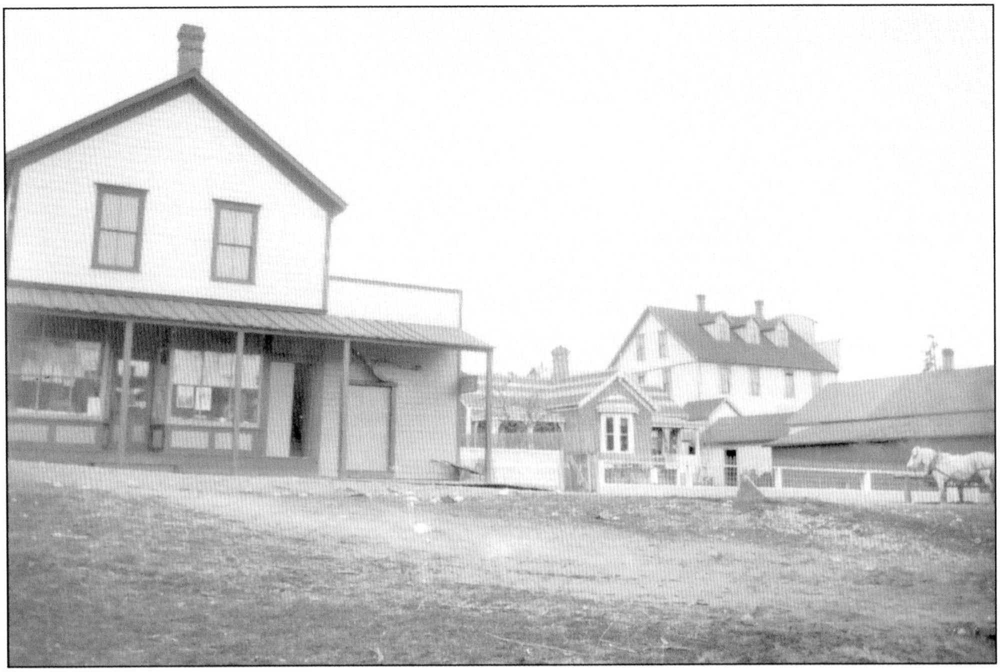

L. B. Carter's first town home sat between his Blue Front Store at far right and the Martin and Jensen store at left. The shortcomings of the town spring became acute for Carter when he had to draw water from his house well to make concrete blocks for his new store building, which would be erected, literally, in his front yard. Compare this with the images on page 25. (WMHA.)

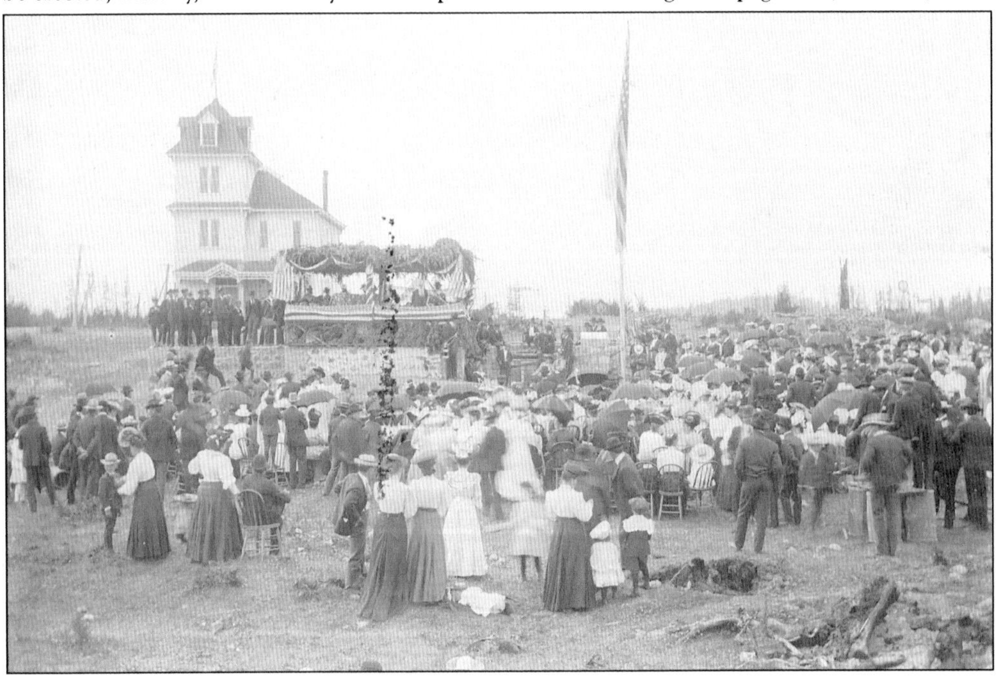

The major local event in 1906 was construction of the new San Juan County Courthouse at Second and Court Streets. Despite the rain, citizens gathered on June 29, when the cornerstone (of Roche Harbor limestone) was laid just below the 1889-vintage all-grades school.

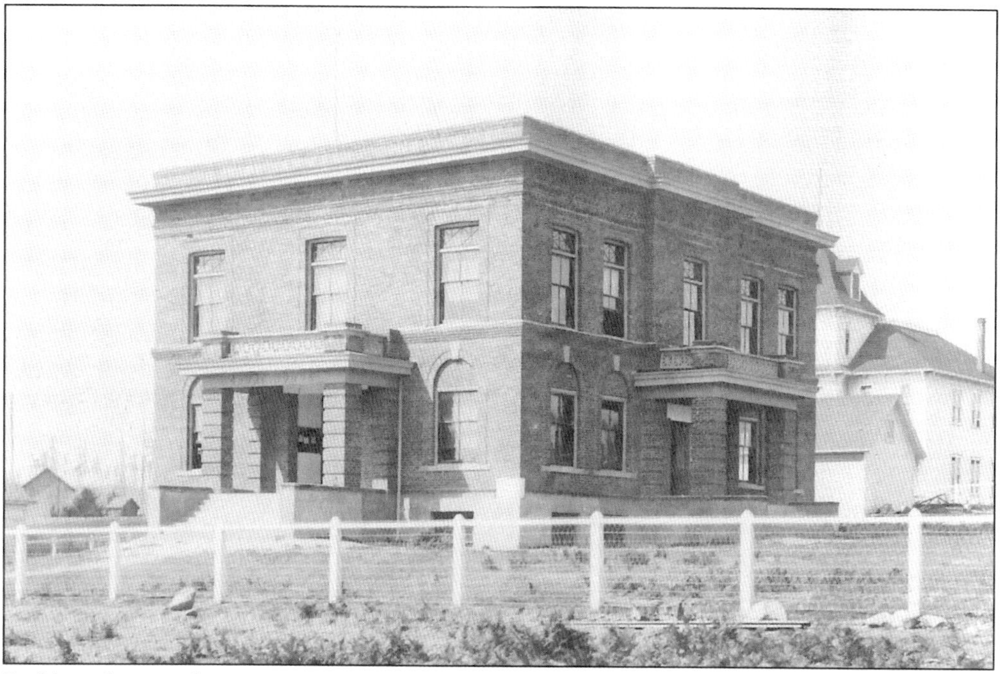

Building the courthouse was not a smooth operation. During construction, the roof fell through the second floor, but the building was finished on December 20 at a cost of $13,950. Unfortunately, the larger rooms were unsuitable because central heating had not been installed, and in February, just two months after completion, the floor collapsed during a county commissioners meeting.

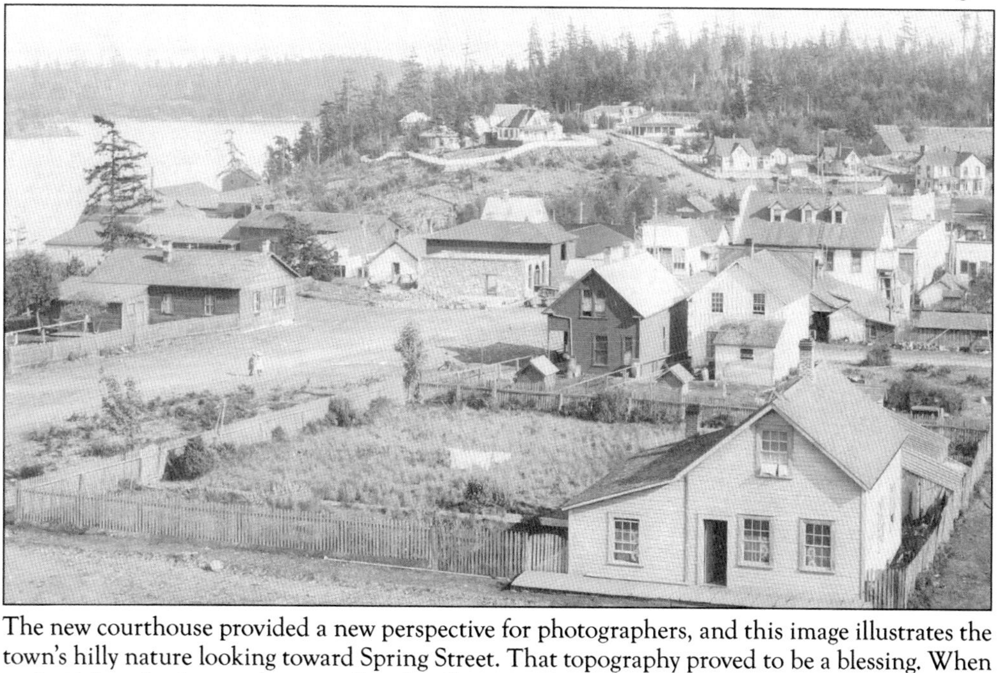

The new courthouse provided a new perspective for photographers, and this image illustrates the town's hilly nature looking toward Spring Street. That topography proved to be a blessing. When typhoid fever broke out due to polluted wells caused by the cesspool method of treating sewage, Mayor Gene C. Gould installed a trunk sewer line that followed the watershed to the bay from the head of Spring Street.

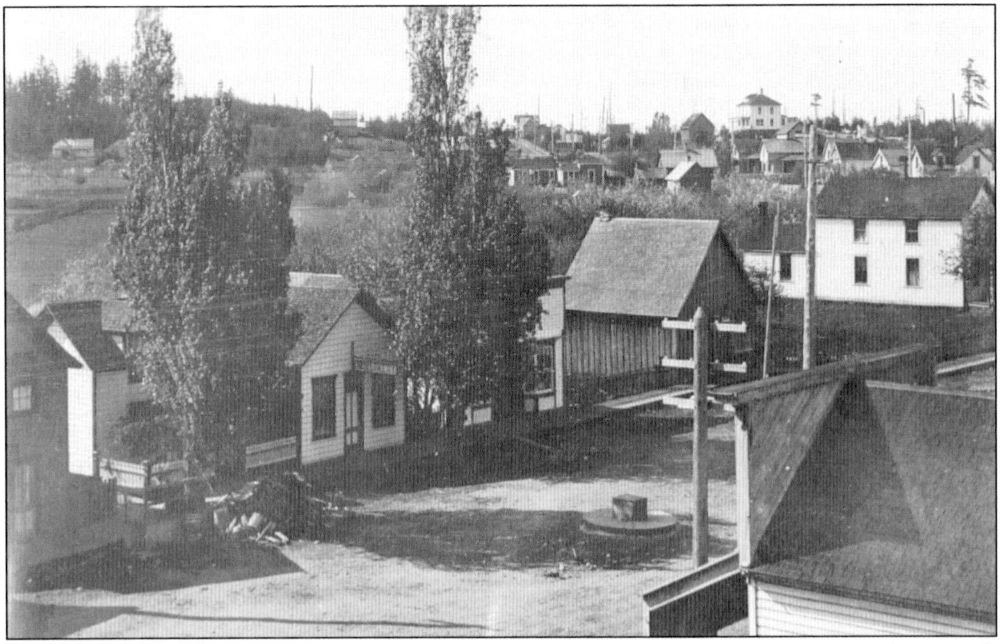

The long-inadequate town pump on Spring Street (right center) was capped when this photograph was taken around 1910. In 1911, the town council approved a gravity system of 10-inch cedar pipe to run from Trout Lake, 5 miles west. Voters approved water and an improved sewer system at a cost of $16,000, and the spring was eventually routed by pipe into the bay.

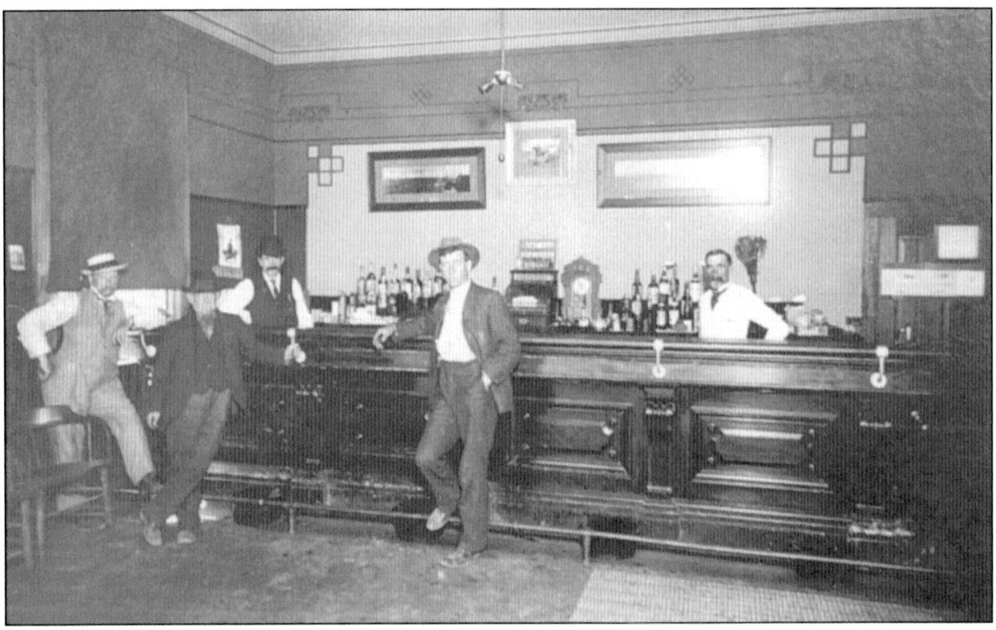

Saloon Best patrons were likely as appalled as owner Jack Douglas (third from left) when, after a stirring, hour-long temperance sermon in 1910 by the renowned Rev. Billy Sunday in the Odd Fellows Hall, the town council voted three to one banning the sale of alcohol within town limits. "Emergency" saloons were soon established in outlying areas.

# *Four*

# A Town on an Inland Sea

Incorporation provided the muscle the town needed to grow through an infrastructure built on fines ("stragglers at night" were fined $5, "bulls running at large," $25) and tax revenues (male dogs cost $2, females, $5). But the waterfront remained its beating heart. Beyond the thriving cannery and mill, the steamers that called daily provided a vital link with the world. Then, as now, waterborne transportation was a grudging fact of life in island living.

Several steamship companies operating out of Seattle, Bellingham, and Anacortes connected Friday Harbor to the mainland by 1910. The vessels included large passenger-freight carriers and smaller launches serving Anacortes and the islands. The steam vessels' boilers consumed two cords of wood at a time, which accounts for numerous photographs of docks stacked high with firewood.

The system was imperfect at first, as passengers and freight handlers could wait through the night for their ships to come in. Seattle captains, in particular, were notoriously cavalier about the island schedule. Moreover, the sole providers—Seattle companies such as Straits Steamship Company and the Puget Sound Navigation Company (the future Black Ball Line)—could charge exorbitant fares.

Capt. Andrew Newhall of Orcas lowered fares by introducing local routes aboard the *Buckeye* and *Islander*. This lasted until he moved to San Juan in 1906 and sold his line south. A second *Islander* was built in 1920 in the Jensen Shipyard to provide local service, but she was sold off after her quirky diesel engine died. She was refitted for steam in Seattle, renamed the *Mohawk*, and thereafter was operated by the competition.

By the 1920s, the old freight-passenger and excursion ships were doomed by increased automobile and truck traffic, which in the end killed Friday Harbor's produce and canning industries because mainland shipping costs were less. Some vessels were retrofitted as automobile ferries. But limited capacity and protracted loading times spurred the Black Ball Line by the 1930s to build or purchase ships specially designed for vehicular traffic. Among the first were the home-built *Vashon* and ferries from San Francisco Bay such as the *Klickitat*.

The ferry line era had begun.

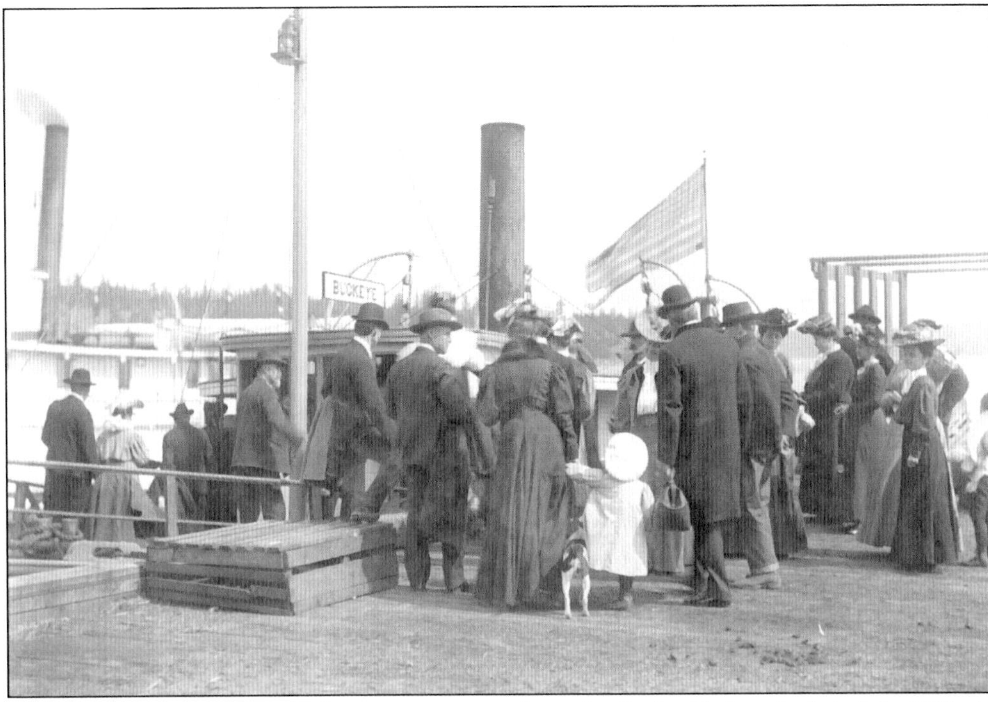


The steamer *Buckeye* (above) takes on passengers from the Friday Harbor dock in July 1903. At 61.5 feet long and 19.8 feet abeam, the ship was stubby in comparison with sleek Mosquito Fleet vessels such as the *Rosalie*. Built in Seattle in 1890, she displaced 80 tons and drew 7.1 feet of water, which enabled her to call at low tide in many harbors. After she foundered in Bellingham Bay in 1895 (one person was killed), she was raised and put back into service as a ferry and charter for hire. But no one seemed leery of coming aboard again, especially not these passengers, dressed to party in derbies and dresses for a Fourth of July outing (with the dog, of course). The bottom view of the *Buckeye* was probably taken that same day.

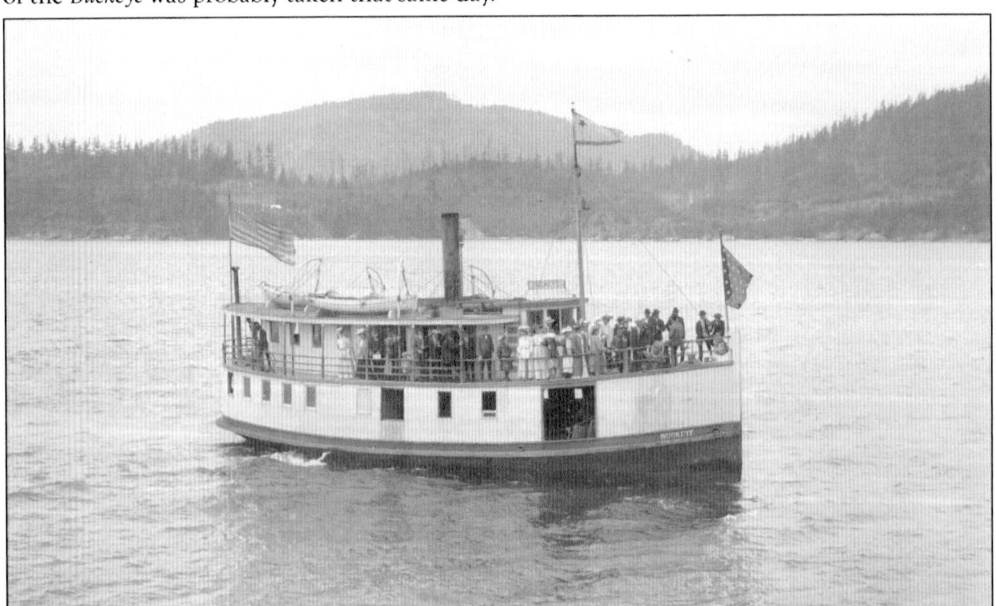

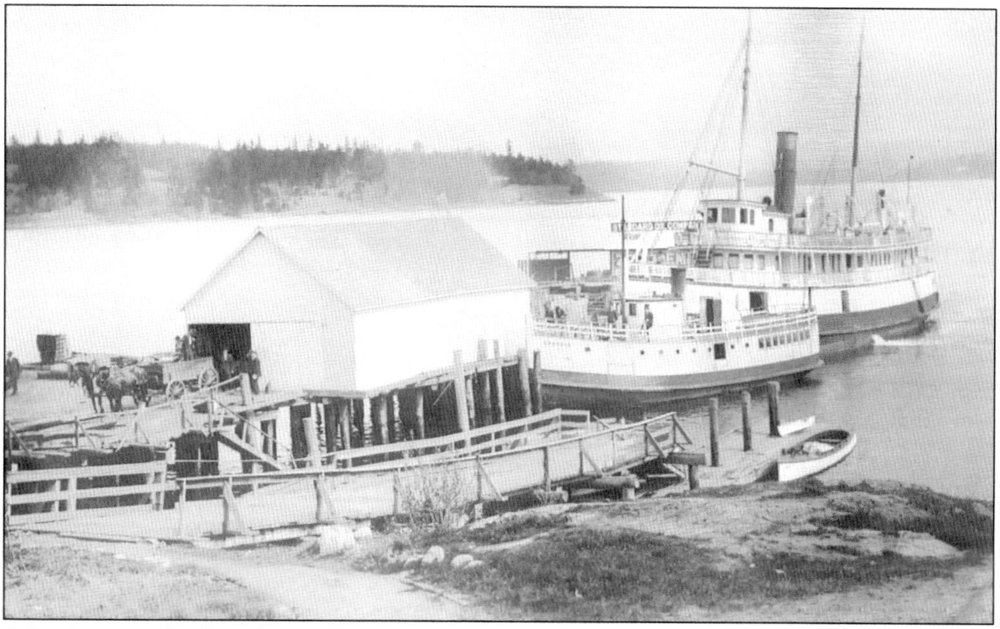

A freight wagon loads at the warehouse on the main dock at the foot of Spring Street in this *c.* 1900 view. The ships are the *Georgia* and *Rosalie*, the latter making regular runs between Bellingham and Seattle, with stops at the San Juan Islands and Anacortes along the way.

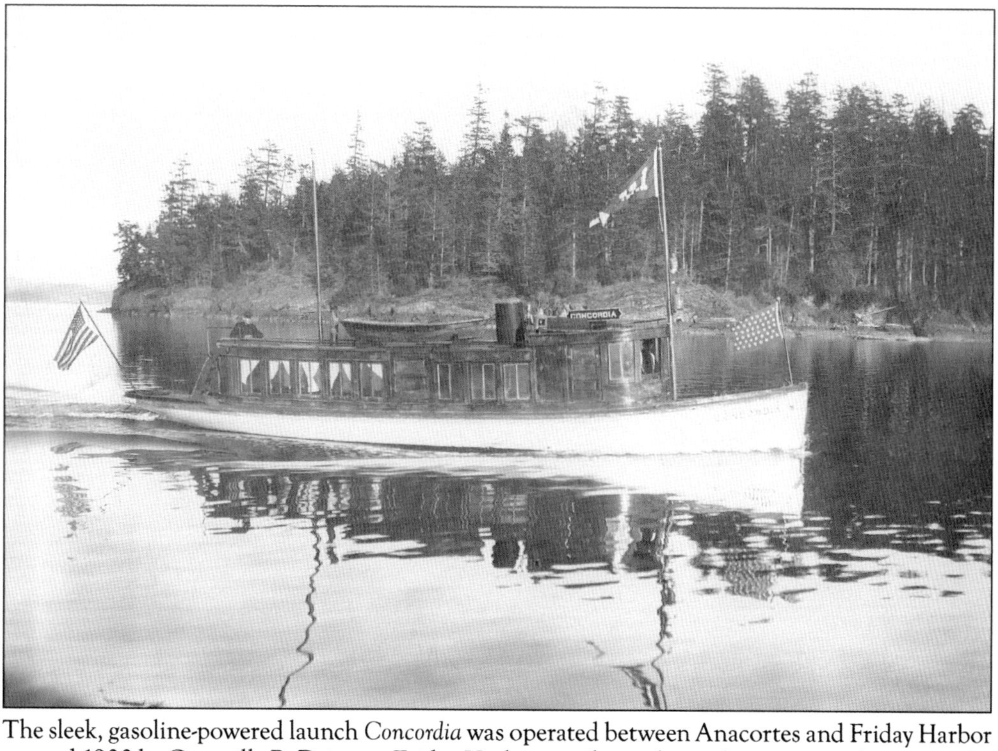


The sleek, gasoline-powered launch *Concordia* was operated between Anacortes and Friday Harbor around 1900 by Granville B. Driggs, a Friday Harbor retailer and strawberry grower known as the "Strawberry King." The vessel called at other islands when required, including Shaw, Lopez, Port Stanley, Thatcher, and Decatur. She was eventually sold and ran charters out of Friday Harbor.

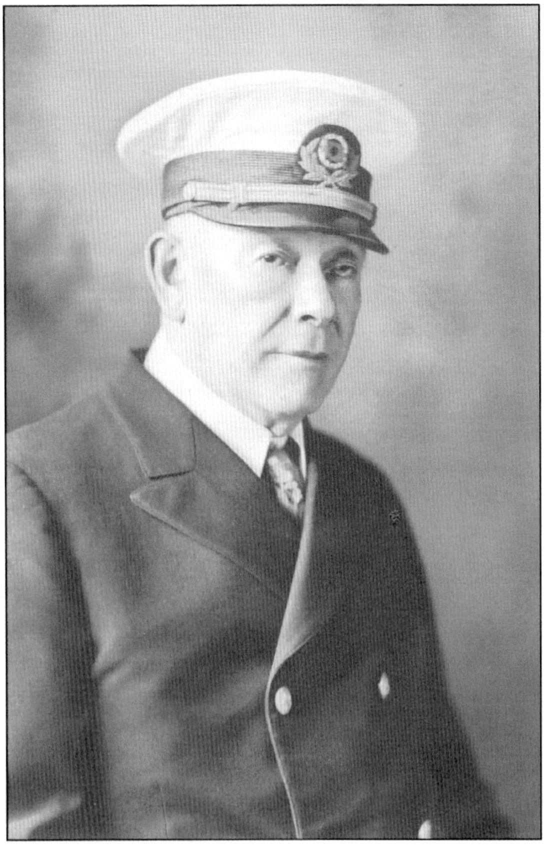

Lopez Island native Capt. Sam Barlow skippered inland steamers for 47 years and carried up to 20,000 passengers without a single major mishap. He was a living legend, in part because he once rode out gale-force winds in the *Lydia Thompson*. As historian David Richardson reports, Barlow was an "independent cuss" and once stopped in the Strait of Juan de Fuca to perform a wedding ceremony.

The *Islander* steams its way through the San Juans around 1906. This was the first vessel of that name to serve the San Juan Islands. Capt. Andrew Newhall built the 87-foot ship in 1904 at his shipyard (near where the Rosario Lodge is today). The ship performed well until Newhall retired to San Juan and sold her to California interests.

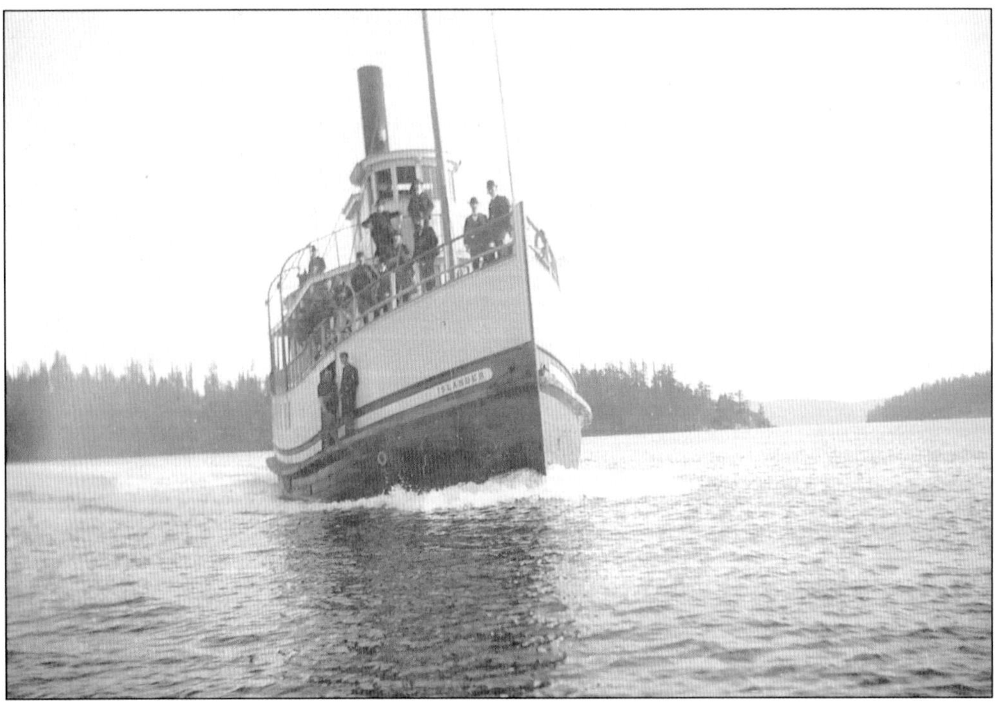

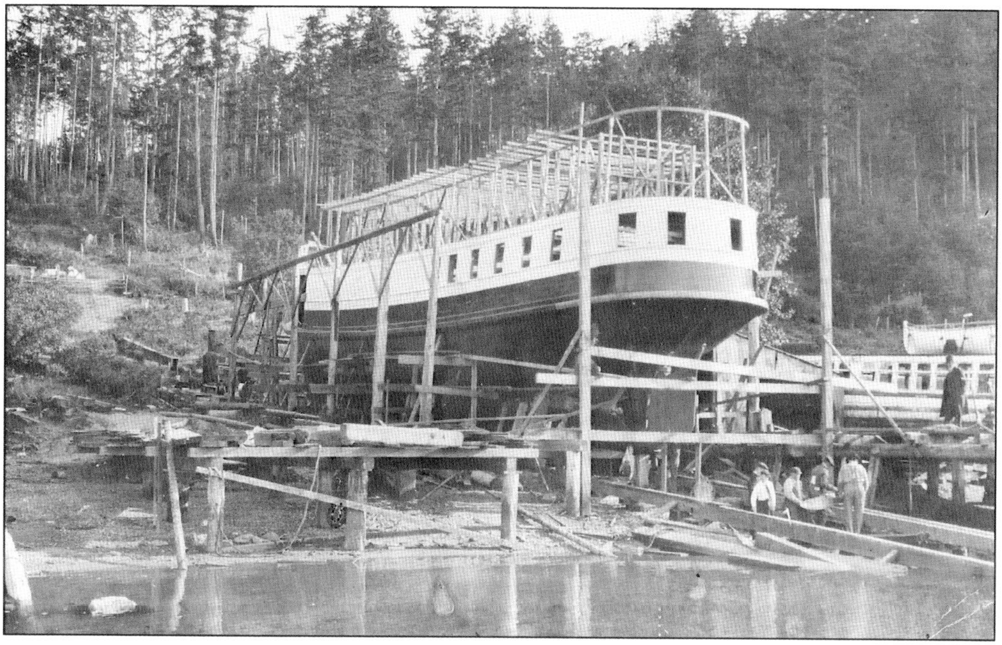

Men prepare the ways below the stern of the second *Islander*, shown here at the Jensen shipyard in Friday Harbor before launching in 1921. At 91 feet, she was the largest vessel ever constructed in the San Juans. Following passenger and automobile ferry service as the steamer *Mohawk*, she served as a tug through World War II. (Jensen family.)

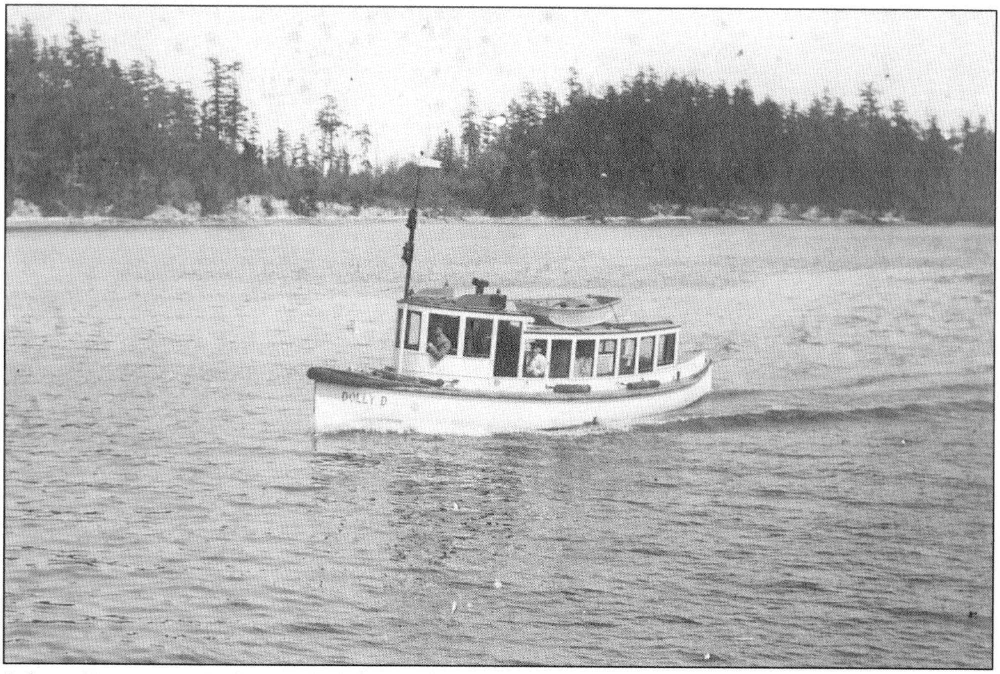

Saloon Best owner Jack Douglas's launch (and sometime smuggler) *Dolly D*, built in 1904, made scheduled runs between Anacortes and Friday Harbor, and for a time served as a research dredge for the University of Washington's biology station. Here she motors between Brown Island and Friday Harbor.

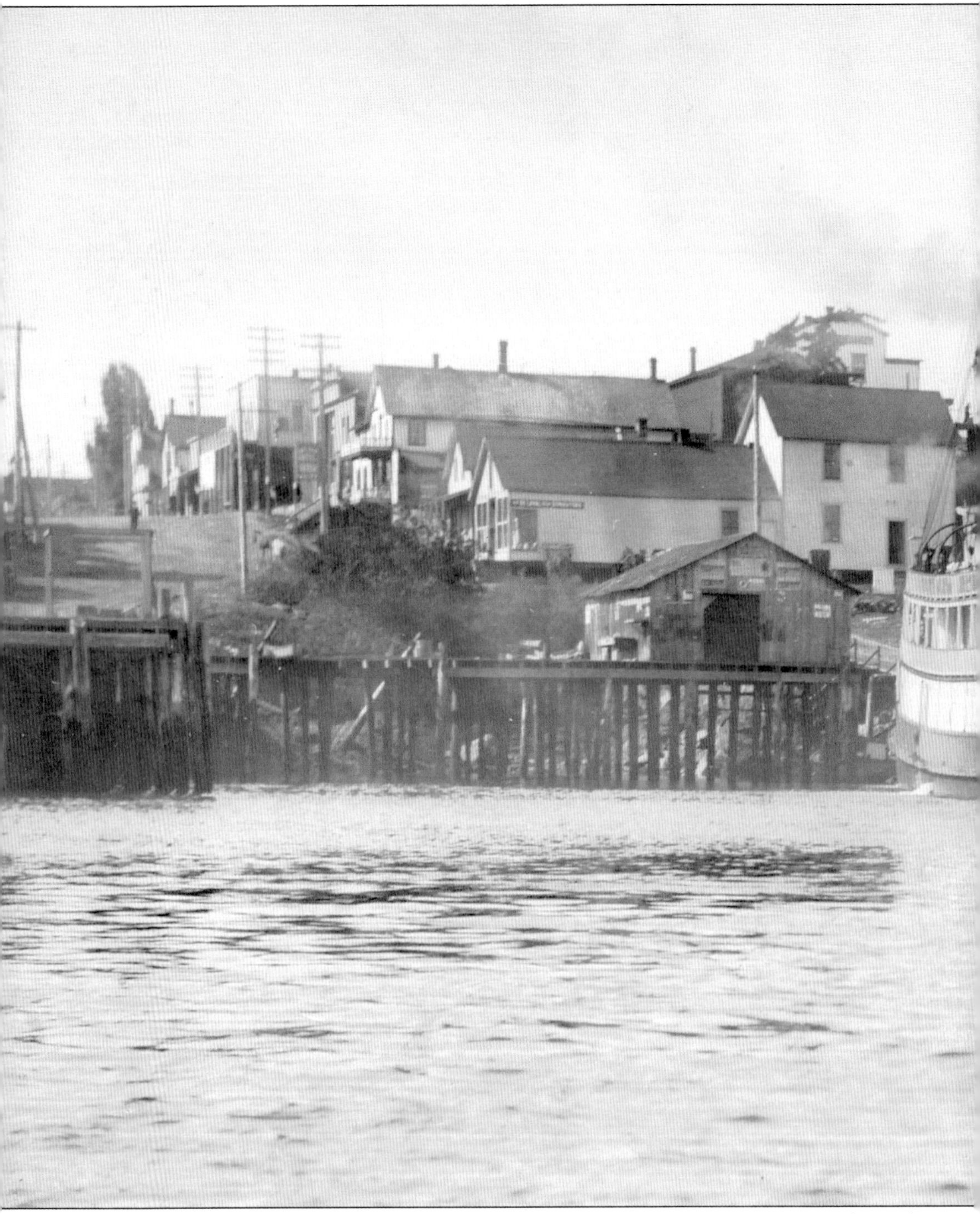

The *Lydia Thompson* (right) and *Rosalie* dock at the foot of Spring Street in 1907. The 91-foot *Thompson*, built in 1893, was a hard-luck ship. Once she nearly exploded when her drunken engine room crew piled so much wood into the boilers that they blazed red-hot. The captain intervened, and fisticuffs ensued. Not long after this photograph was taken, she struck a sandbar heading up Hood Canal, rolled onto her beam end, and was filled by the flood tide. The 136-foot *Rosalie*, also

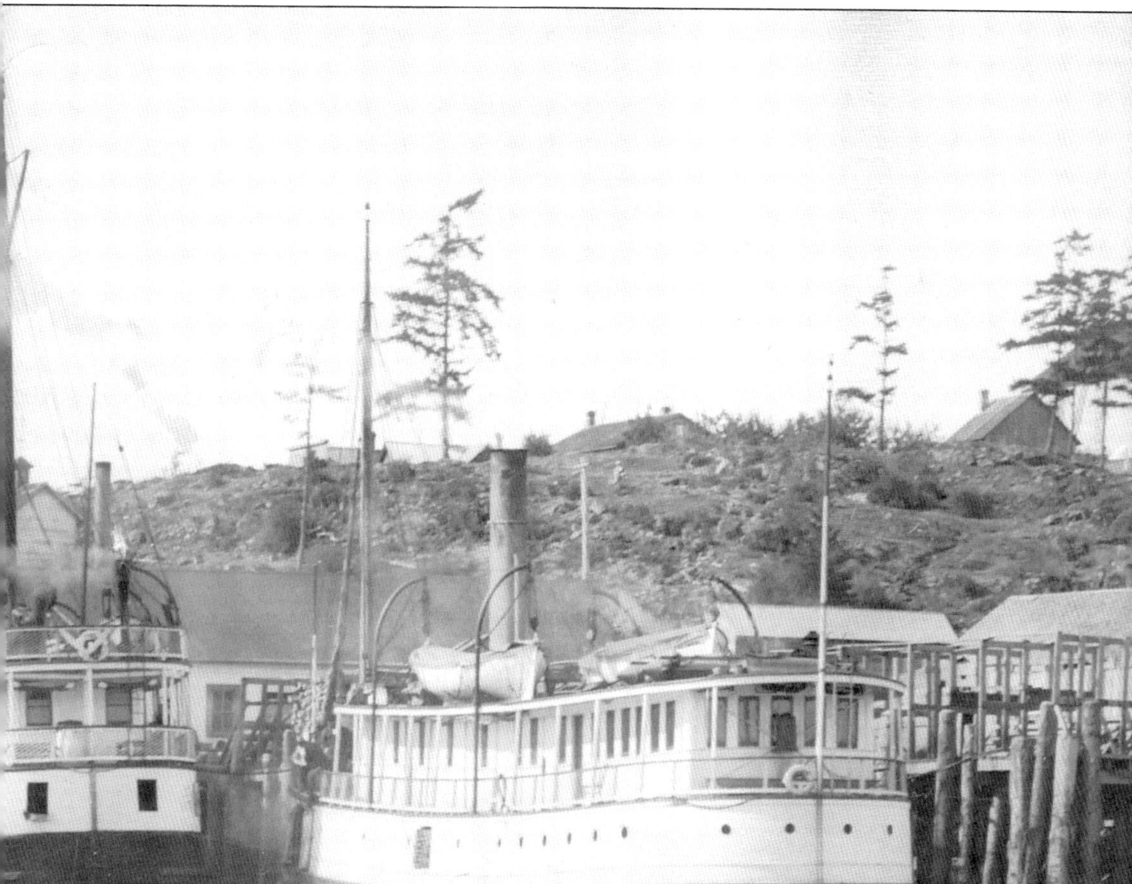


built in 1893 in Alameda, California, was far more durable. The ships kept a punishing schedule on the Seattle-to-Bellingham run. In the early years, they slowed at scattered landings and gave a blast of the whistle. Sometimes rowboats hailed them, loaded with fresh produce and flowers bound for the Pike Place Market.

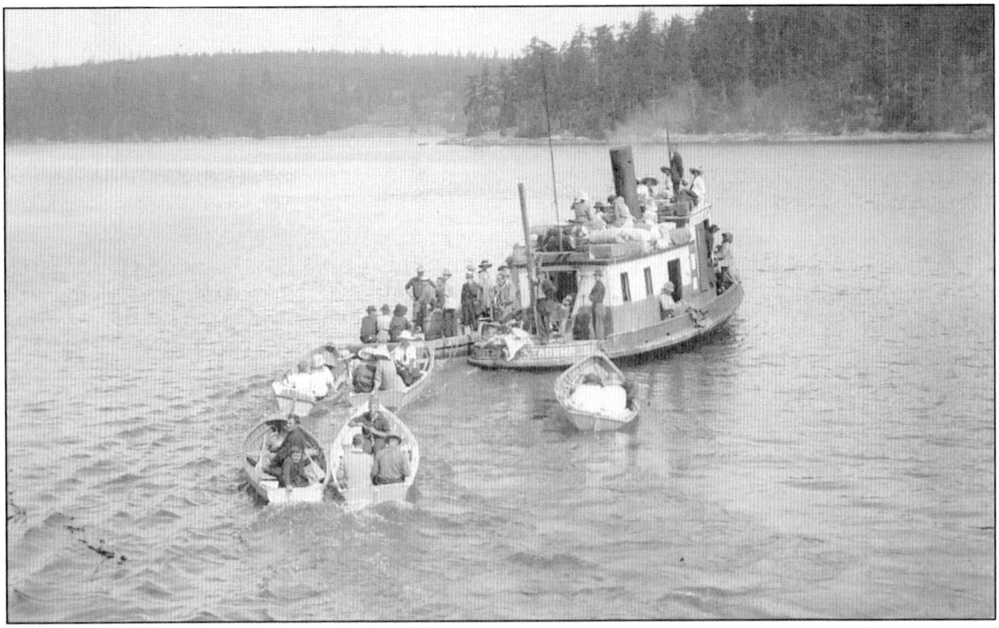

The steamer *Violet* is loaded fore to aft (and atop) with University of Washington students on their way to harvest marine biology specimens for study in the Friday Harbor Laboratories around 1911. The *Violet* served the labs—then located near the cannery—for three summers primarily to dredge for specimens but also, as shown here, to tow skiffs used for collecting close to shore.

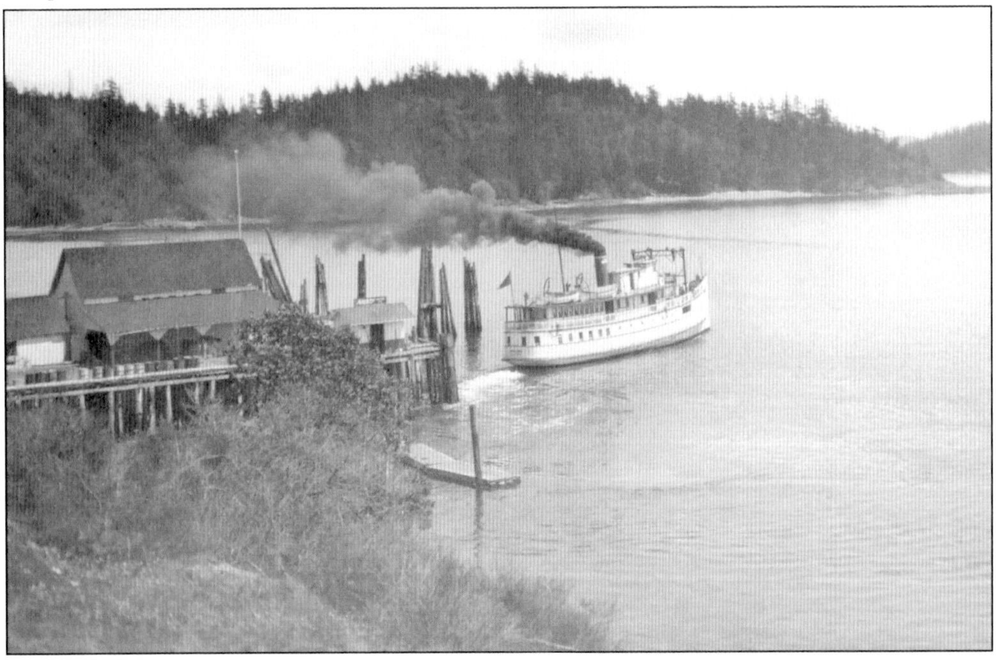

Black smoke billows from the *Mohawk* as she pulls away from a dock in the San Juan Islands. The apparatus on the ship's bow is a Barlow steam elevator. Heavy cargo, including automobiles, was pushed onto the elevator from the dock and lowered to the deck. The process was time-consuming, but islanders preferred it over "transfer boards"—two-by-sixes lashed together that made for a tenuous ride over the water.

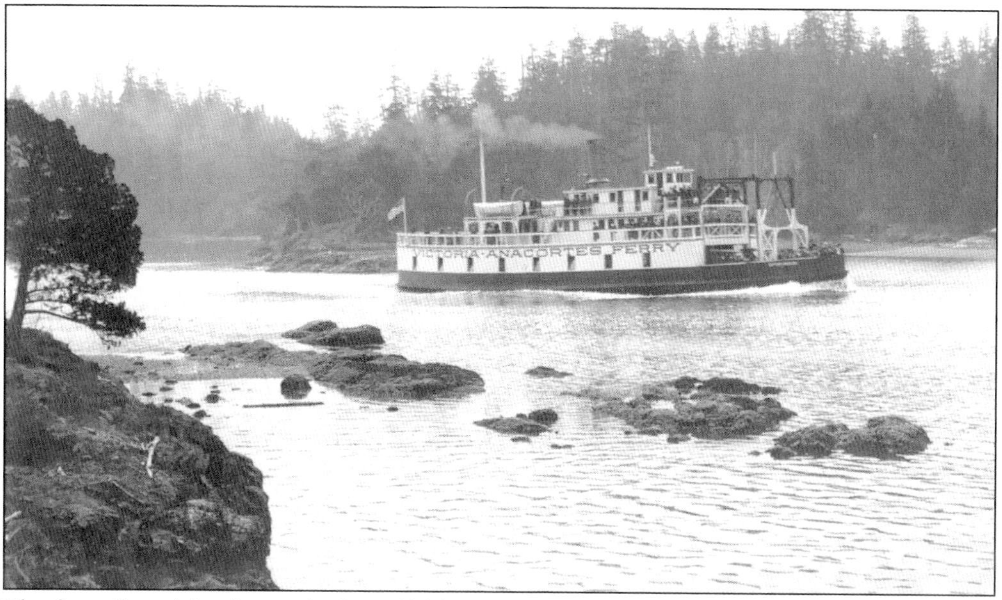


The ferry *City of Angeles* was built in 1906 as a passenger steamer. Its Anacortes–Sidney route, under the ownership of Harry Crosby (related to Bing), initially stopped at Roche Harbor. In 1930, it switched to Friday Harbor and added Shaw Island. In 1928, the fare from Anacortes to Sidney was $5 each way, $8 round trip. The route closed during 2020 pandemic.

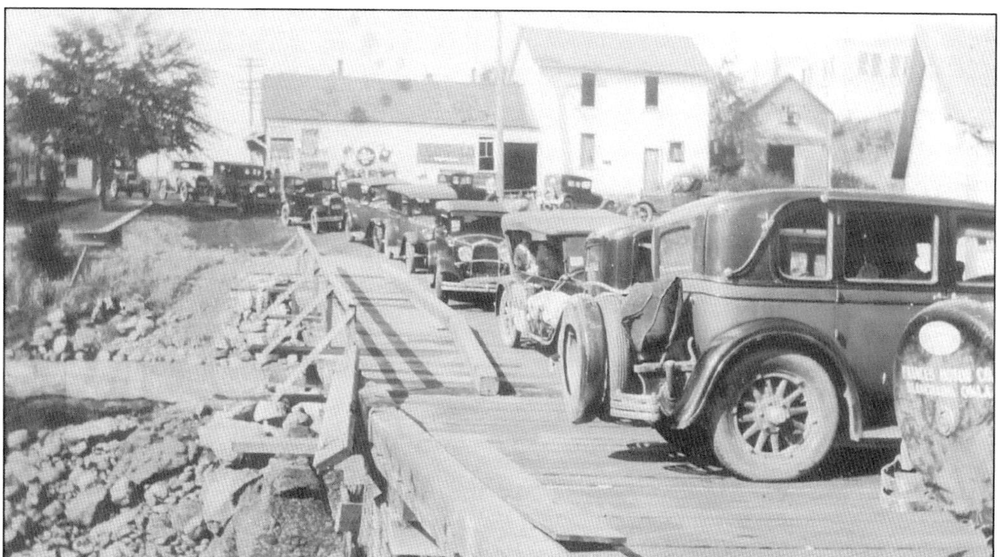

Waiting for the ferry was a pastime even in the 1920s. The increase in automobiles boosted tourism and brought part-time residents, which resulted in long ferry waits. As early as 1906, the *Friday Harbor Journal* warned that as wealthy part-time residents and tourists continued to arrive in increasing numbers, "the man of moderate means will become dispossessed through the purchasing power of wealth."

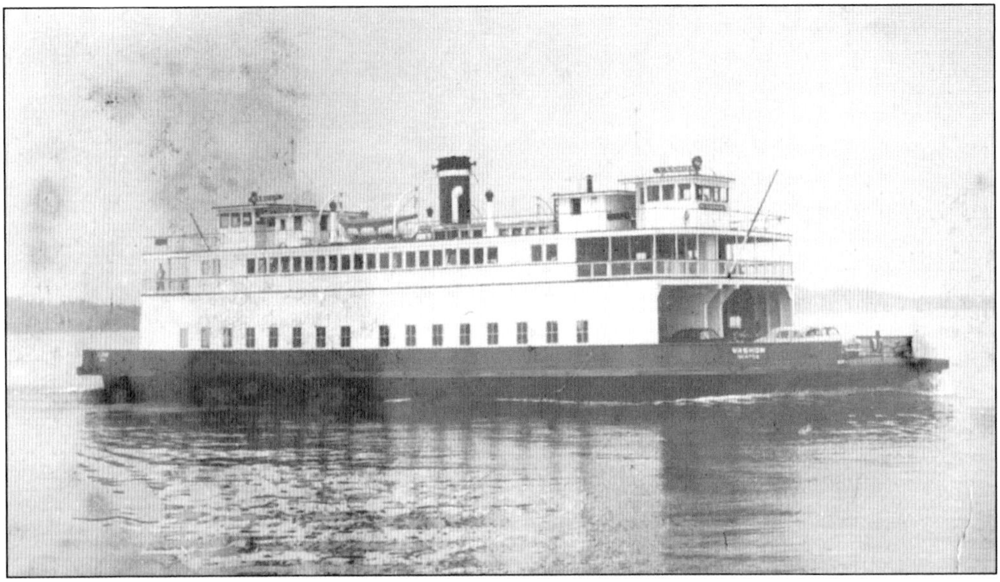

Built in 1934 on Seattle's Lake Union, the trusty *Vashon*, with its diesel engines and distinctive wooden superstructure, took over the run from *Rosario* and served Friday Harbor as the principal ferry into the 1960s. The *Vashon* came into the possession of Washington State Ferries in 1951 after the state bought out the Puget Sound Navigation Company, which had held a ferry service monopoly since 1929.

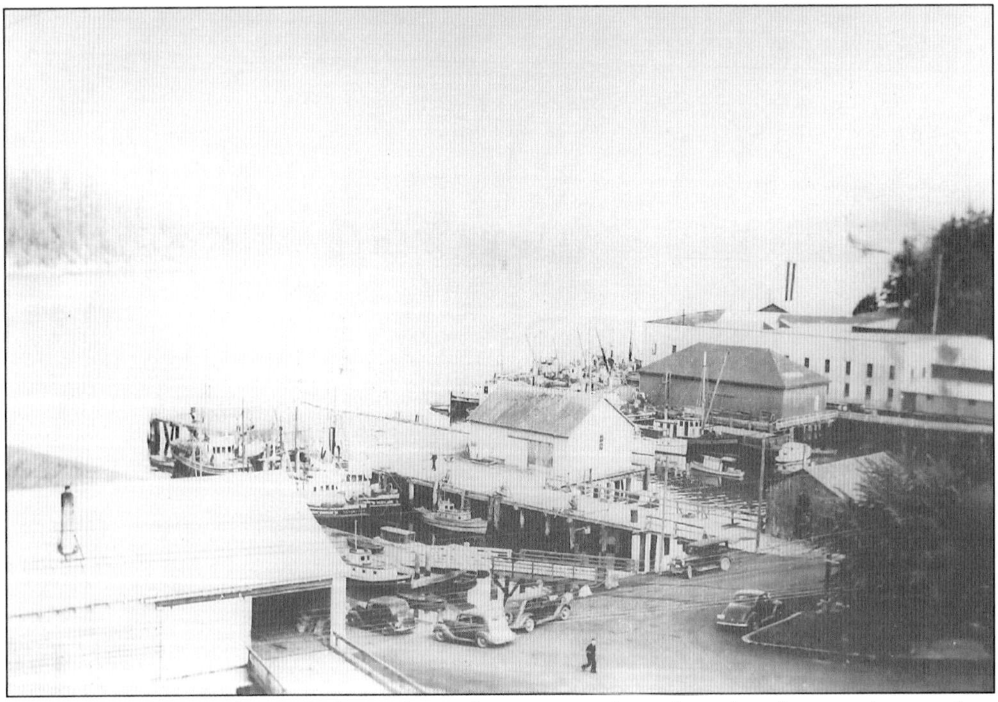

Memorial Park was at last a shady rest beneath two giant elms when this photograph was taken in the 1930s, possibly from the bluff at the end of West Street. Two automobiles at lower center queue up to board the ferry at the foot of Spring Street, and masts bristle from the fleet of purse seiners and the *Nereid*, tied up at the net house at center right.

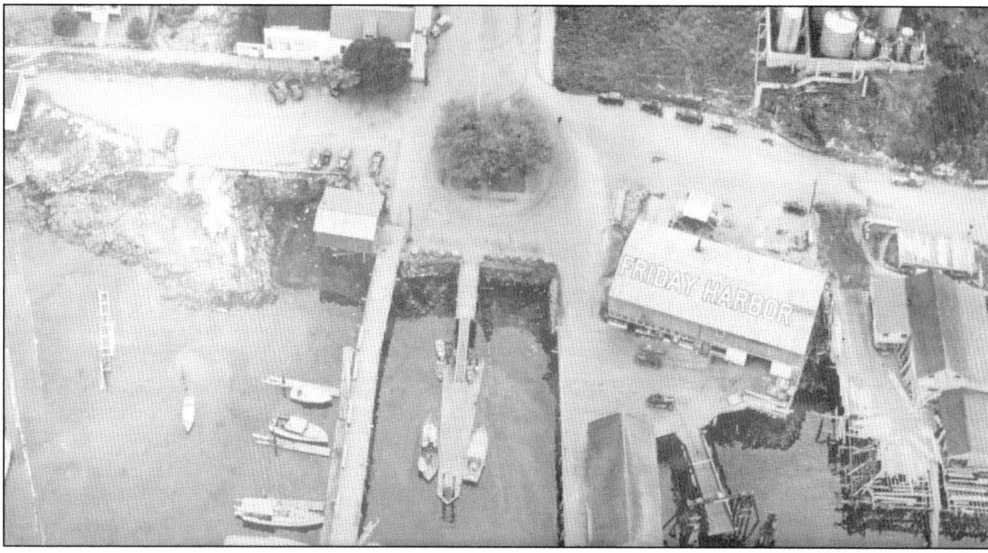


This detailed aerial view reveals the dock system at the foot of Spring Street as it existed in the mid-1940s. The ferry dock is at lower center right, just below the warehouse with "Friday Harbor" emblazoned on the roof. Through 1968, motorists queued up Spring Street around Memorial Park, spilling over onto First, Second, and Court Streets on weekends. The only breaks in the lines were at intersections.

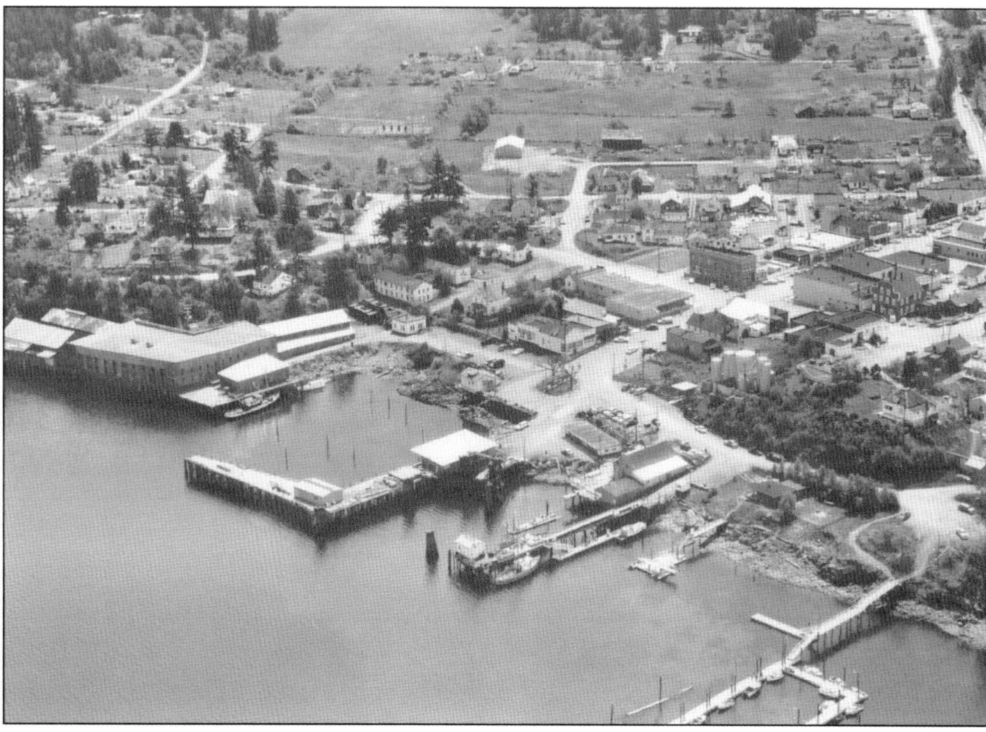

This 1950s photograph captures a blend of old and new. The city float had been removed and replaced with the L-shaped dock partially in use today. The marina at lower right was primarily for fishermen, and the cannery structures were still in place on the site of future ferry operations. Pea shelling machines, parked below the dormitory at center left, indicate a revived pea industry.

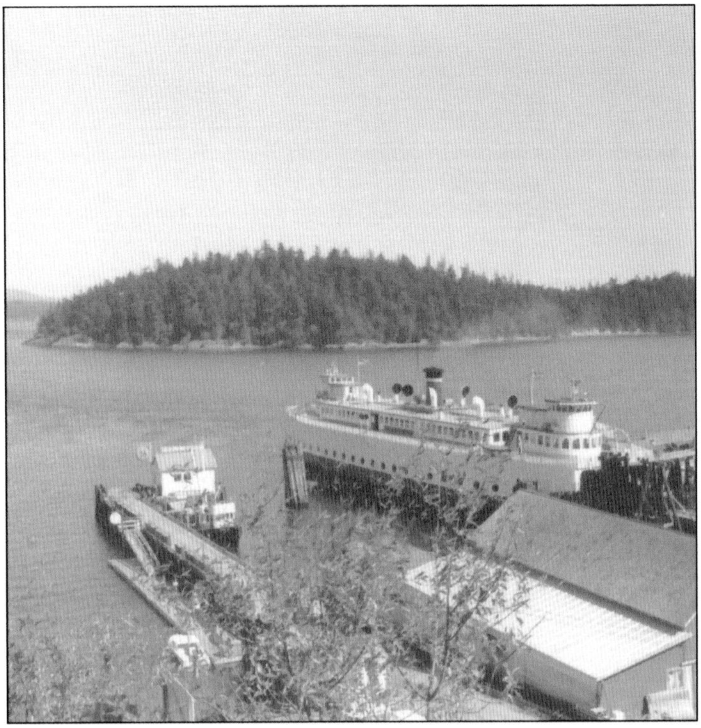

The MV *Klickitat*, shown here at the old ferry dock, was one of several steel-electric class ferries purchased from the San Francisco Bay system in 1940. She was a fixture on the Anacortes-Victoria line until—along with the other 1927 vintage steel-electrics, including the locally beloved *Nisqually* and *Illahee*—her wooden deckhouse was replaced in the mid-1980s by an oddly proportioned modern superstructure. They were removed from the system in 2008.

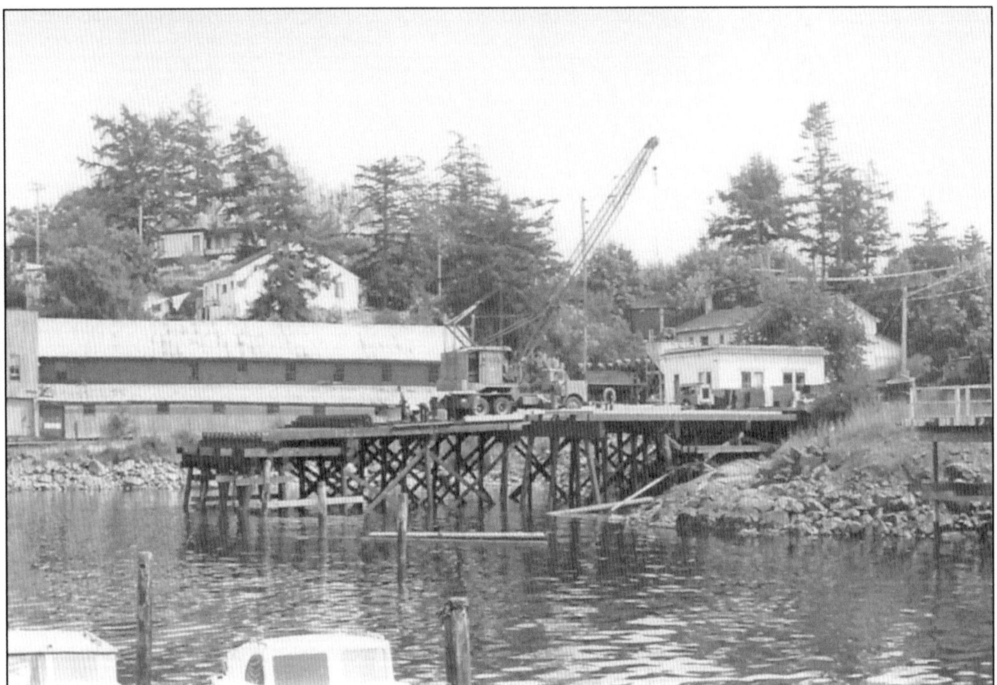

Work is underway on the new Washington State Ferries dock on Front Street just below the old cannery office, center right, and the manager's house, now an espresso bar. The cannery had yet to be removed, but plans were already afoot to build condominiums and shops on the site, which sold for $200,000 to real estate developers.

# *Five*

# A Town at Heart

As in most frontier towns, a struggle arose over Friday Harbor's soul in the early years. The influx of good jobs and disposable income encouraged men to bring or start families and build neighborhoods, churches, and schools, mainly on the hills that gently ascended to Joe Friday's old grazing lands. The opposite was true nearer the docks, where the workday was washed away as it had been from the time of Israel Katz—in the saloons and poolrooms (and the unmentionable bordello) crammed into the first block of Spring Street.

The town ban on alcohol sales in 1910 and Prohibition in 1919 effectively stymied the legal saloon trade on the island until 1933, but this had little impact on the quality of life of most of the town's citizens. Friday Harbor became not only a forum for business and government, but also an ideal place to be entertained, make friends, and help one another through church, civic, and fraternal organizations.

In the late 1870s, Catholic and Presbyterian ministries, on the island from the 1860s, built churches across the road from one another on Madden Lane. Then looking to expand their congregation (and collection plate), the Presbyterians built a new church at the corner of Spring and Blair Streets in 1897. The Methodist church (now the Grange Hall) had been on First Street since 1889, though a miniscule congregation made its future tenuous at best.

On the fraternal side, the Odd Fellows, Masons, and Loyal Order of the Moose established lodges to have fun while raising money for charities, and veterans found comradeship through the Grand Army of the Republic and later the American Legion. Women organized to promote temperance, education, civic improvement, and the home through groups such as the Women's Study Club and church guilds.

Summers were filled with activities. The town spared no effort to celebrate Independence Day, conducting parades with floats and crackerjack bands to rival any in the country. Town baseball games drew big crowds. Farmers, dairymen, and home gardeners celebrated the island's bounty every August, beginning with the first San Juan County Fair (in September) on the waterfront in 1906.

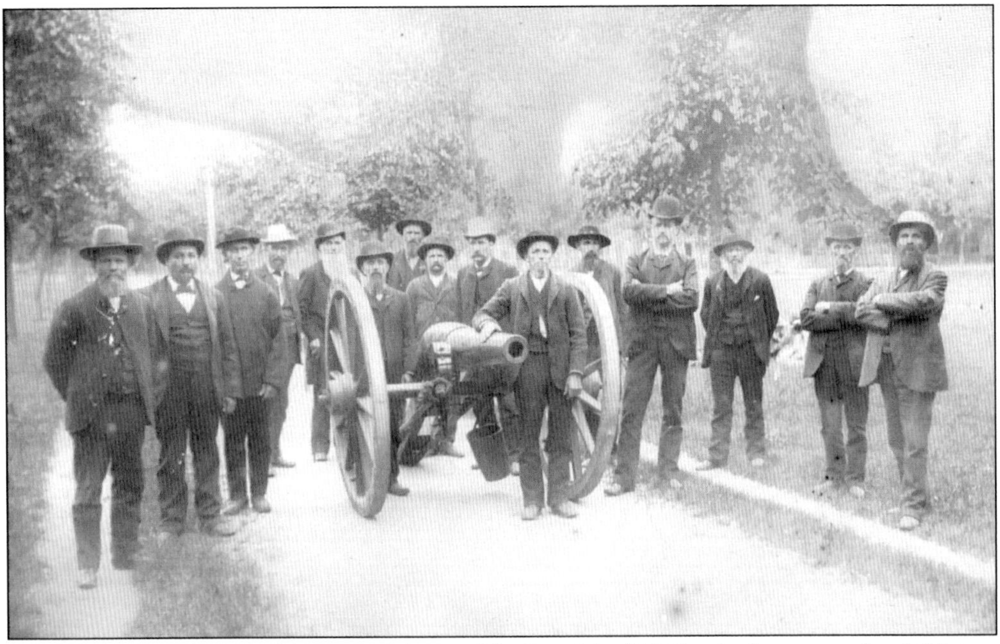

The Silas Casey Chapter of the Grand Army of the Republic (GAR) soberly surrounds a fieldpiece (cannon) around 1880. Founded in 1866, the GAR was a fraternal order composed of Union army veterans of the American Civil War and served as a template for all veterans groups thereafter. This is one of the few photographs of Ed Warbass as a younger man (far right).

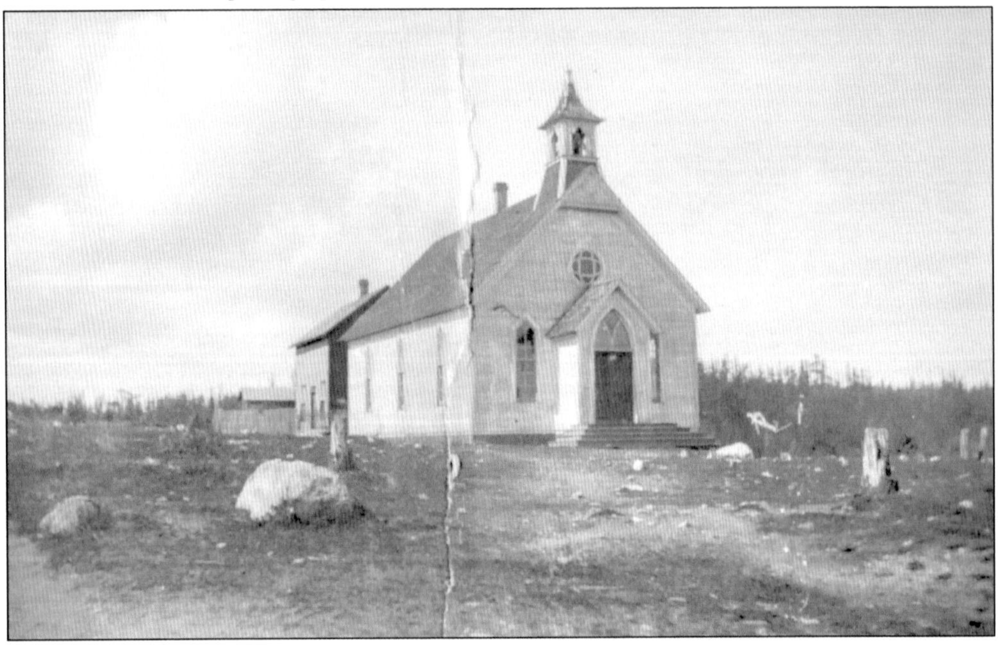

The Reverend Andrew McNamee arrived from Port Townsend in the late 1880s hoping to establish a Methodist church. Unfortunately, his fire-and-brimstone temperance views in a town with upper, middle, and lower saloons so curtailed the growth of his congregation that he went into debt to build the church. It finally closed in 1911 (ironically after the town alcohol ban) and became the Grange Hall in 1975.

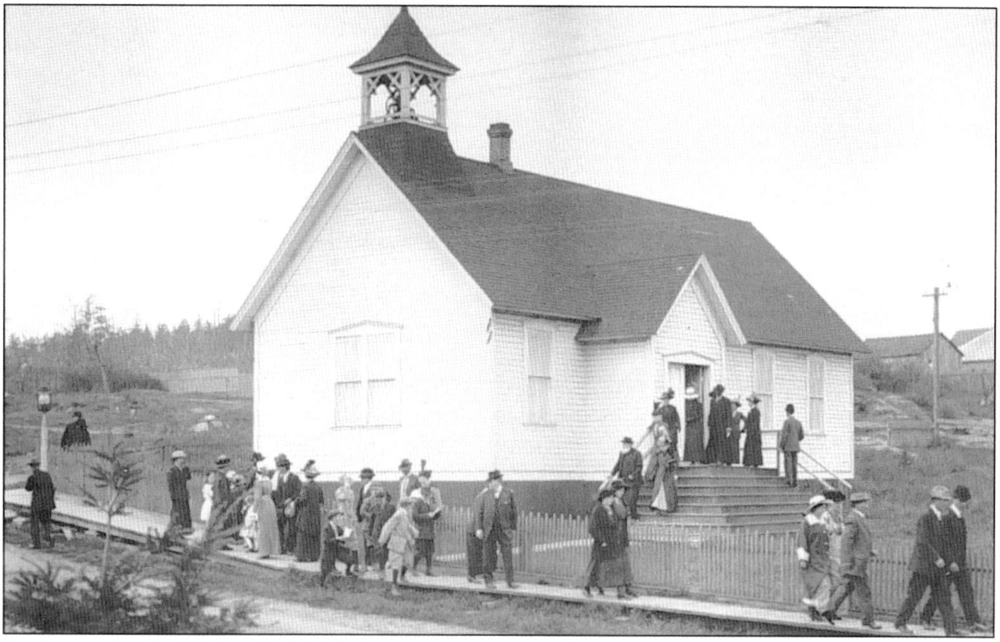

Built in 1897, the Emmanuel Presbyterian Church at Spring and Blair Streets replaced the original sanctuary established by Rev. T. J. Weekes on Madden Lane in 1878. The new church expanded in 1925 and was replaced in 1988 by a new building across the street. The structure was remodeled as a professional office complex, which is still in use.

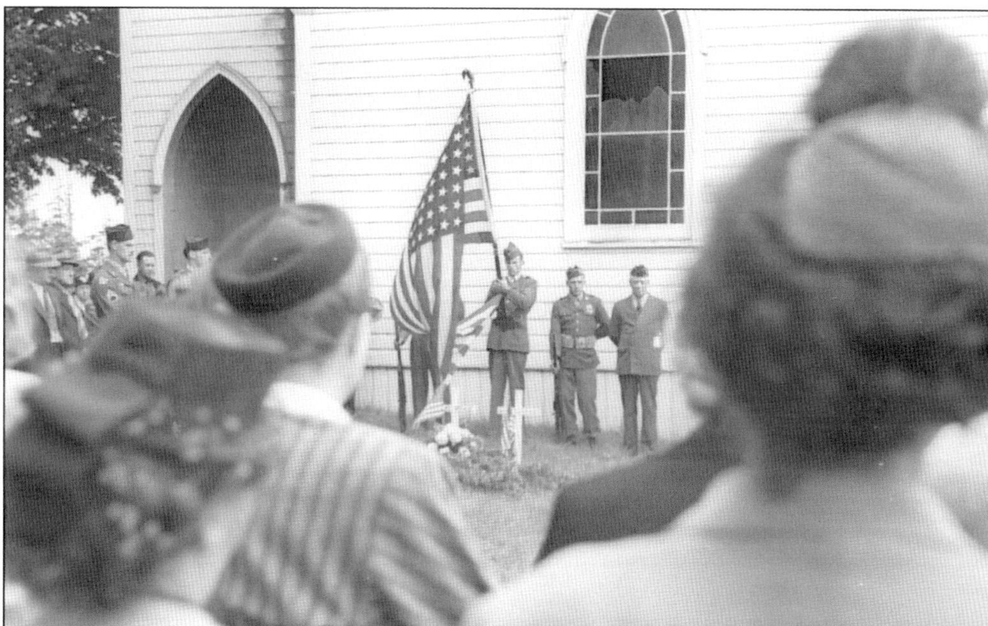

A memorial service is conducted at the Valley Church on Madden Lane, probably during World War II. The oldest church on the island, it was built in 1878 with funds donated by the Seattle Presbytery along with $150 raised via a community bazaar, still an essential activity in the island community. It was in danger of being demolished until Ella Erickson Dightman launched a preservation campaign.

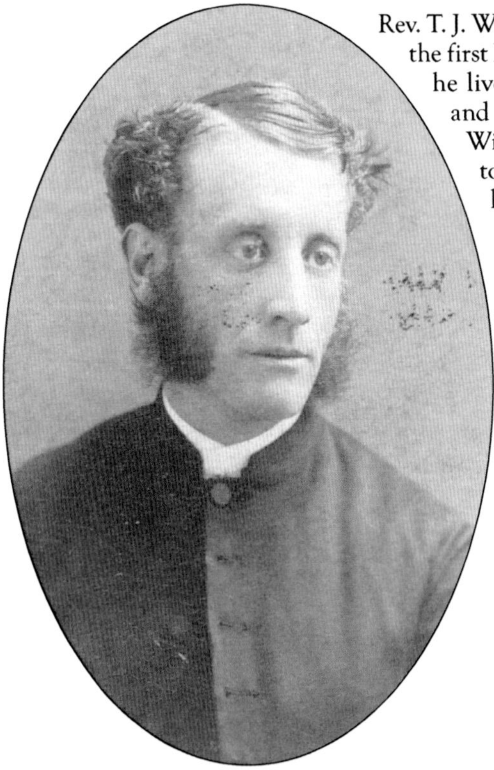

Rev. T. J. Weekes came to San Juan Island in 1870 to serve as the first Presbyterian minister. After the joint occupation, he lived in one of the abandoned officers' quarters and married Margaret Naylor, a local schoolteacher. With no salary save for the collection plate, he had to scratch for a living as a postman, teacher, and lighthouse keeper at Cattle Point.

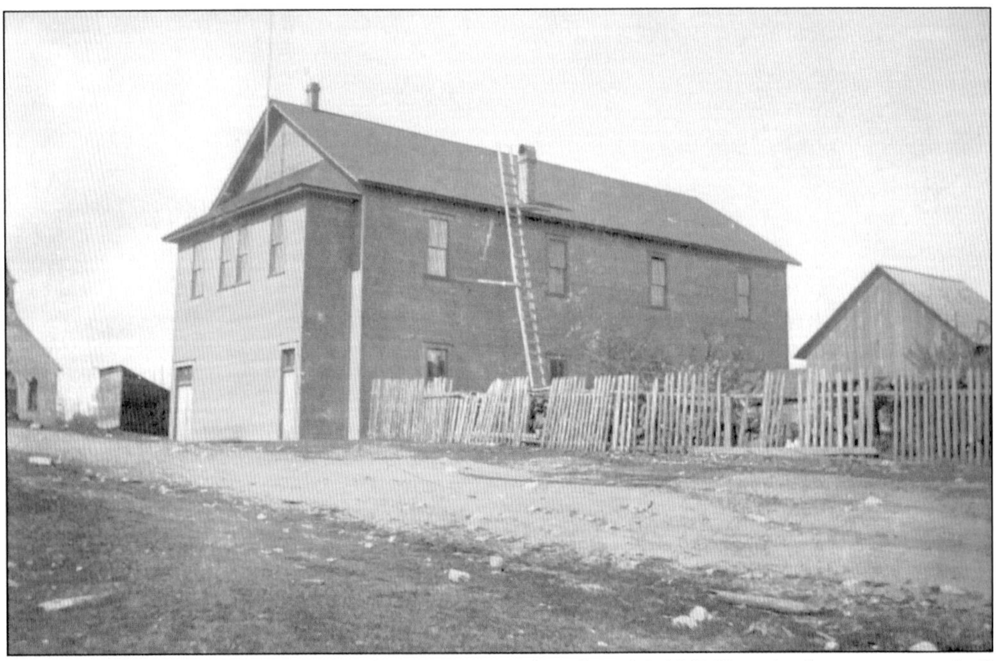

The Mount Dallas Lodge No. 95 of the International Order of Odd Fellows built its two-story hall on First Street in 1892. The ground (maple) floor and stage hosted a murder trial, basketball games, and a nationally renowned evangelist. In the mid-1950s, Milton and Emilia "Lee" Bave converted it into a theater. It became the Whale Museum in 1979.

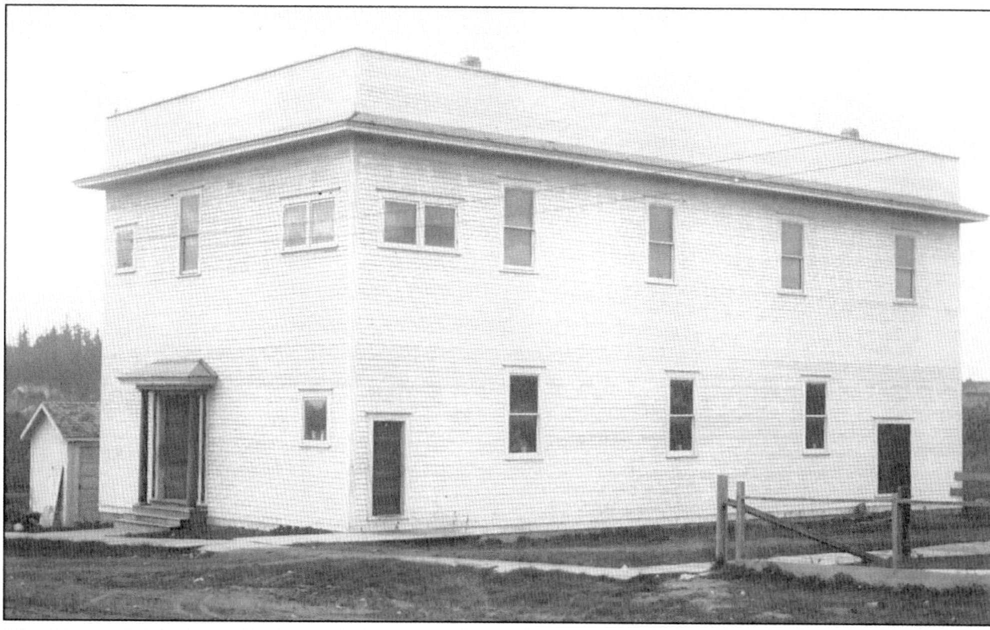

The Masonic Hall was built in 1914 across from the new county courthouse on Second Street. Several events took place on the second floor, including the Century Ball in 1924. For $1.50, patrons enjoyed supper and dances such as the Henry Shimmy, Willy's Night-Crawl, and Buick Bustle. "Attention Bachelors," the handbill read, "Ladies Free."

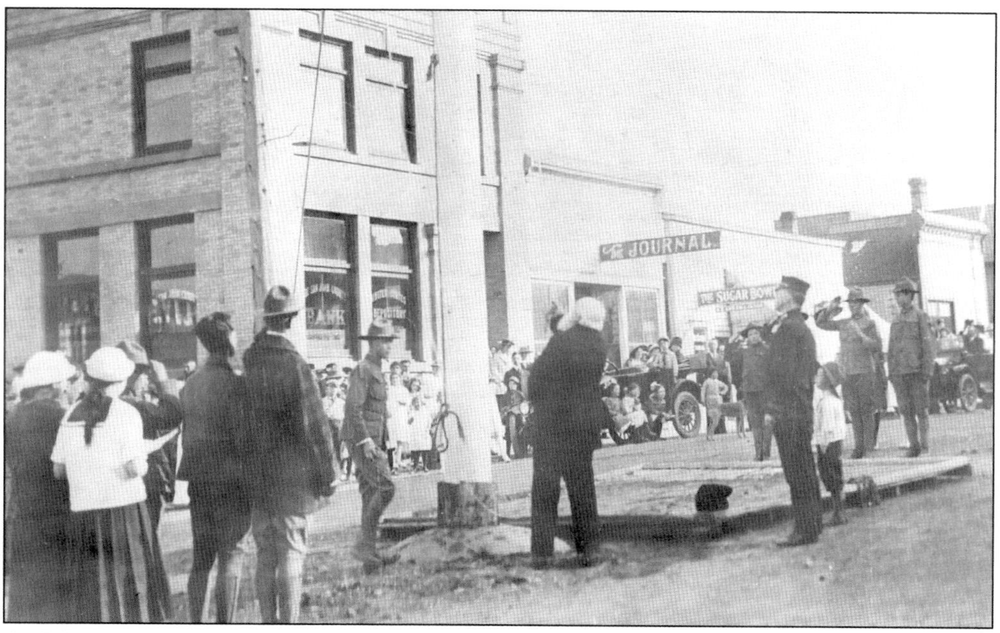


On May 30, 1917, pioneer blacksmith Charles McKay (white hair and beard) raised the American flag on the new pole erected at Spring and First Streets. McKay was honored as one of the last living participants in the Pig War crisis of June to November 1859, when he rowed to Bellingham for a U.S. flag to raise on the island in defiance of Great Britain. He died the following year.

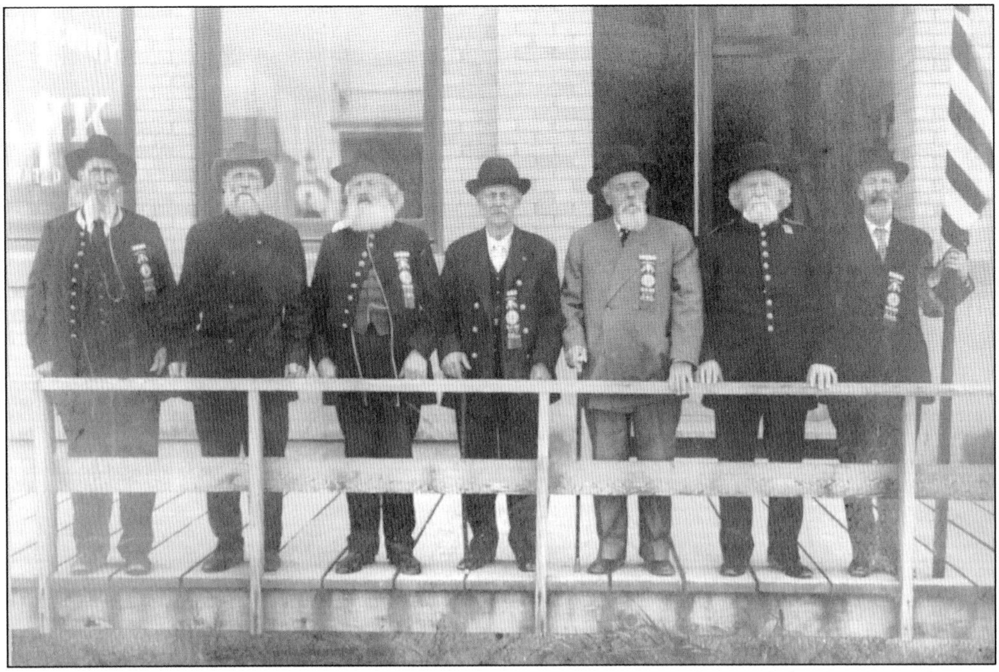

The renamed Hardin Smoots Chapter of the GAR congregates in front of the San Juan County Bank around 1910. From left to right are Thaddeus Smith, William Cooper, George M. Dightman, John L. Blair, John Hankinson, George Smith, and S. J. Croft. The 45-star flag is on display in the San Juan Historical Museum.

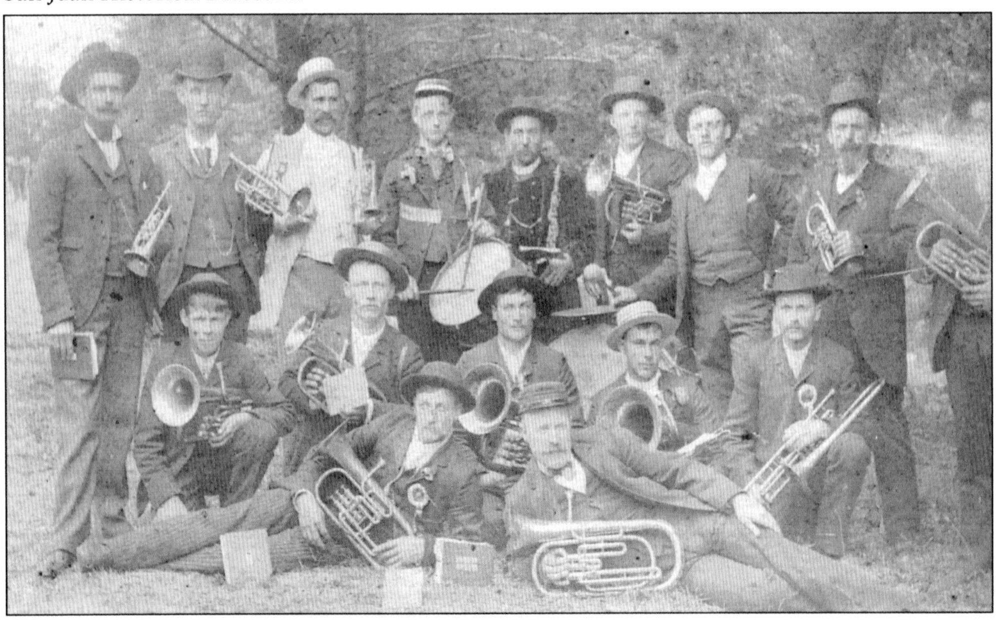

One of the first bands on San Juan Island played for many occasions, including school festivals. The sound must have been rich with so many baritone horns. From left to right are (first row) George Stewart, Aug Wold, Henry Banna, Ben Hanna, Bob Firth, S. B. Boyce, and Paddy Mile; (second row) John Dougherty, Ole Wold, Frank Boyce, unidentified, John Stamm, Jim Firth, Joe Jensen, and Ed Ziegler.

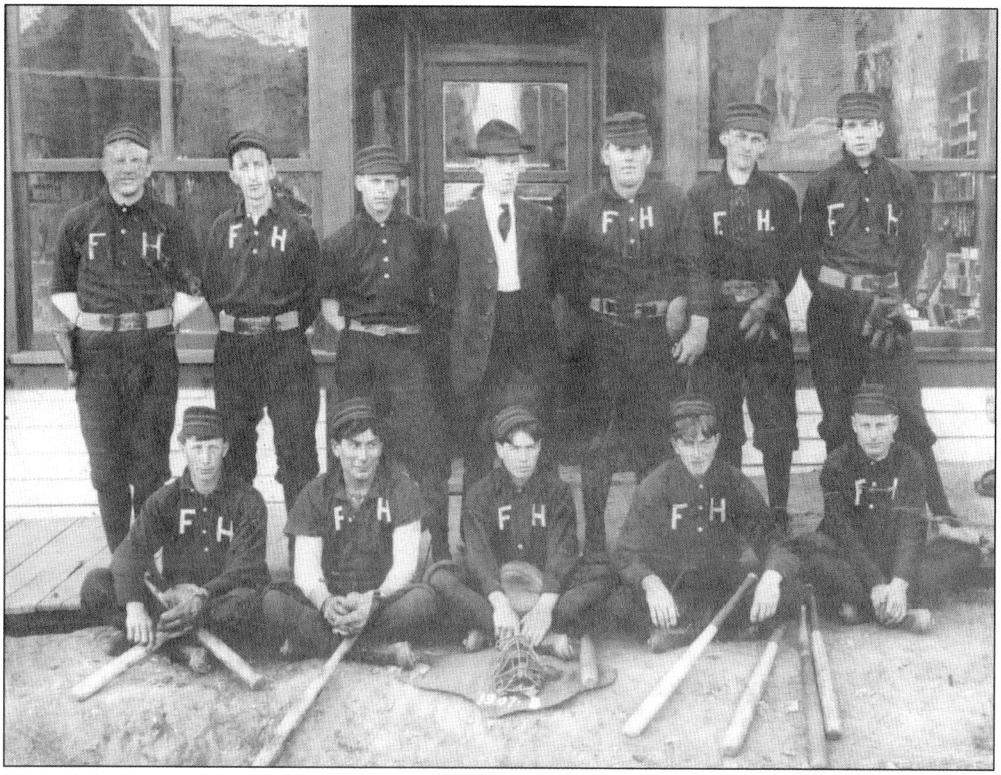

The 1905 edition of the Friday Harbor Baseball Club poses after splitting a doubleheader with the U.S. Army team from Fort Worden. From left to right are (first row) Bill Schuman, Bill Rosler, Bruce Blaine, Dick Worthington, and Carl Templin; (second row) Steve McNamee, Clarence Workman, Bill Trimble, unidentified manager, Art Erickson, Martin Nichols, and John Douglas.

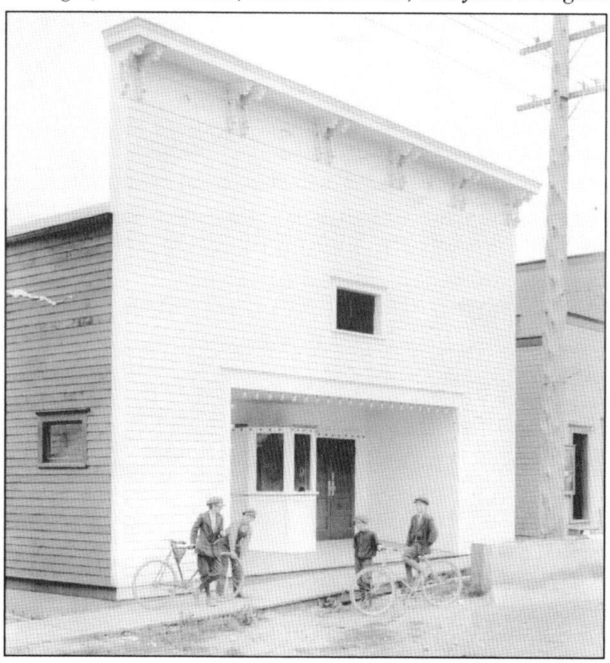

The 250-seat Fribor Theater (FRIday HarBOR), now the Palace, opened on July 4, 1914 as a silent film theater and live playhouse. One traveling Broadway show that played twice on a Sunday in 1915 was *Just Jim*, featuring Hollywood western star Harry Carey. Admission was 10 and 20 cents.

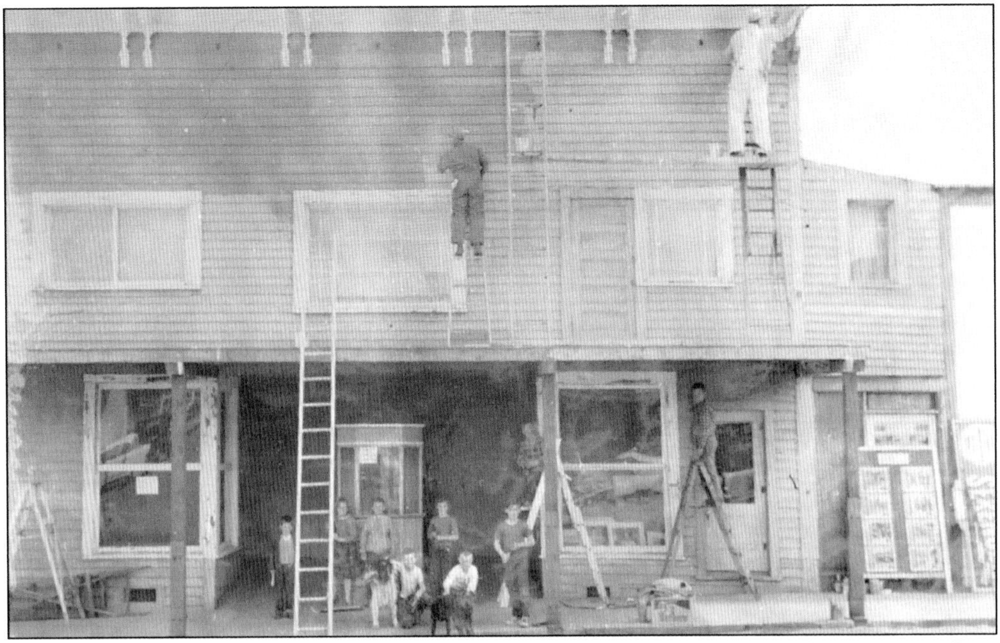

The renamed Royal Theater undergoes renovation, presumably in 1959 after another rescue purchase by Lee and Milton Bave. It was renamed the MADD Playhouse (Music, Art, Drama, Dance) and hosted community theater productions and feature films. It is said that Lee Bave stood by in the projection booth, ready to cover the lens to protect patrons from what she deemed unseemly material.

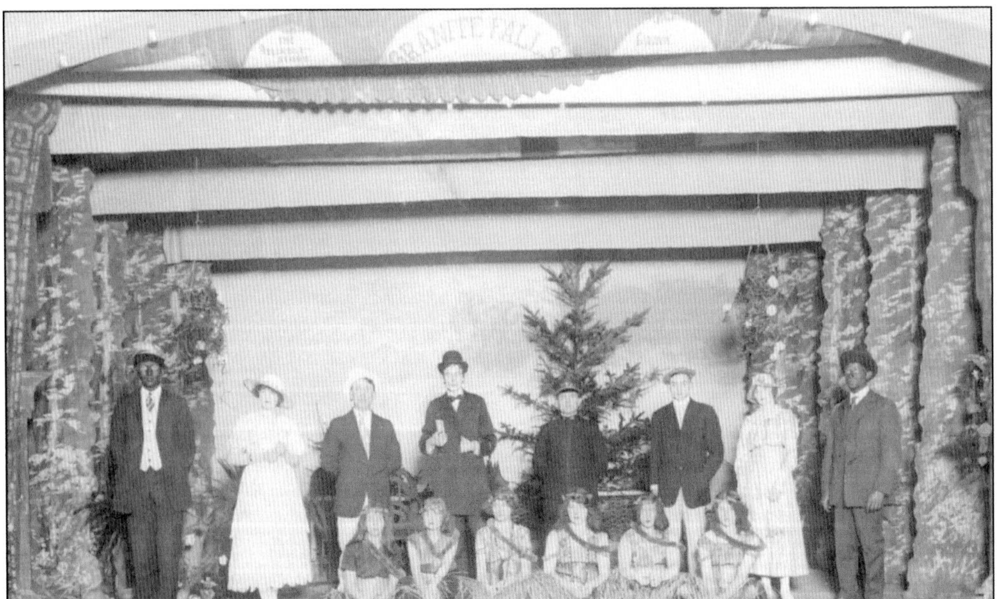

San Juan Island has always been fond of amateur theatricals, as this turn-of-the-20th-century image attests. With its proscenium arch and stage, the Odd Fellows Hall was a natural. But no production rivaled the performance of William Ashley (Billy) Sunday, a baseball player turned evangelist who orated here on the perils of demon rum.

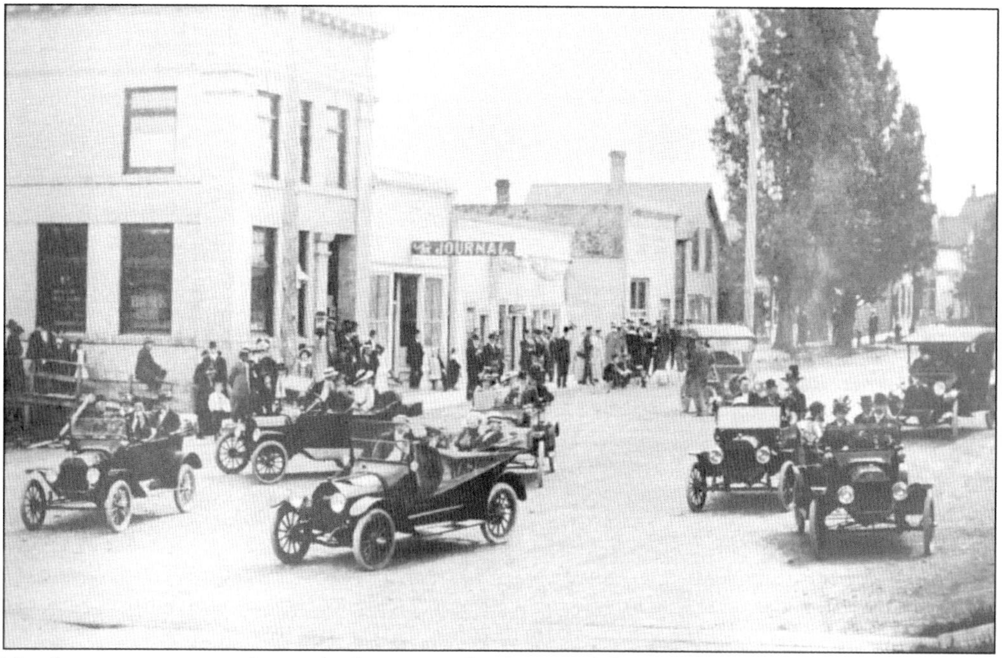


Nearly everyone sports a hat in this happy tangle of automobiles cruising down Spring Street around 1914, perhaps to a University of Washington football rally judging from the pennant displayed on the lead car. At far right is the original county courthouse, replaced in 1906 and moved from the future location of the bank.

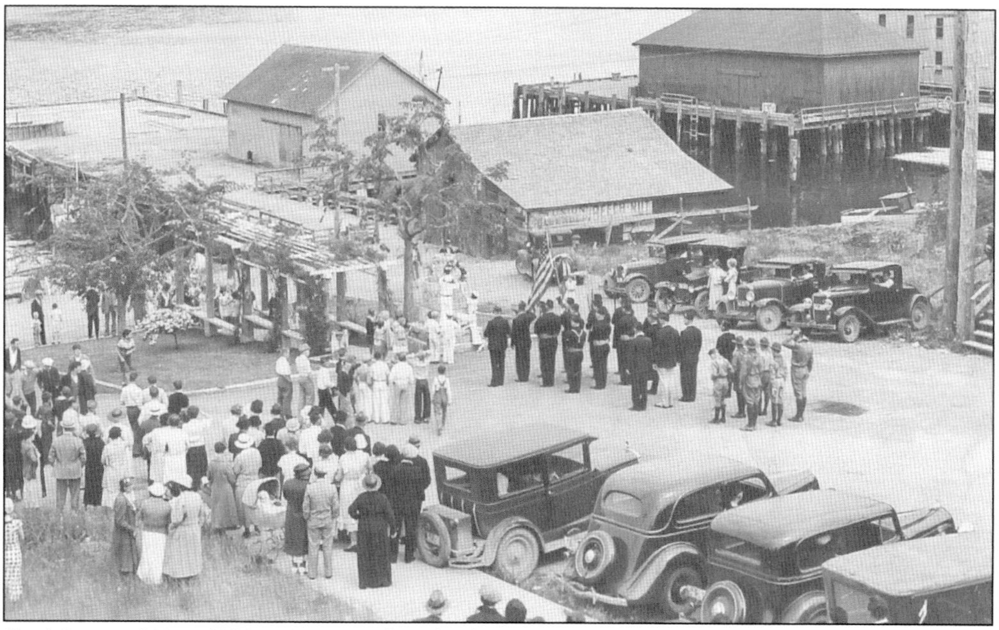

On Memorial Day 1938 in Memorial Park, the American Legion firing squad and color guard prepare to pay a salute to the fallen, while children in sailor suits drape floral wreaths around the monument. Installed in 1921 following a fund-raising campaign launched by the Women's Study Club, the cenotaph honors nine San Juan County residents (three from Friday Harbor) killed in World War I. (Jensen family.)

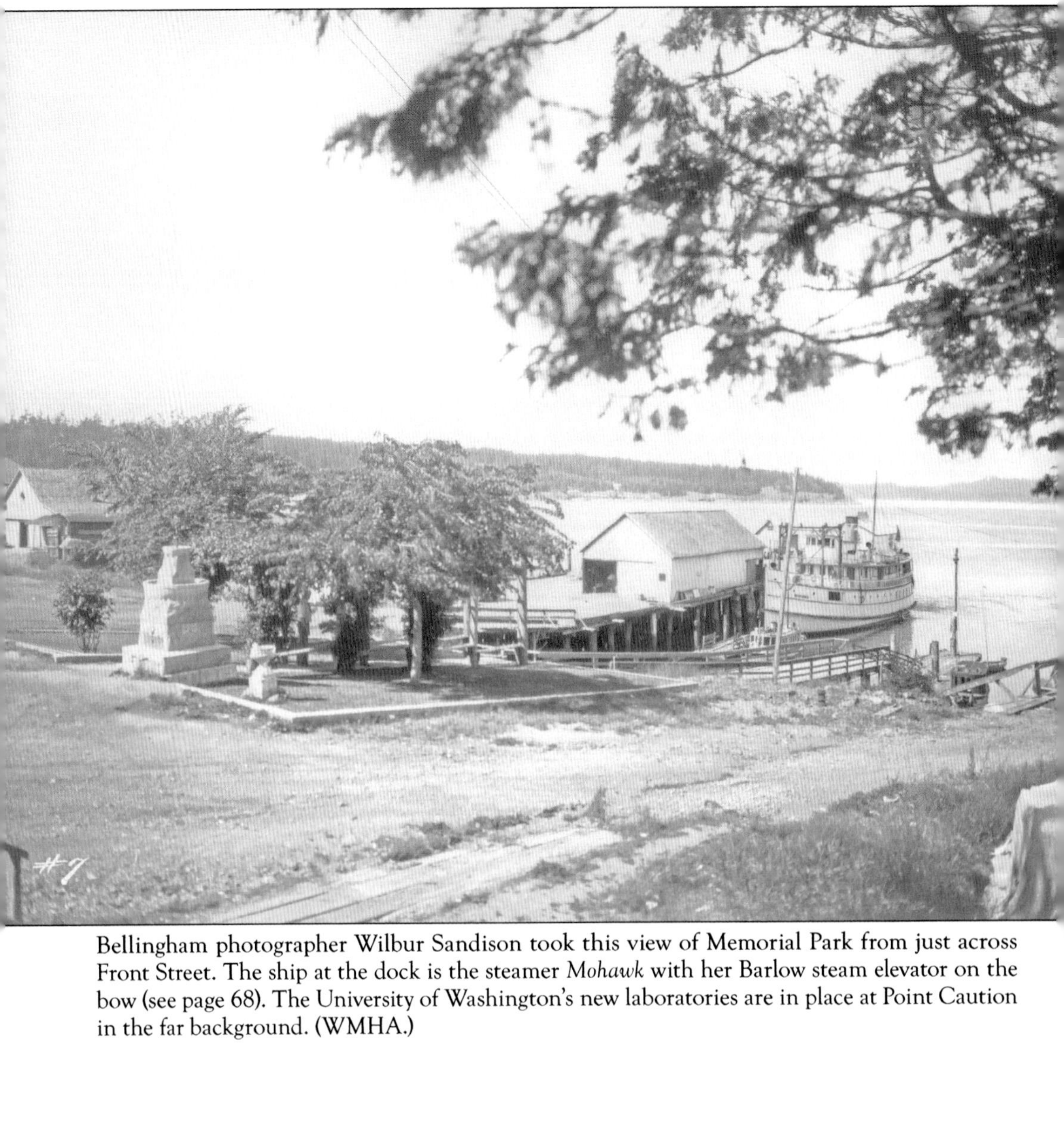

Bellingham photographer Wilbur Sandison took this view of Memorial Park from just across Front Street. The ship at the dock is the steamer *Mohawk* with her Barlow steam elevator on the bow (see page 68). The University of Washington's new laboratories are in place at Point Caution in the far background. (WMHA.)

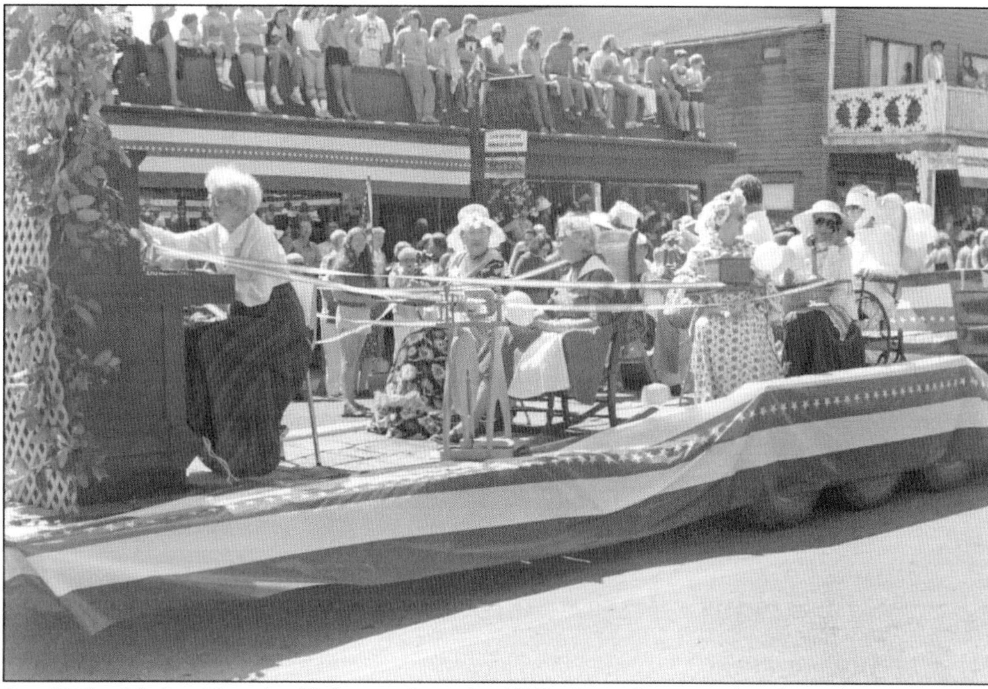

At a Friday Harbor Fourth of July parade in the 1970s, Lucy Storm replays her role as one of the town's telephone operators for more than 40 years. "If you called for someone and that person wasn't at home, she knew where to find him," one islander reports. "She knew everything about everyone."

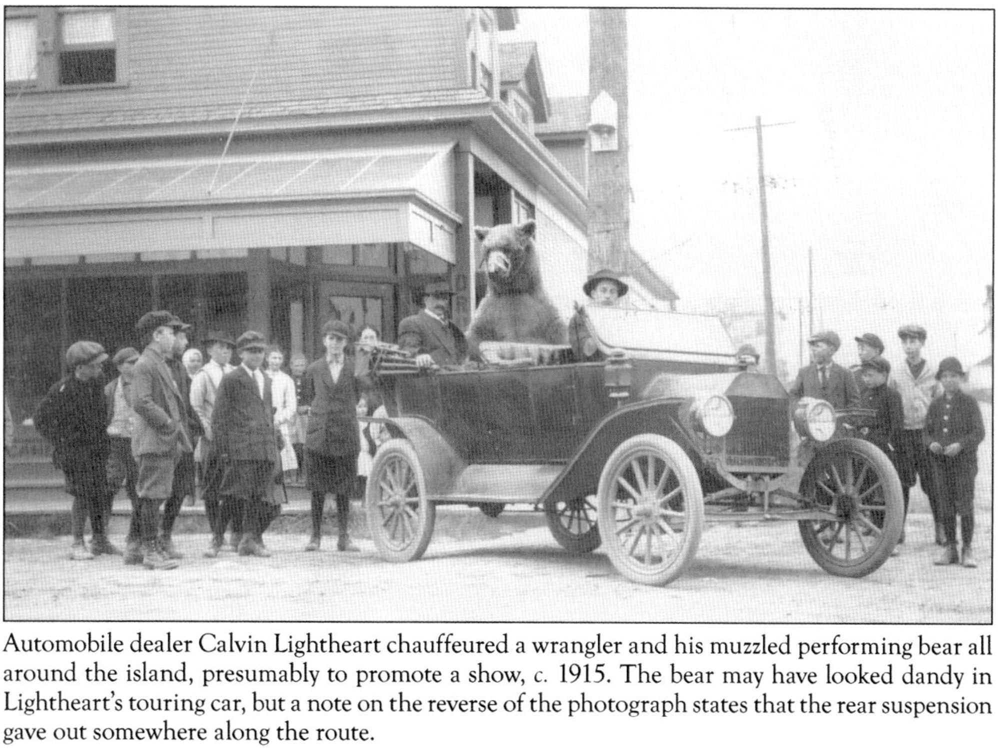

Automobile dealer Calvin Lightheart chauffeured a wrangler and his muzzled performing bear all around the island, presumably to promote a show, *c.* 1915. The bear may have looked dandy in Lightheart's touring car, but a note on the reverse of the photograph states that the rear suspension gave out somewhere along the route.

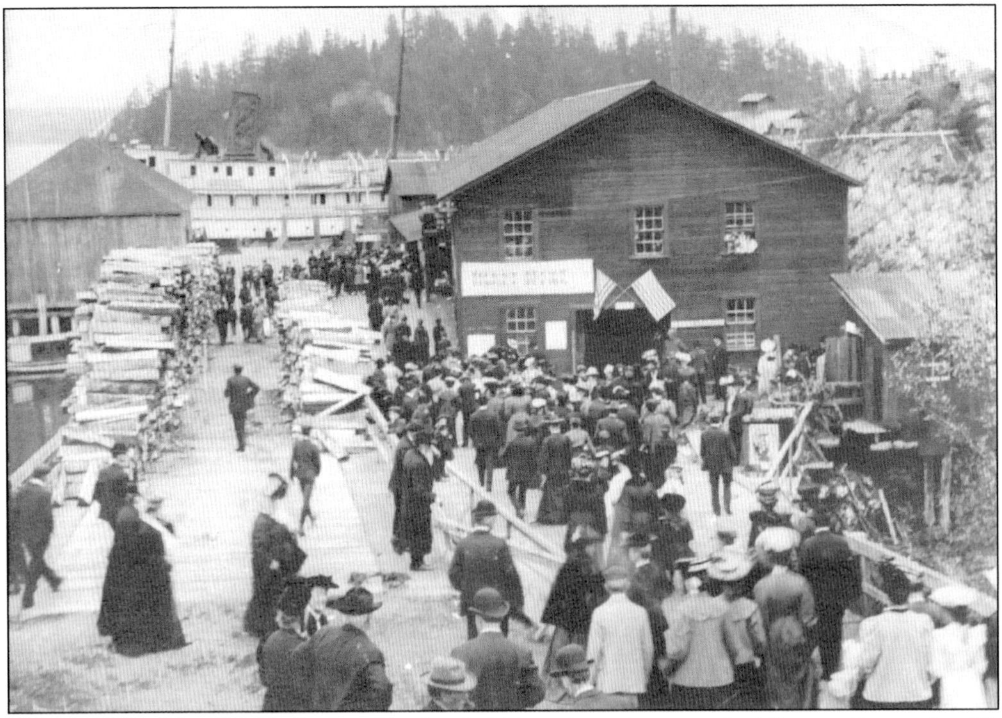

The town turned out for the first county fair, held in a cleared cannery building, on September 27, 1906. The *Friday Harbor Journal* worried that not all attendees would find lodging: "It should be the duty of Friday Harbor to see that all who attend the fair are comfortably sheltered and have enough to eat. To this end our homes should be opened if necessary."

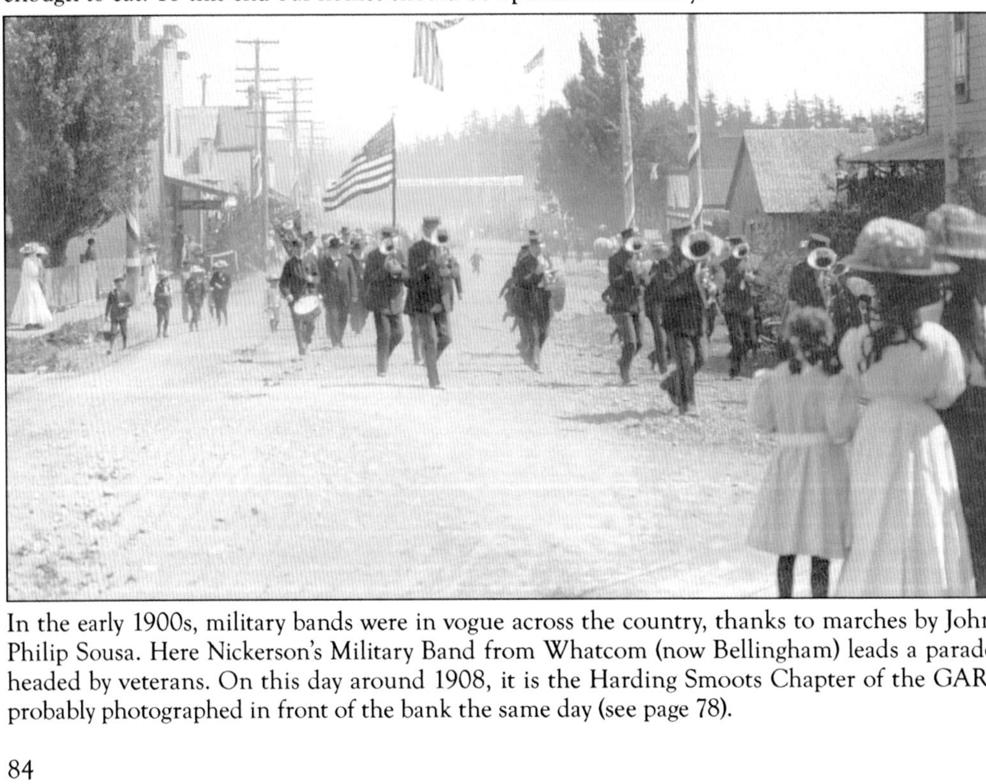

In the early 1900s, military bands were in vogue across the country, thanks to marches by John Philip Sousa. Here Nickerson's Military Band from Whatcom (now Bellingham) leads a parade headed by veterans. On this day around 1908, it is the Harding Smoots Chapter of the GAR, probably photographed in front of the bank the same day (see page 78).

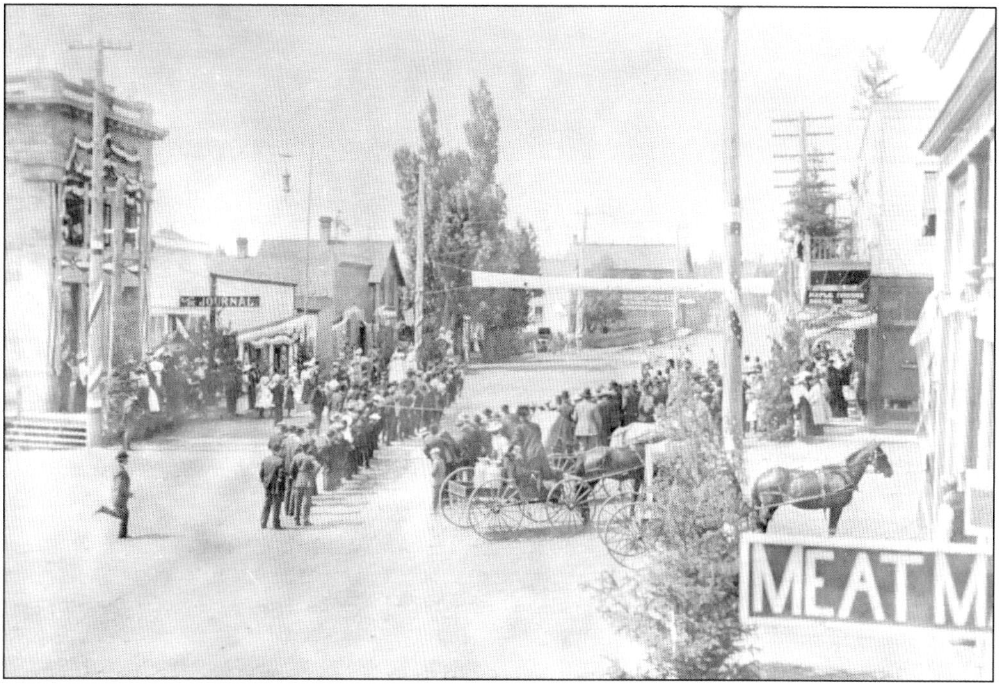


Each Fourth of July, several Chinese workers at the cannery sponsored running races for the children. In this post-1907 view (the bank is complete), a crowd gathers for the finish. The Maple House hotel and hardware store are open for business on the corner of Spring and First Streets.

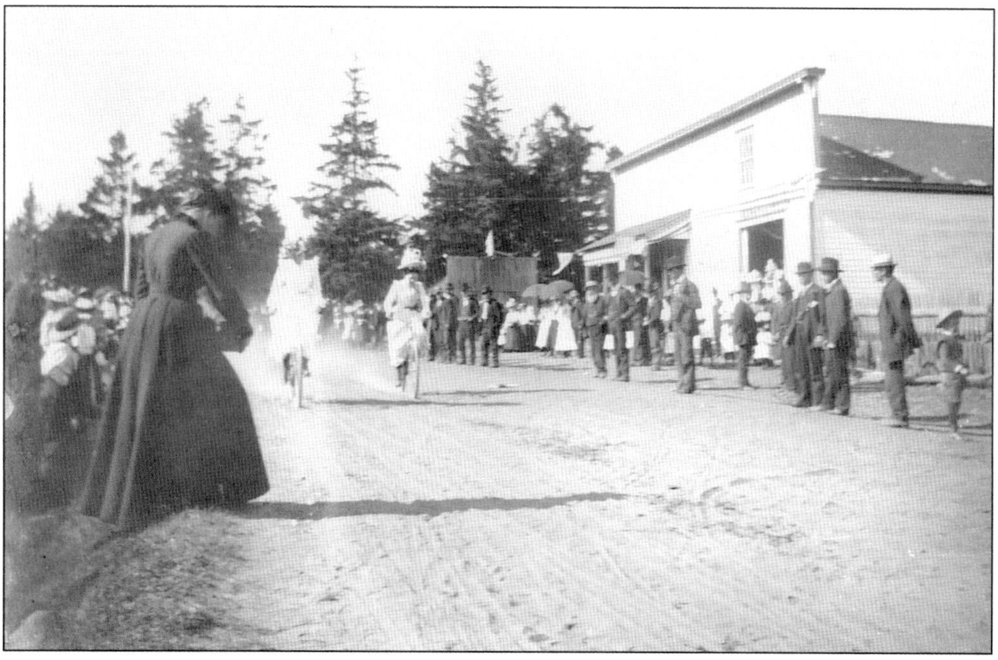

The men—all in hats—may be wondering why these women have not lost theirs by now as they pump furiously—in voluminous skirts—toward the finish line. In 1913, the county fair venue was split between a field at Madden's Corner and the James King farm, and automobiles shuttled people for 20¢. A woman in the foreground records a Kodak moment (see page 99).

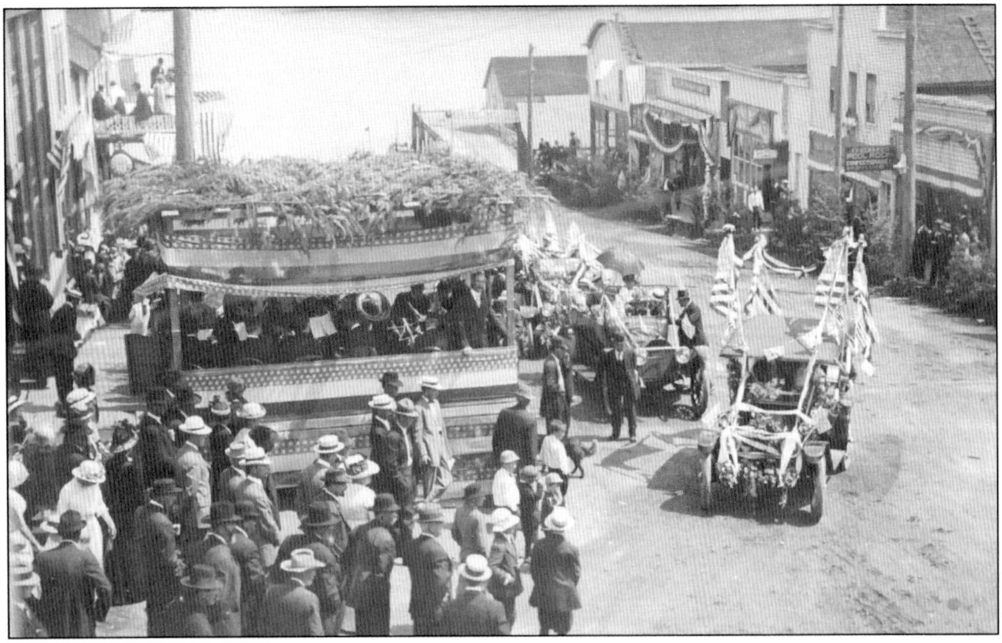

Friday Harbor has long celebrated the Fourth of July with a spirited parade. The whole town turns out to cheer for bands, community groups, politicians, and friends in decorated cars and floats. Above, musicians play airs from the bandbox, which is festooned with evergreen branches and red, white, and blue bunting, as are the wooden sidewalks and "upper pool hall." Below, after the parade, family, friends, and visitors await the passenger ship on the MacKenzie (or main) dock and city float around 1914. Note the virtually empty Point Caution Federal Reserve, where the University of Washington labs would be relocated in 1924.

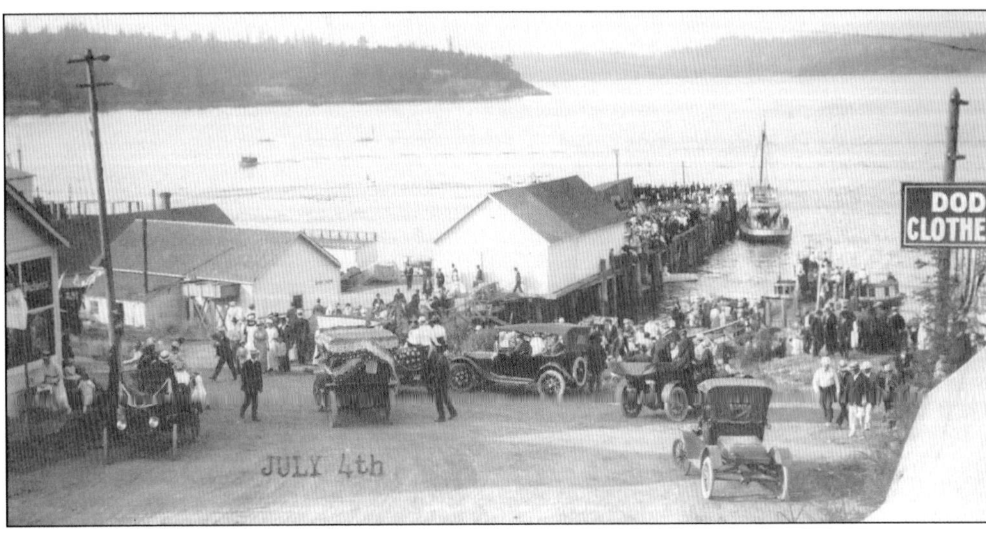

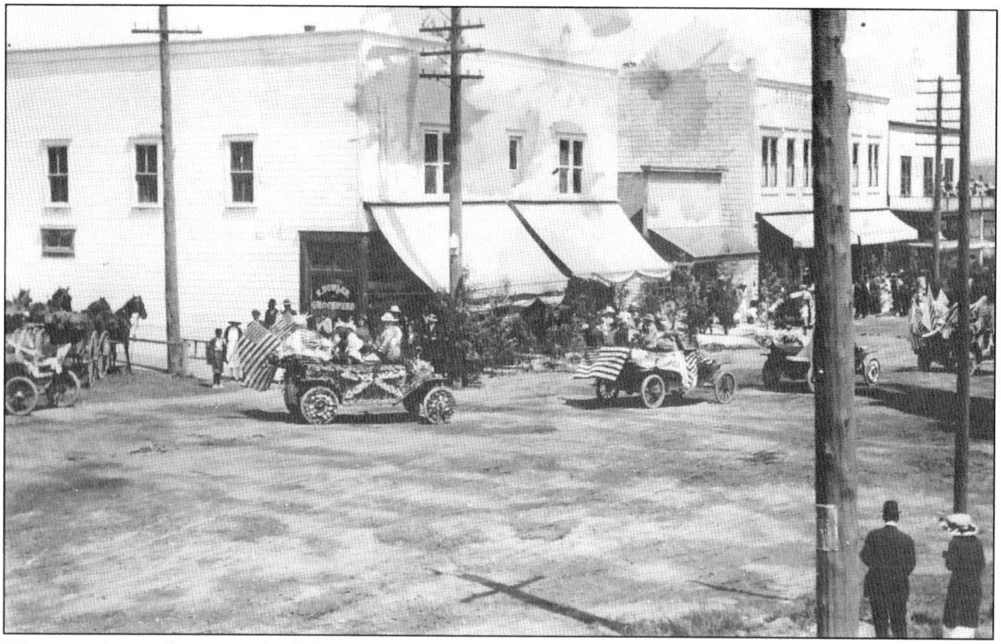

The parade is photographed (see page 86) rounding the corner at Second and Spring Streets, revealing the major structures that would one day form two-thirds of King's Market. From right, the Tulloch's Hardware/Maple House hotel and Carter's Department Store. The R. Bowler grocery building and the old Blue Front Store (the tiny wooden structure) were demolished and replaced to form the current store.

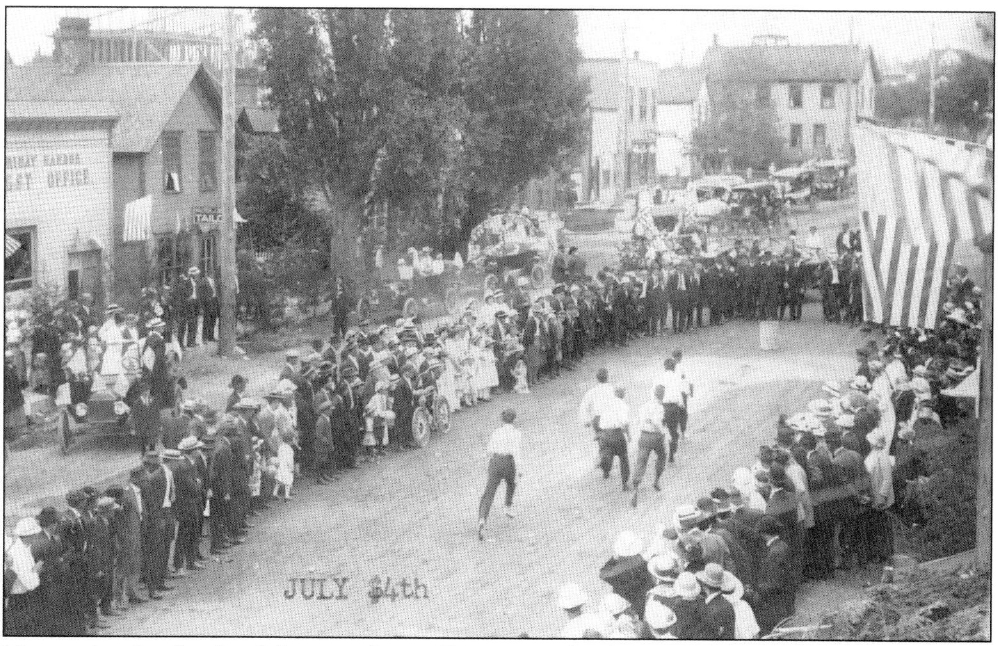

Men sprint for the finish line in this *c.* 1914 race. The date can be roughly verified because automobiles were introduced that year. The old county courthouse is visible at upper right, as is the millinery owned by the Mullis sisters. They must have had a booming business: it seems every spectator is wearing a hat.

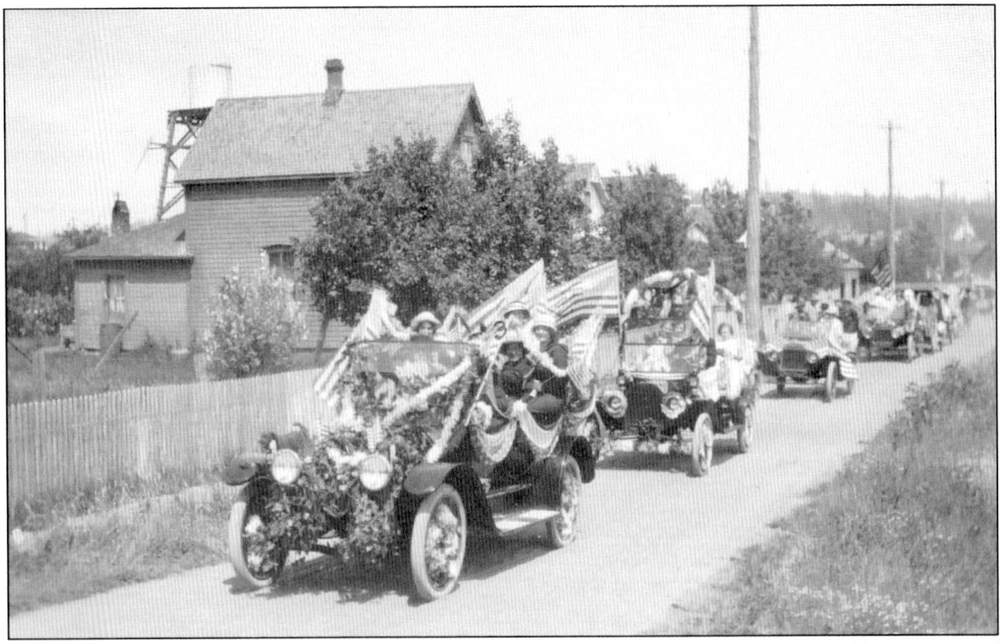

The 1915 Fourth of July parade cruises up Argyle Avenue, still rural in 1915. Sheriff Jones owned the house nearest the foreground, which eventually became the home of Friday Harbor historian Etta Lightheart Egeland. Today the viewer would be looking toward Spring Street and the retail block that includes the health club.

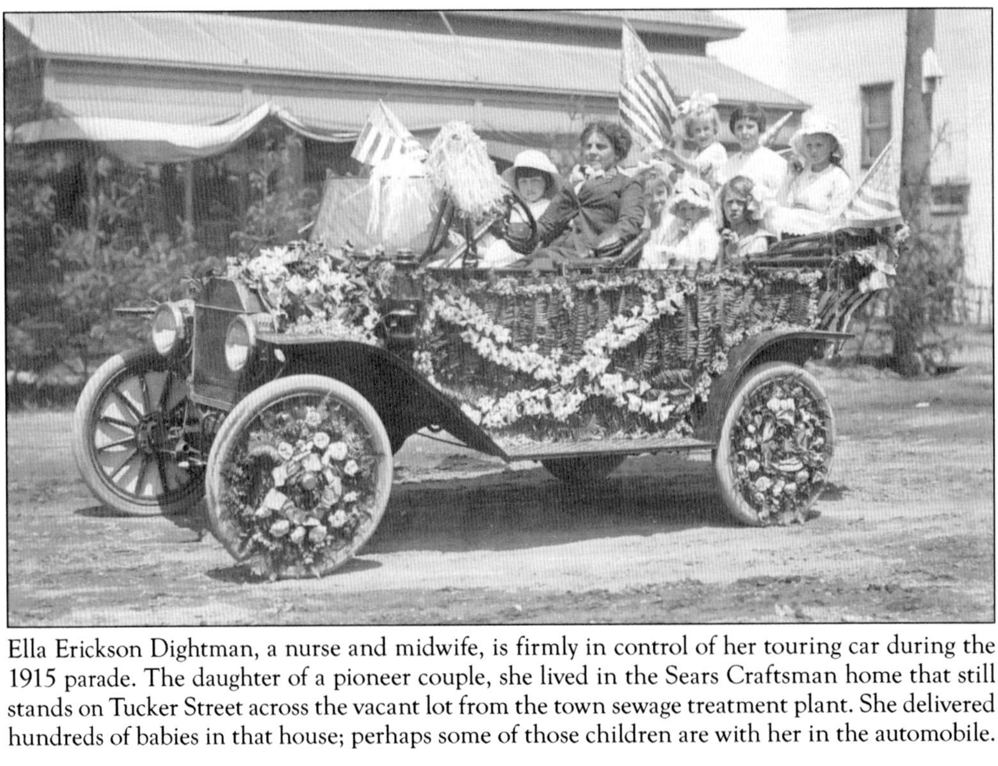

Ella Erickson Dightman, a nurse and midwife, is firmly in control of her touring car during the 1915 parade. The daughter of a pioneer couple, she lived in the Sears Craftsman home that still stands on Tucker Street across the vacant lot from the town sewage treatment plant. She delivered hundreds of babies in that house; perhaps some of those children are with her in the automobile.

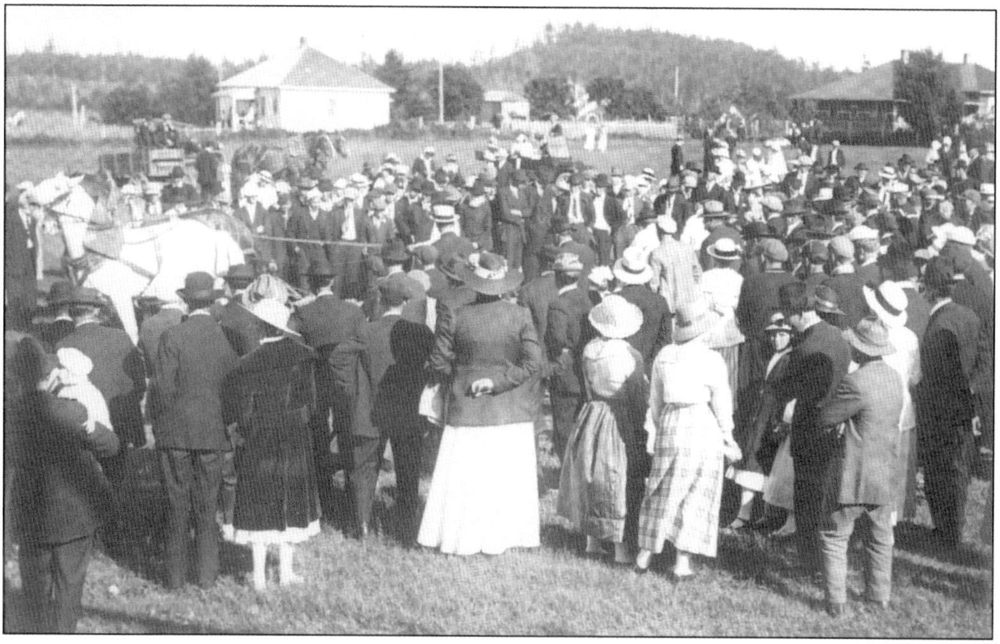

One popular county fair event was the horse pull. The teams were harnessed to a rock-filled stone boat, a flat sled that farmers used to clear rocks from their fields. The team that hauled the most weight over the prescribed course (27 feet) won. This replaced horse racing, banned in many counties because of gambling (which is not to say no one gambled on the pulls).

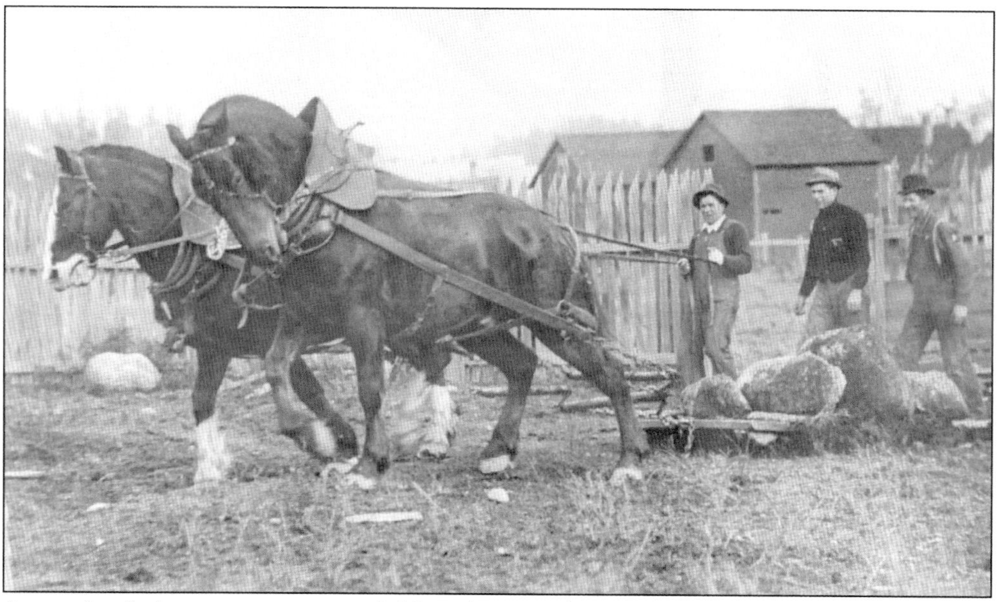

A typical rock clearing operation, probably within town limits, illustrates how a stone boat worked. The horses, usually French Percherons, weighed up to a ton and could haul loads of two tons or more. A visitor to American Camp can view rock piles likely created through this process.

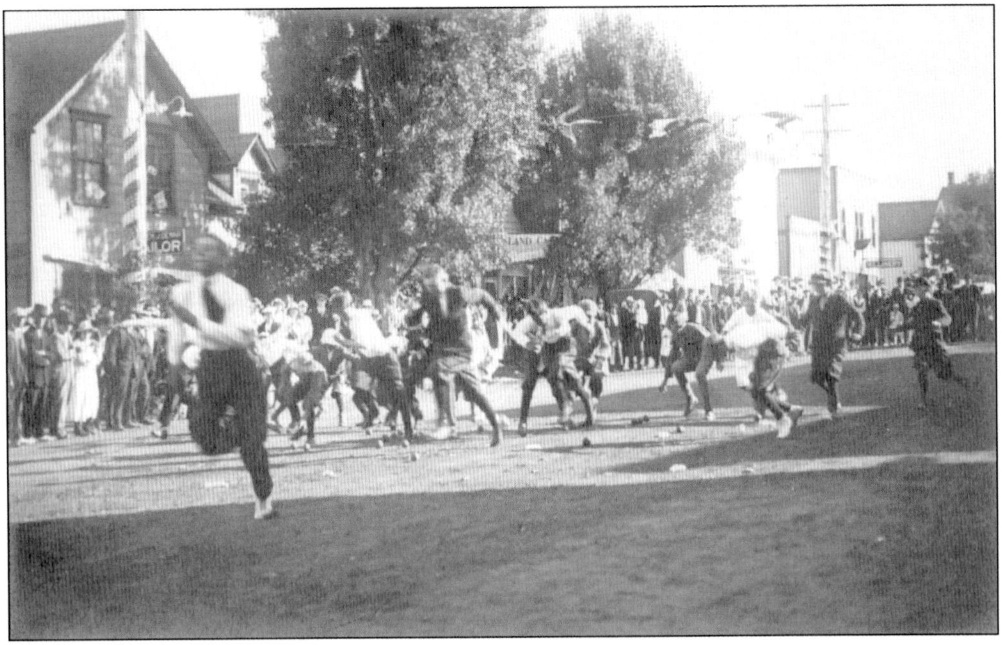

In these action shots from July 4, 1916, boys race toward the bay, kicking and reaching for balls skidding along among them. In the image below, the race seems to have been reduced to a pushing and shoving match—though all in good fun. The 1916 celebration was the largest ever in Friday Harbor to date, with more than 3,000 people showing up for the parade, including a capacity load of 1,200 who arrived from Seattle aboard the steamer *Chippewa*.

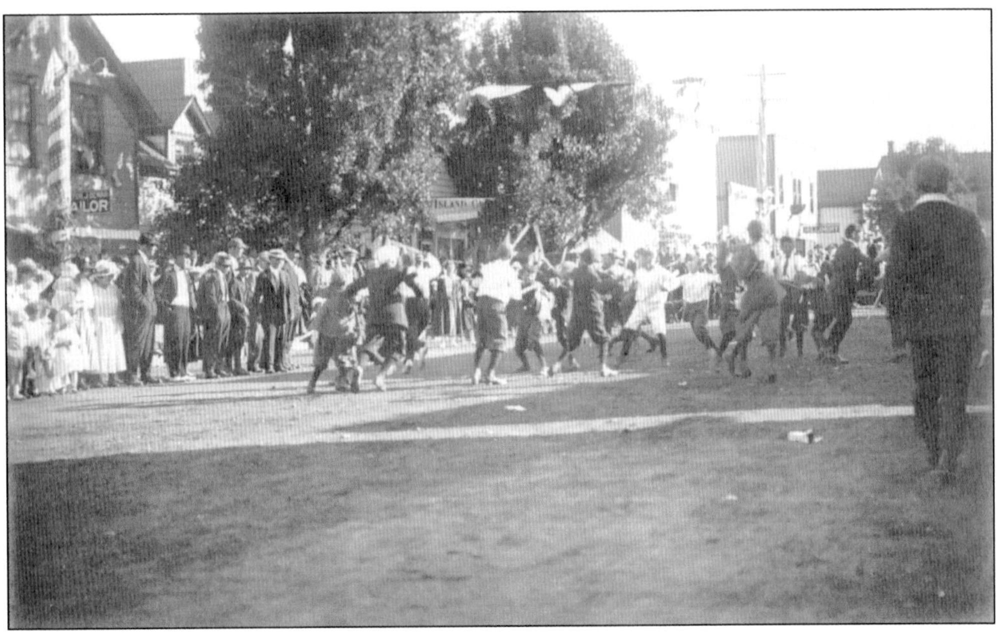

# *Six*

# A Town in Class

Late in the 19th century, many island children still attended one-room schoolhouses around the island, often at county crossroads. Classrooms were Spartan and utilitarian. "We had a furnace, and it'd get cold on one side of the room and hot on the other," wrote teacher Juanita Egeland Rouleau. "Our restrooms were in a building outside . . . boy, were they cold in the winter-time!" Children ate their lunches, often bread and lard packed in metal tobacco boxes or lard pails, on wooden benches along the walls.

The new, two-story consolidated "belfry" school was built in 1890 with a $3,000 bond at the south end of what is today the courthouse parking lot. With only two teachers and more outlying schools closing, the district leased the adjoining church (which still stands) for grades one to three in 1899. Off-island children were charged 50¢ and 75¢ for primary and secondary grades, respectively.

In 1912, overcrowding and the need for a four-year accredited high school spurred voters to approve a $10,000 bond for a new consolidated school. Also located in today's courthouse parking lot, it opened in February 1913. The old school was converted to a lunchroom and was moved from the road to the future community theater site.

During the Depression, married women were not allowed to teach because it was assumed their husbands could support them. "We had a number of teachers living in sin then," Rouleau said.

The new school housed grades one through 12 until 1936, when islanders approved a modern, two-winged elementary school to be built on Blair Avenue (now the middle school). A concrete building with bathrooms and another building with a small gym (but bigger than the one on Orcas) were built behind the high school's main buildings.

In the early 1950s, it was decided that a new school would cost less than repairs, and the new high school opened in 1959 adjacent to the elementary school. The old school was torn down in 1961 by Sam Bridges, who won a bid ($267.58) to dismantle it. Bits and pieces of the building are scattered around town, with the most visible being the portico pillars that now support the balcony of the two-story Friday Harbor Drug building.

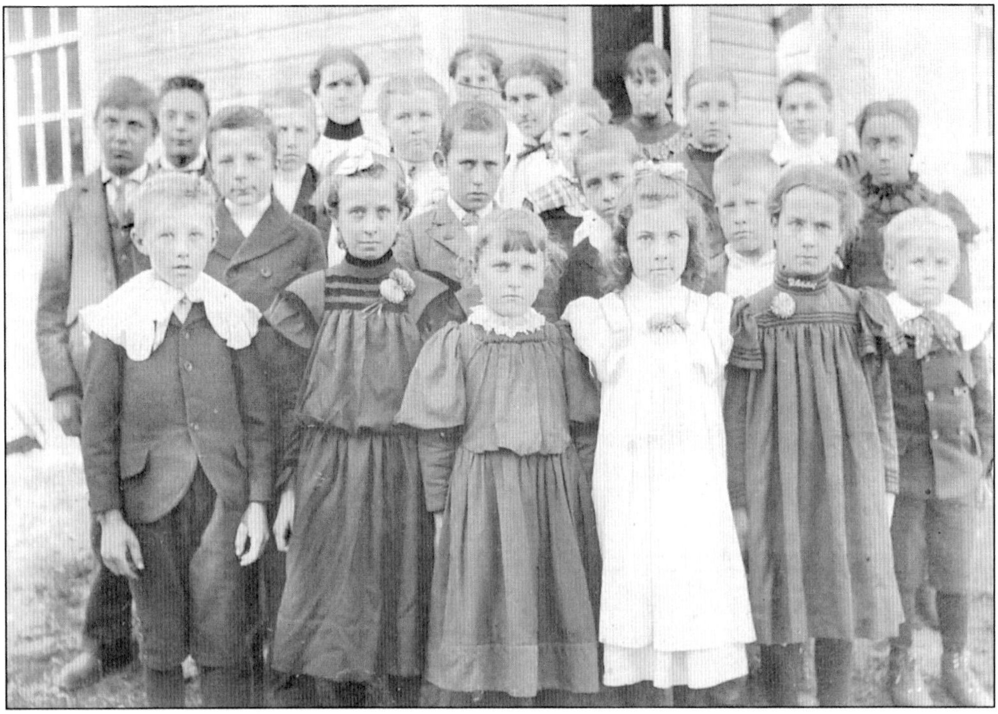

Sober pupils stand still for the photographer in front of the No. 2 Schoolhouse, once located near the corner of Schoolhouse and San Juan Valley Roads. Note the two especially grim boys in "Little Lord Fauntleroy" collars at opposite ends of the first row. No doubt the older boy at far left administered a noogie afterwards.

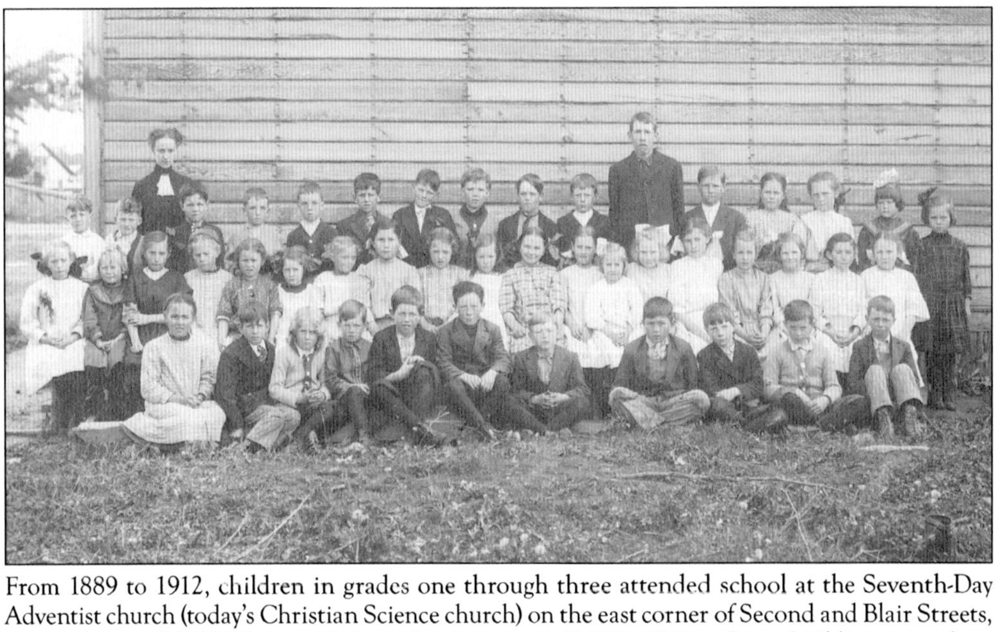

From 1889 to 1912, children in grades one through three attended school at the Seventh-Day Adventist church (today's Christian Science church) on the east corner of Second and Blair Streets, pictured around 1911. The town's first school was a small, 20-by-32-foot frame building near where the Masonic Hall stands today. The drinking fountain was a bucket of water fetched by students from the town spring.

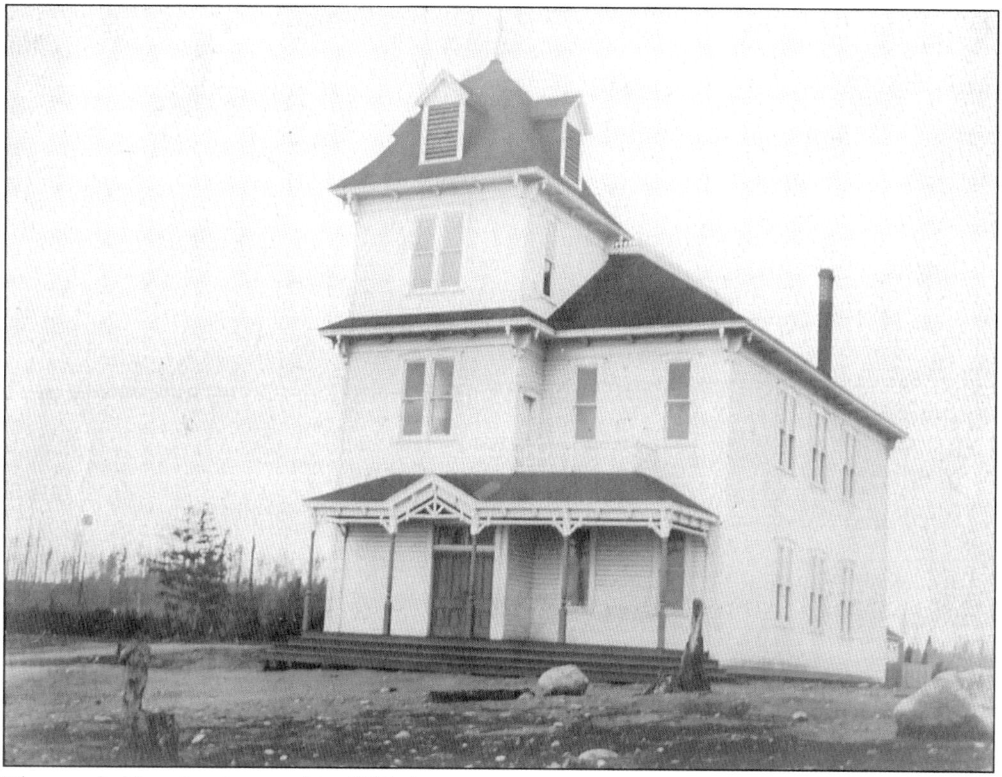

The new belfry school opened in 1890. It was too small from the start, as the eight rural districts on the island were closing and transferring students. In 1900, the $190.47 budget included a new privy, repairs on the old privy, inside painting, refinishing desks, wood for heating, books, supplies, and janitors.

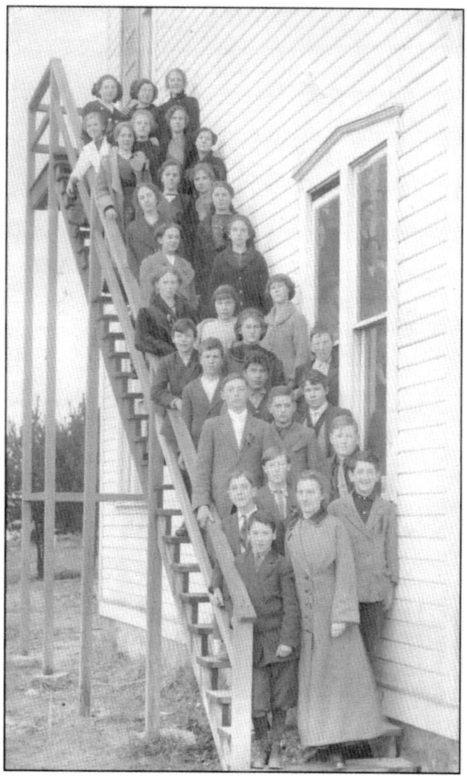

These middle school students squeezed together on the stairs of the old belfry school for the photographer. From about 1910 to 1912, the teachers of this school were Laura Carter, who taught fourth, fifth, and sixth grades and shared the ground floor with Julia Jensen, who taught seventh and eighth grades. Future island historian Etta Egeland is listed as sixth from top.

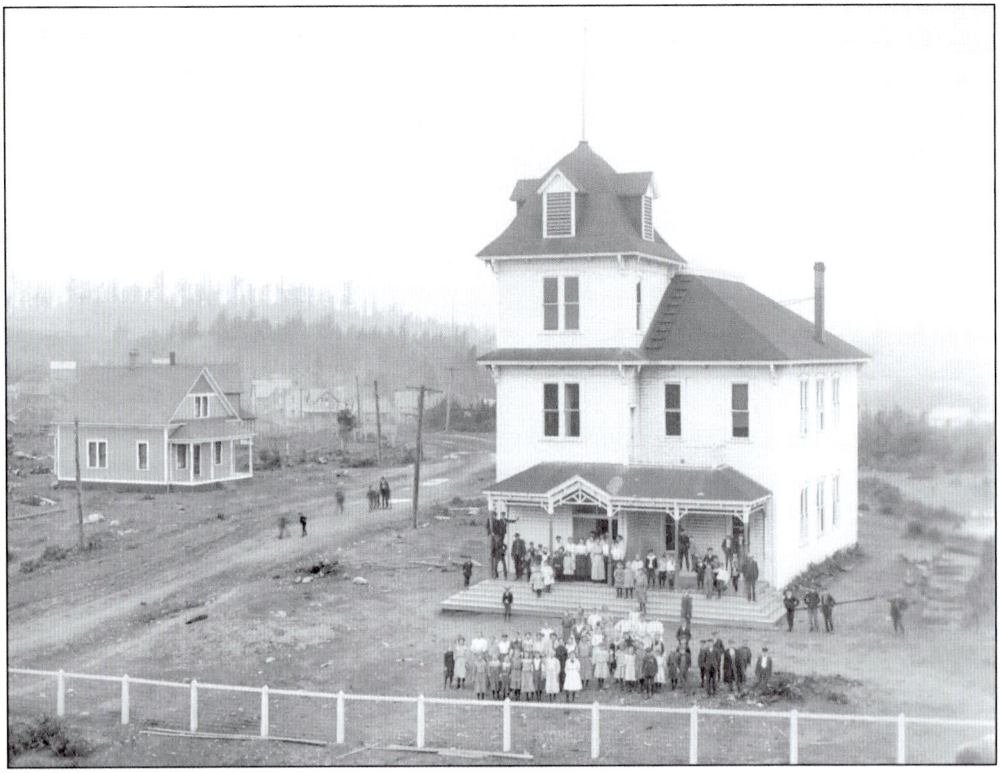

The Ken Nash home (now the law offices of Judge Carla Higginson) appears newly completed in this post-1906 image taken from the roof of the county courthouse. Note the way Guard Street drops in elevation on its way through the woods. A ninth-grade class was added to the school in June 1901, creating the island's first high school. Walter Nichols taught upstairs.

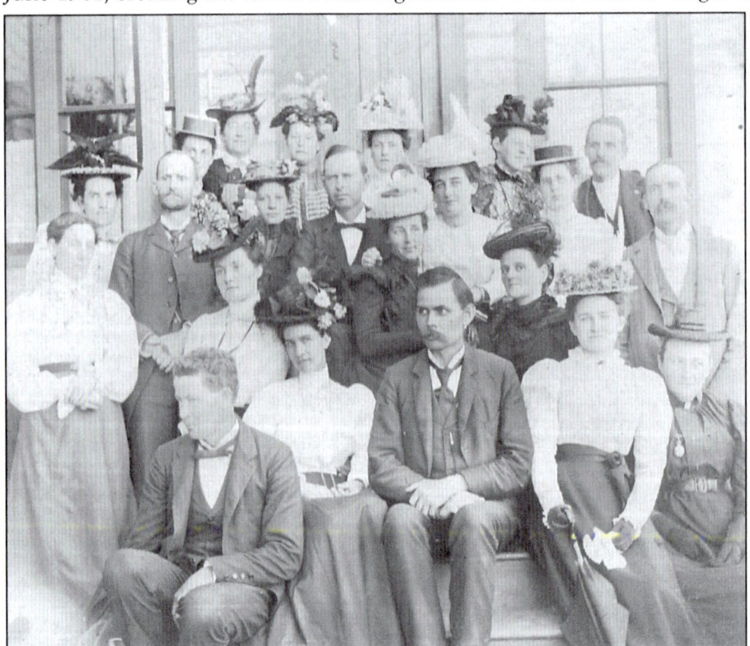

Friday Harbor teachers gather in front of Dr. George Wright's office on Spring Street around 1900 during a meeting of the Teacher's Institute. No identification key is given, but Wright is at the far top right, and his wife, Laura, is seated at far left in the second row, above the man sitting far left. Albert Jensen, who taught school before opening his shipyard, sits at center with bow tie. (Jensen family.)

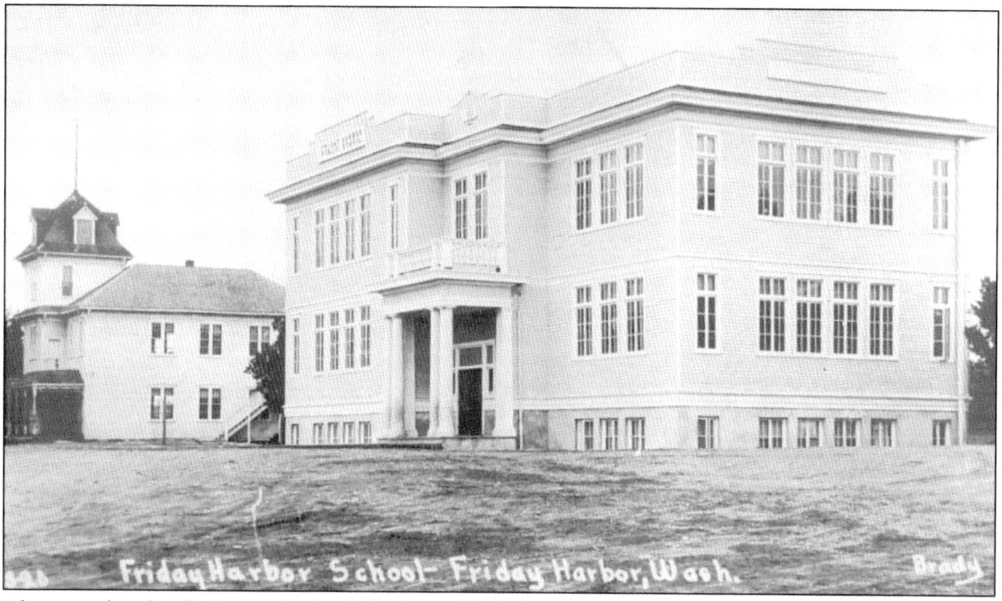


The town's school district looked flush in 1913, but the second floor of the belfry school was considered unsafe. The bell tower was removed and the building relegated to a lunch hall until it was torn town in the 1930s. The largest of the bells weighed more than 200 pounds.

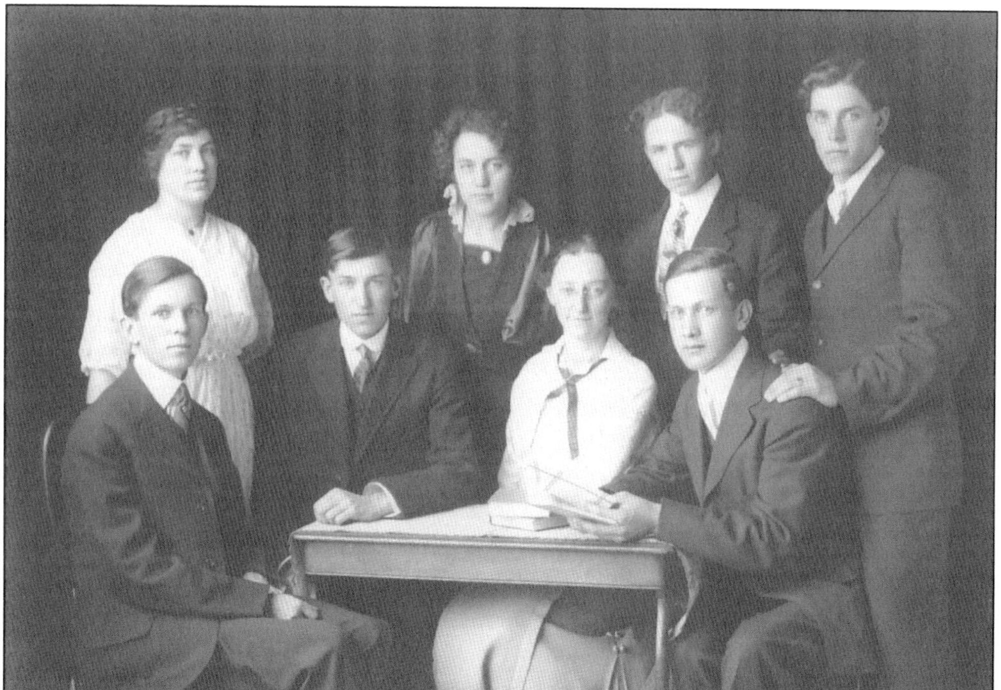

Friday Harbor High School's first graduating class gathers for commencement in June 1915. From left to right are (first row) George Higgins, Norman Churchill, Loretta Newhall, and Arthur Groll; (second row) Leda Culver, Louise Nelson, Albert Nash, and Richard Wotton. Most of their fathers were prominent in the town business directory.

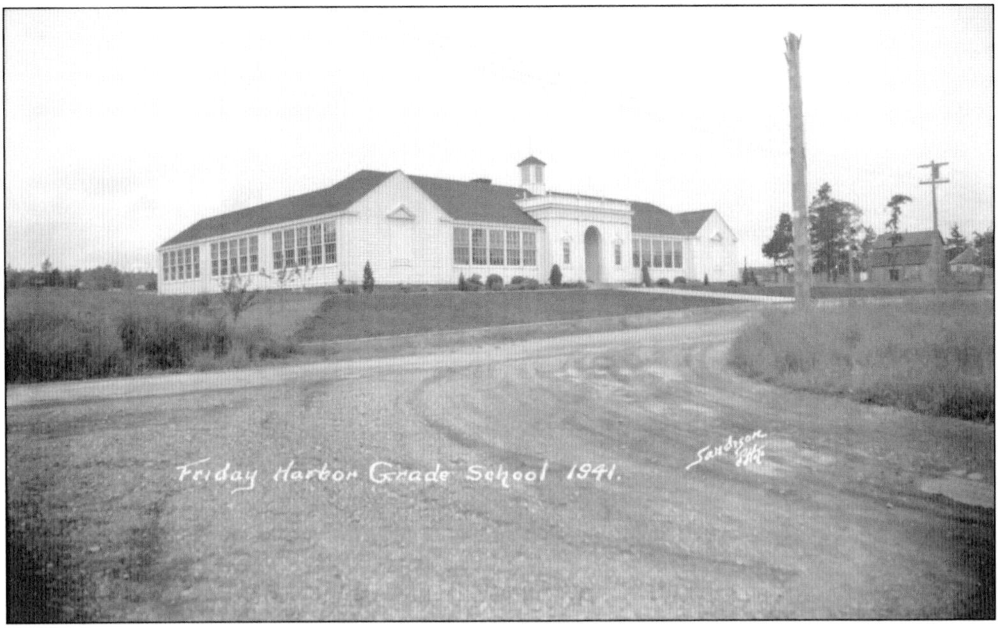


Friday Harbor's new elementary school stood alone in 1941 when photographer Wilbur Sandison attended its dedication. The school had been completed three years earlier at a cost of $31,686. It now serves as the district's middle school. The new high school would be sited where the barn is at right. (WMHA.)

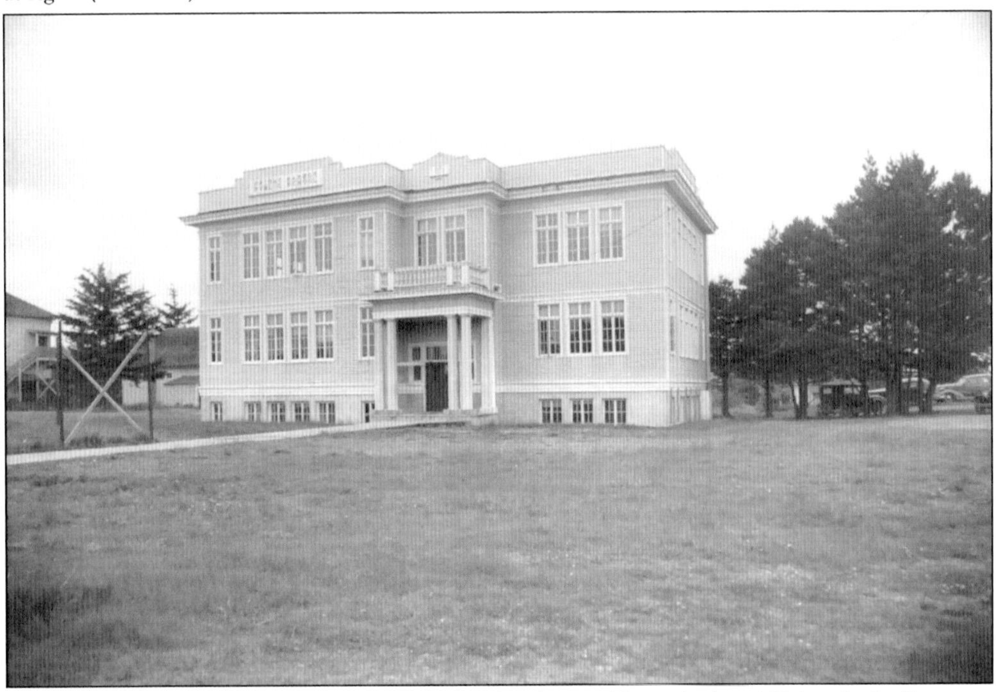

Sandison also recorded this image of the high school, possibly in the late 1930s, which illustrates how far the building was set back from Second Street. To the right is the parking area, roughly in the same spot as today's courthouse lot. At left is the small gymnasium, and at far left is the old belfry school that had yet to be torn down. (WMHA.)

In this c. 1912 image, a school official hands out awards to students of the new public school. High school teacher Walt Nichols stands at far left. According to Juanita Egeland Rouleau, the high school rated well in the state. Subjects included Latin, French, and "a good music program." Note the boy in the Boy Scout uniform at far right. International scouting was founded in 1910.

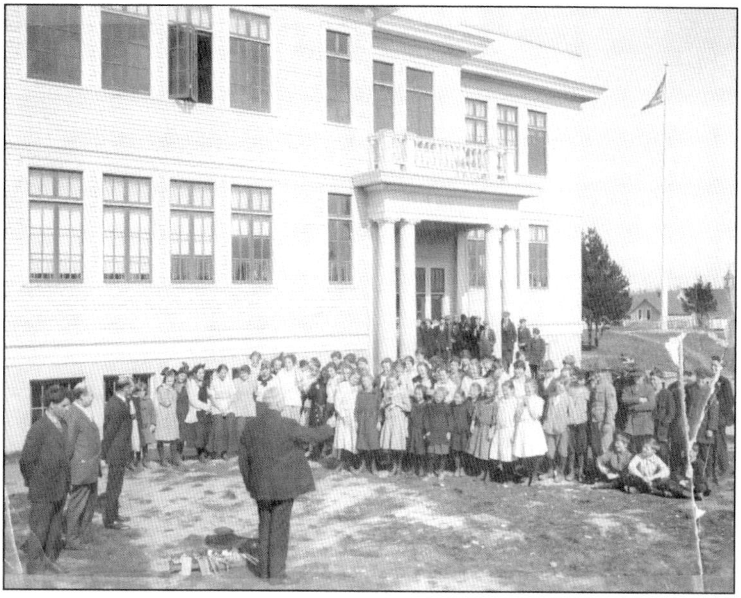

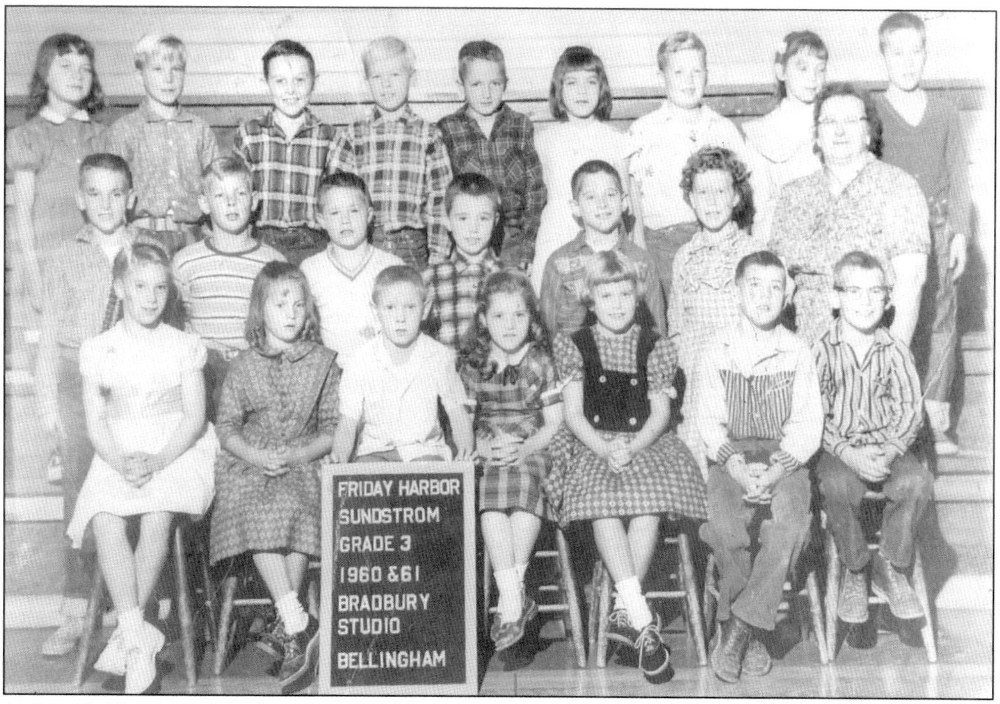


A cheerful lineup of students sits for this c. 1960 photograph of Winnie Sundstrom's third-grade class at Friday Harbor Elementary. Debbie Hudson is standing in the third row at far left. Standing in the third row fourth and fifth from left are Sam Buck Jr. and Bob Murray; at far right is Scott Bell. Seated second from right in the first row is Dennis Wilkes.

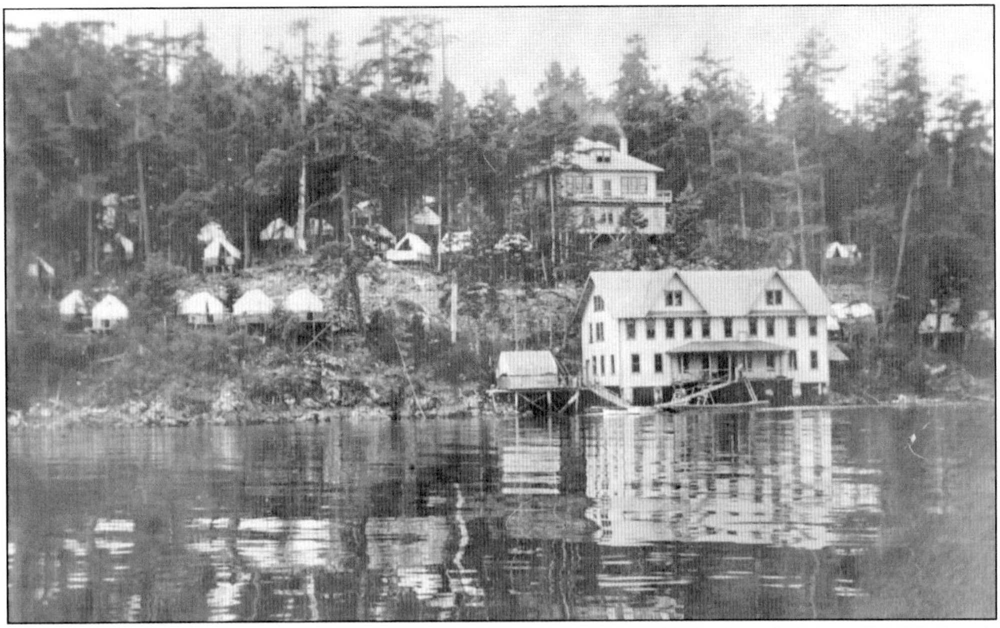

The original University of Washington biology station was established in 1904 on Ed Warbass's property just south of the cannery. It then moved into the closed cannery until 1909, when Capt. Andrew Newhall donated 4 acres contiguous to the site that was to become known as Kwan Lama. The structure on the water, built in 1910, housed the labs and lecture halls, and the top building, built around 1911, housed additional lecture spaces, administrative offices, and a dining hall. Students slept in tents with wooden floors. The new labs, opened in 1924 at the old Point Caution Federal Reserve site, were 24-by-56-foot, one-story structures that housed offices, storage, research rooms, and a general laboratory. Each could accommodate about 20 students. By 1928, four more labs and a lecture hall were added. The total cost, including dormitories and a splendid dining hall, was $75,000.

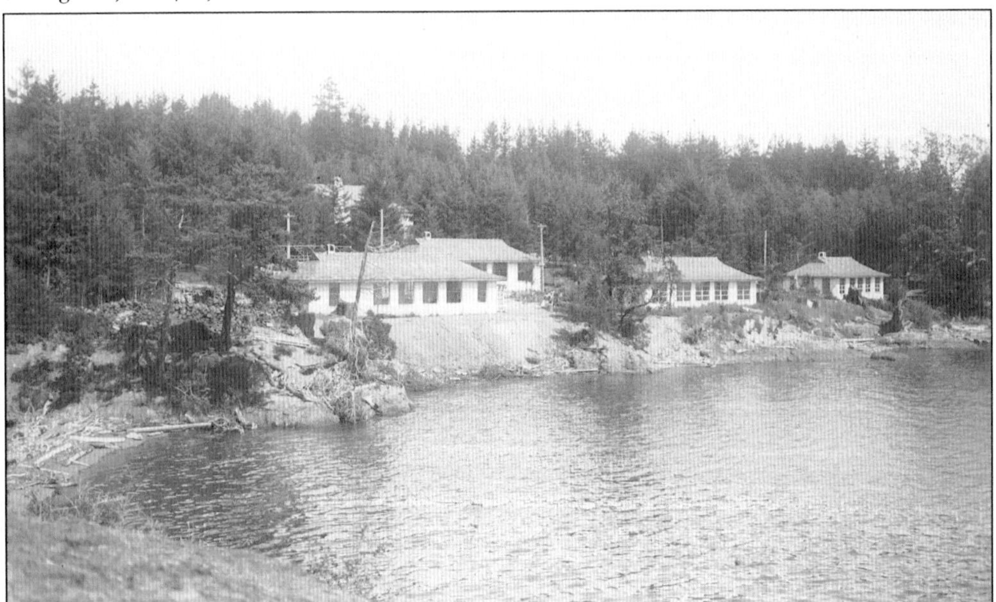

# *Seven*

# A Neighborly Town

J. A. McCormick was a small-town photographer with a big heart. In his photographs of Friday Harbor in the early 20th century, on view at the San Juan Historical Museum, he captures families in party hats, children on bicycles, friends, lovers, graduating classes, and family homes. Thanks to him and countless amateurs with a love of photography, a lost world comes to life and the subjects live again, if only in the imagination.

Photography was coming into its own simultaneous with the growth of Friday Harbor's neighborhoods. Only two years before volunteers cut the Argyle Wagon Road in 1890, which would soon become the principal avenue of one of the town's first residential neighborhoods, George Eastman released his first Kodak box camera. With its single shutter speed and fixed-focus lens, almost anyone who could afford the $25 price tag could be a photographer and do what studio photographers could not: capture spontaneous action.

The only problem was that customers purchased the Kodak pre-loaded with 100 frames of celluloid film, and the camera then had to be returned to the factory for developing. Not surprisingly, most of these early domestic photographs in Friday Harbor depict well-to-do families. But all that changed when, in 1900, Eastman refined (and simplified) the technology with the Kodak Brownie. Now anyone with the urge to record daily and special occasions could do so with a simple snap of the shutter—therefore the "snapshot" and, by 1907, "real photo" picture postcards. The San Juan Historical Museum has several hundred of these 3.5-by-5.5-inch "divided back" (greeting on one side, address on the other) sepia cards. Some capture domestic scenes as described above, and others document public buildings, industry, special events, and disasters.

Most of the latter images were taken by professional photographers and sold over the counter in drugstores and photo studios. One of these, an image of a small boy posing with a salmon nearly twice his size, brought McCormick national renown. A copy now resides in the collection of the New York Public Library, where McCormick is honored among 1,500 other pioneer photographers.

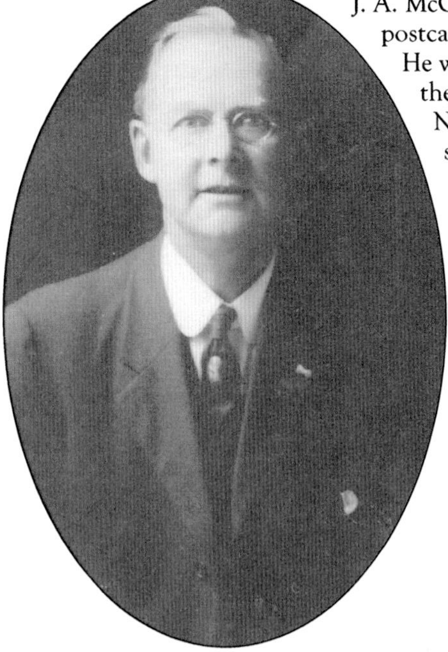

J. A. McCormick circulated his own 3.5-by-5.5-inch real-photo postcards when he ran for county engineer in the 1920s. He was a professional photographer, clerked for a time in the drugstore during World War I when owner Albert Nash was in a pinch, and helped design the town's sewer system. He took many of the portraits of town families in this book.

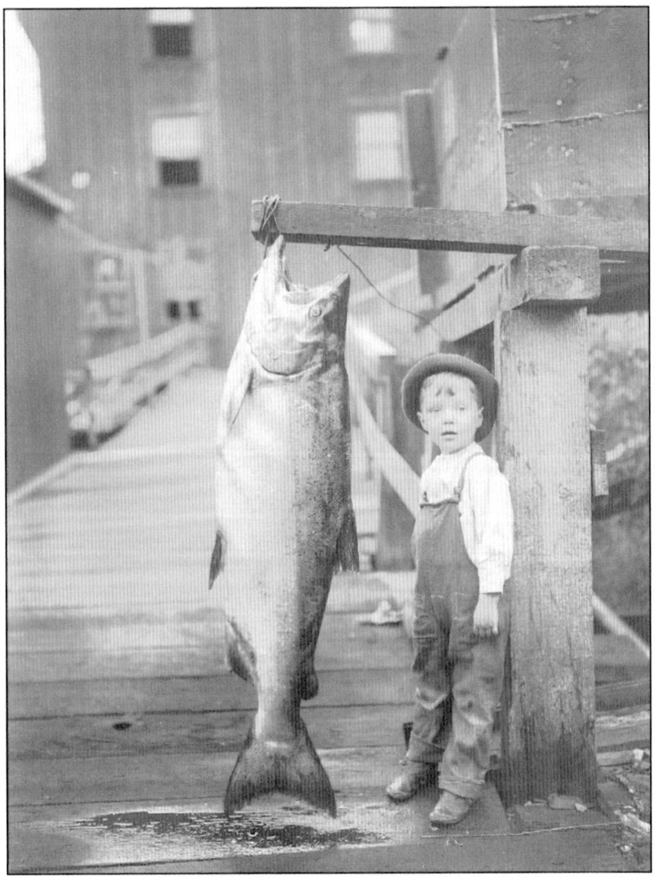

In this nationally famous McCormick portrait, three-year-old Calvin Washburn, son of the Friday Harbor Packing Company's accountant, stands next to a salmon that weighed in at more than 46 pounds—5 pounds more than young Calvin.

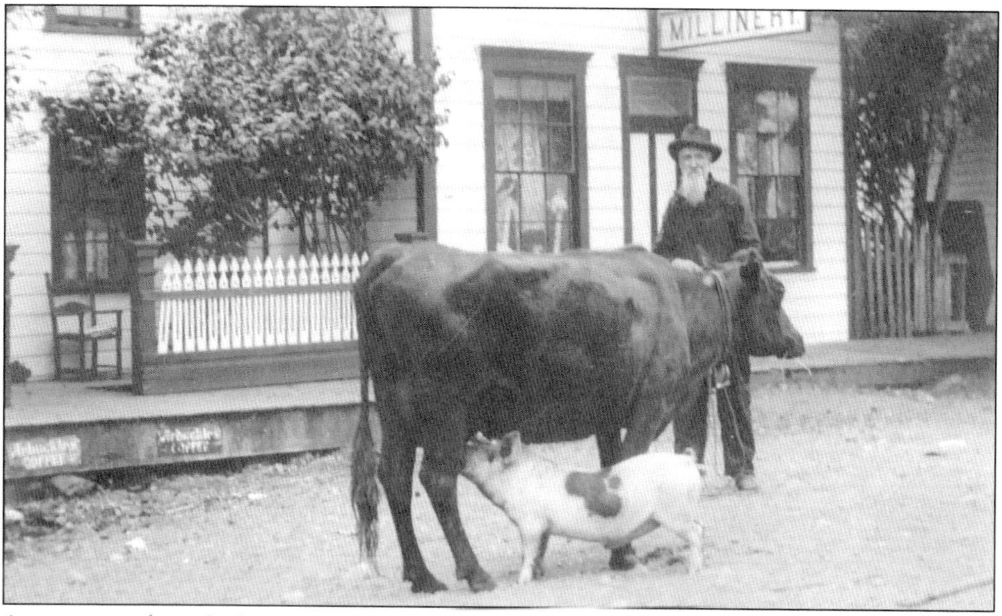

A pig pauses for refreshment in this McCormick photo, shot in front of Ella and Ada Mullis's millinery on Spring Street, *c.* 1910–1917. The man with the cow is Charles McKay, who led the temperance charge in the 1910s, writing, "I have seen liquor sold on this island for 50 years and have seen the curse and poverty it caused to mothers and their families."

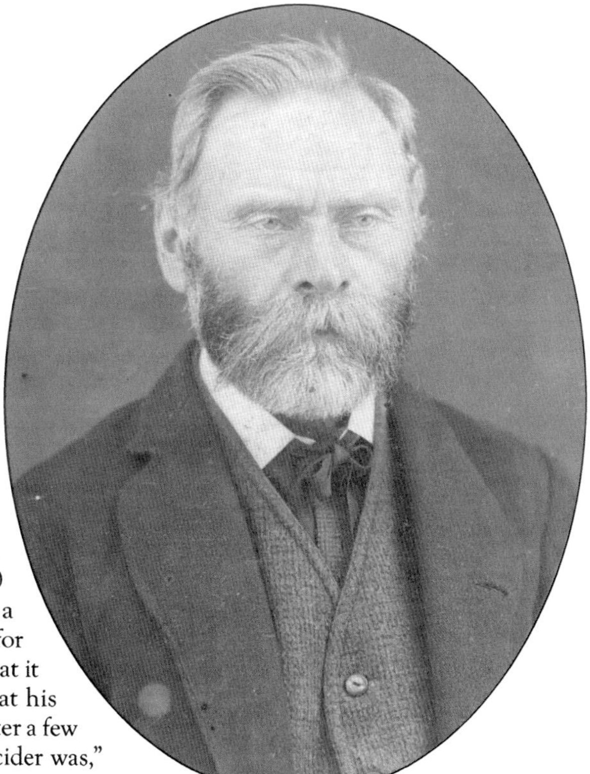

Henry Penshaw was quite the opposite of McKay. He is entered in the 1870 census as a 38-year-old farmer and a native of Maine. But he is best known for his homemade cider. It has been said that it was fermented just hard enough so that his guests could still find their way home after a few drinks. "He knew just how potent his cider was," recalled one islander.

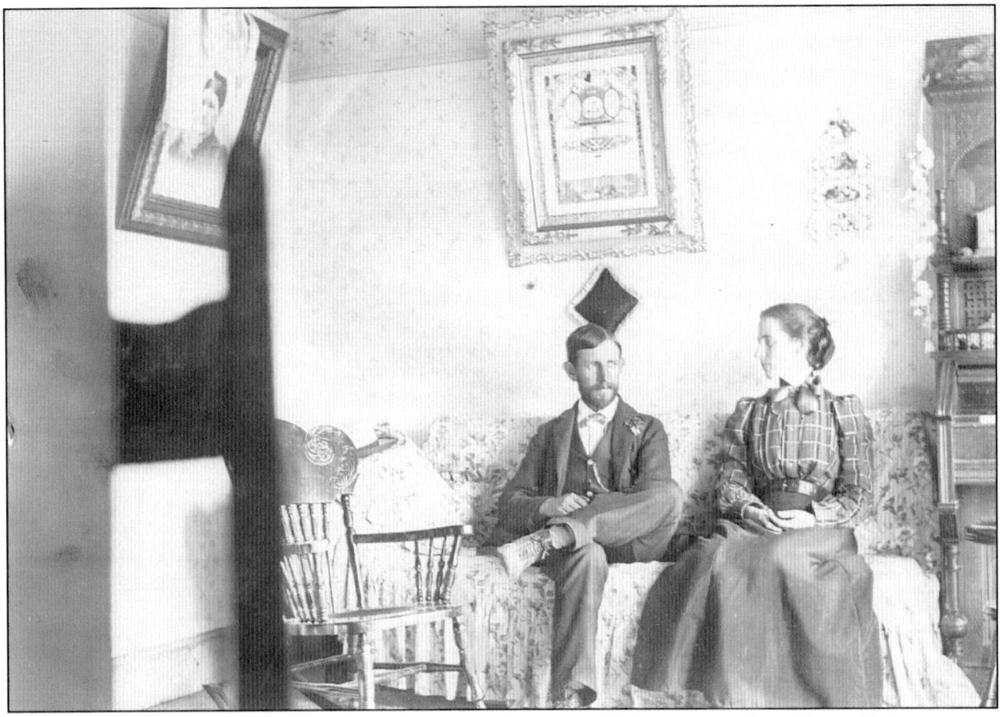

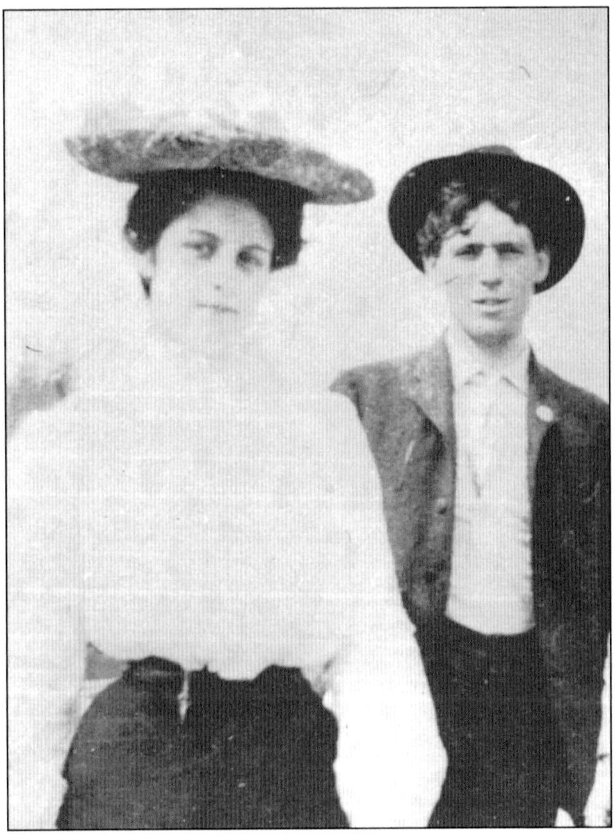

Capt. Herbert H. and Mary Crook Davis relax in the home of William Douglas. Mary was the daughter of William Crook (and sister of Jim), who settled at English Camp in 1875. Married in 1897, Davis retired from the sea and in 1920 founded the H. H. Davis Lumber Company on the waterfront, now Browne's Home Center on Mullis Street.

Walter and Grace Nichols were Friday Harbor schoolteachers who lived in the house across from Spring Street School. Walter taught high school and became principal before retiring. Al Sundstrom remembers: "Old Walter had the pix punch. He'd walk down aisle and poke you in ribs with a pencil. You didn't even have to say anything!" Nichols owned one of the last cows in Friday Harbor.

From left to right, Walter Scribner, John Nash, and Henry Lightheart left no doubt as to their loyalties in this splendid image probably taken in McCormick's studio. All three boys' families were among those who helped build Friday Harbor, representing farming, retail, and transportation. Lightheart's cousin Etta Egelund lived into her hundreds.

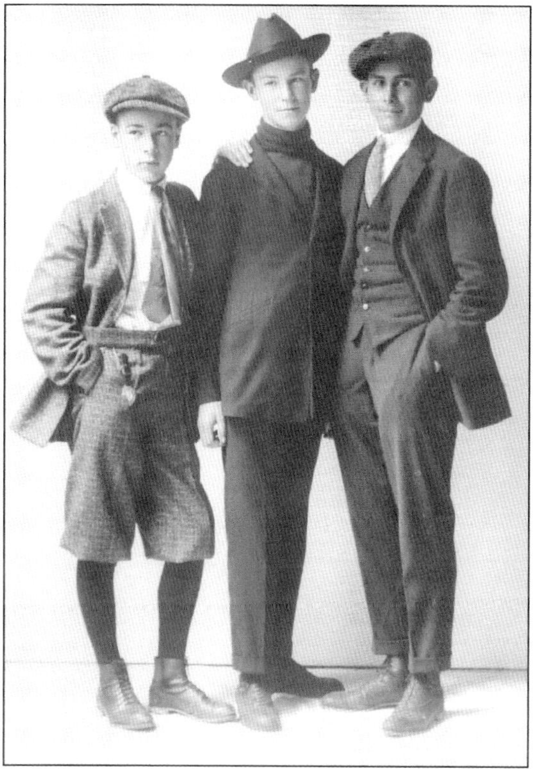

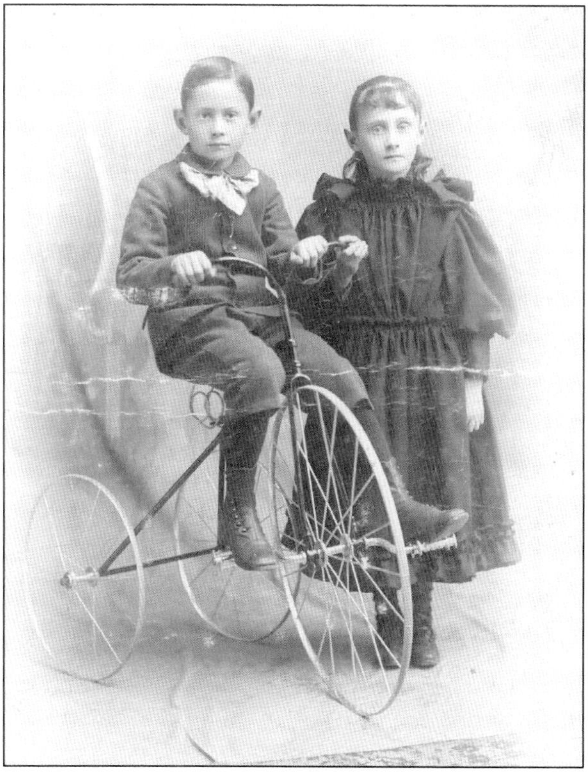

Alvie and Lettie Carter were the children of Launor B. and Emma Carter, owners of Carter's Blue Front Store and later Carter's Department Store. L. B. built houses for both his children on Argyle Avenue, Lettie's in 1912 when she married contractor George Nicholson. She later married William "Billy" Roark.

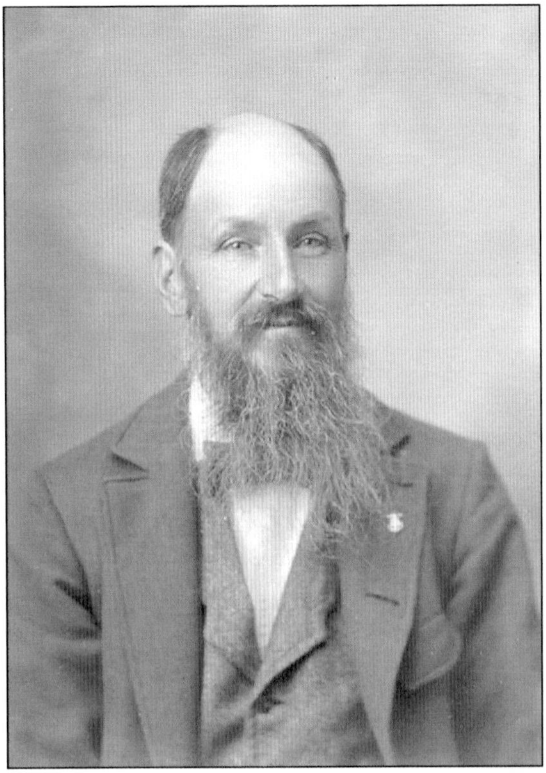

Englishman George Mullis arrived on San Juan Island in 1894 with his wife, Emma, and their children, Ada, Frank, and Ella. A master carpenter who learned his trade at Buckingham Palace, he built a house in 1905 at the corner of Argyle Avenue and Caines Street, which still stands. Frank followed him in the trade, and Ada and Ella opened a millinery on Spring Street. (Peggy Sue McRae.)

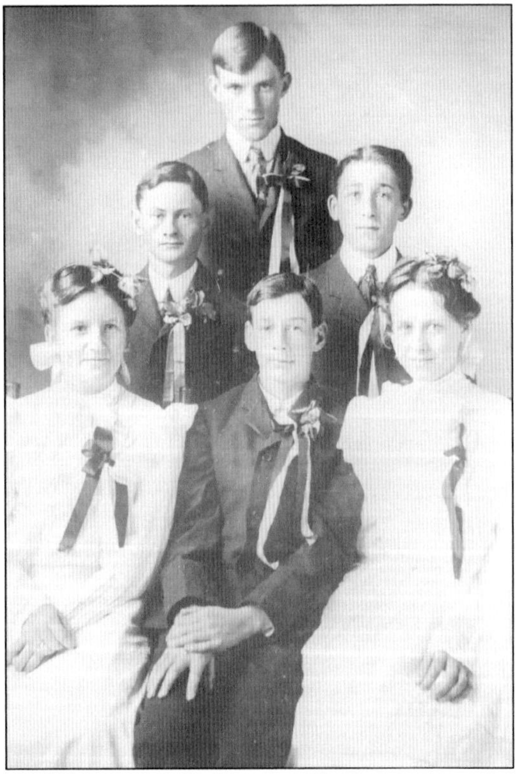

The 1907 graduating class of the belfry school are, from left to right, (first row) Agnes Wright, Cecil Carter, and Gladys Guard; (second row) Alvie Carter and Norman Driggs; (third row) Colin Sandwith. Cecil Carter, son of San Juan pioneer Cornelius L. "Kirgy" Carter, started as a clerk and janitor with San Juan County Bank in 1906 and remained for 61 years before retiring as chairman of the board.

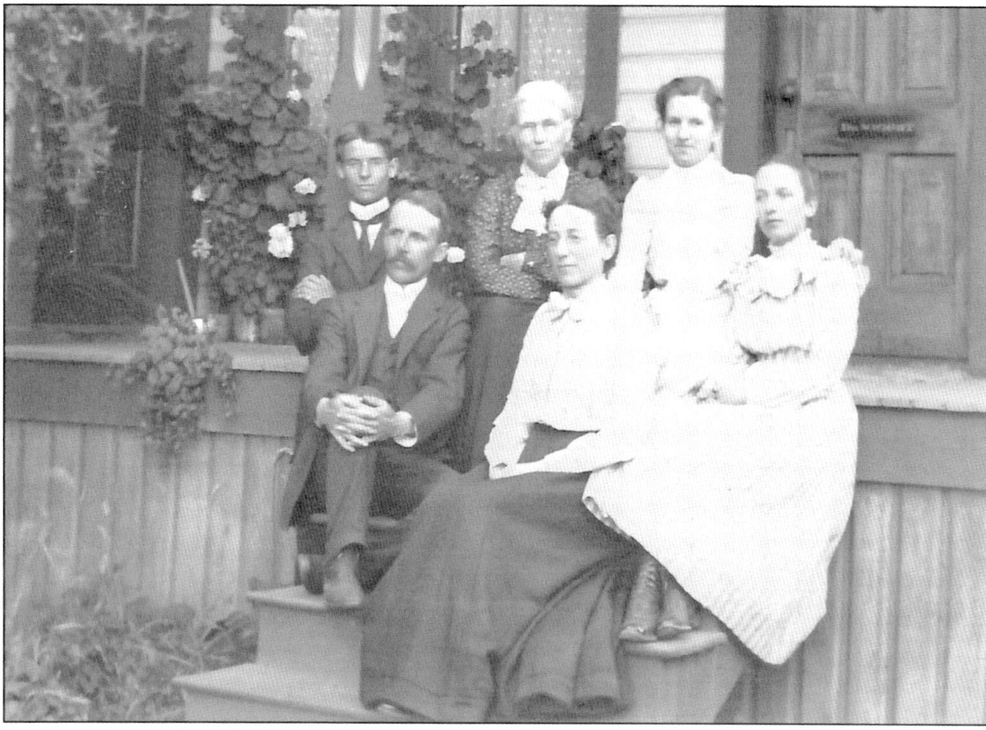

Dr. George Wright and his family relax on the steps of the family home on Spring Street, c. 1900. From left are Leon Little (Wright's cousin who managed and eventually bought his drugstore next door), Dr. Wright, his mother Blair, wife Laura, and daughters Agnes and Louise. Wright's office was in the rear of the house.

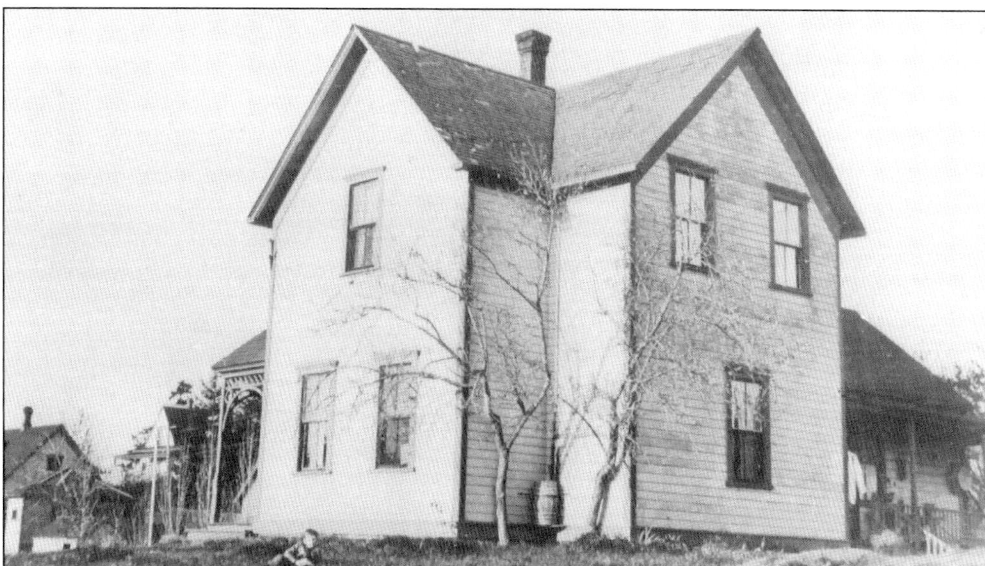

This elegant house on Nichols Street was built in 1898 by O.H. Culver. It was later occupied by William H. Higgins, and then passed through several owners, including Bob and Mildred Hartzog, former publishers of the *Friday Harbor Journal*. It is still standing today between the ferry overload waiting areas.

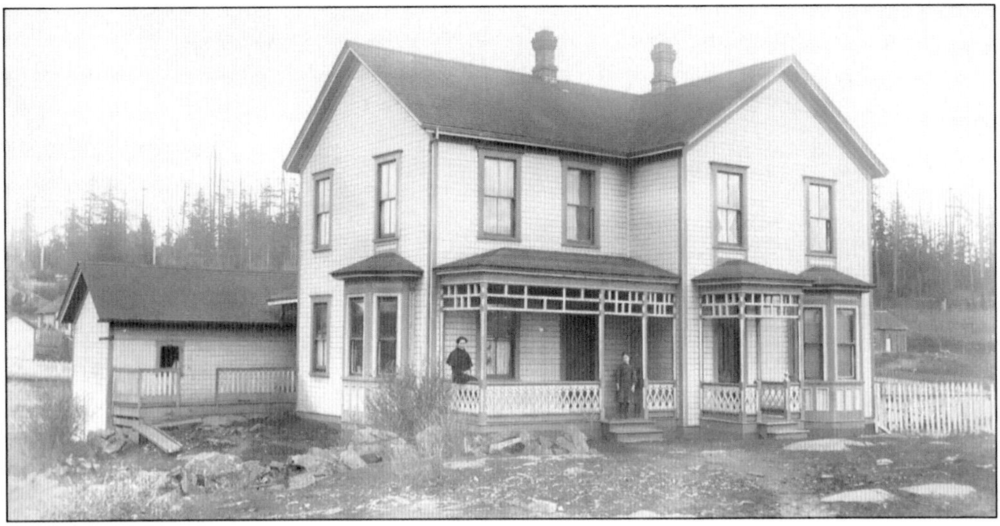

In 1889, Norman Churchill, a retail grocer, built this house at First and A Streets. He claimed to be a distant relative of the Churchills, as in Winston S. (the latter making world headlines just a few years later during the Boer War). The house served for years as a restaurant with shops, then moved to Argyle Avenue to make way for condominiums.

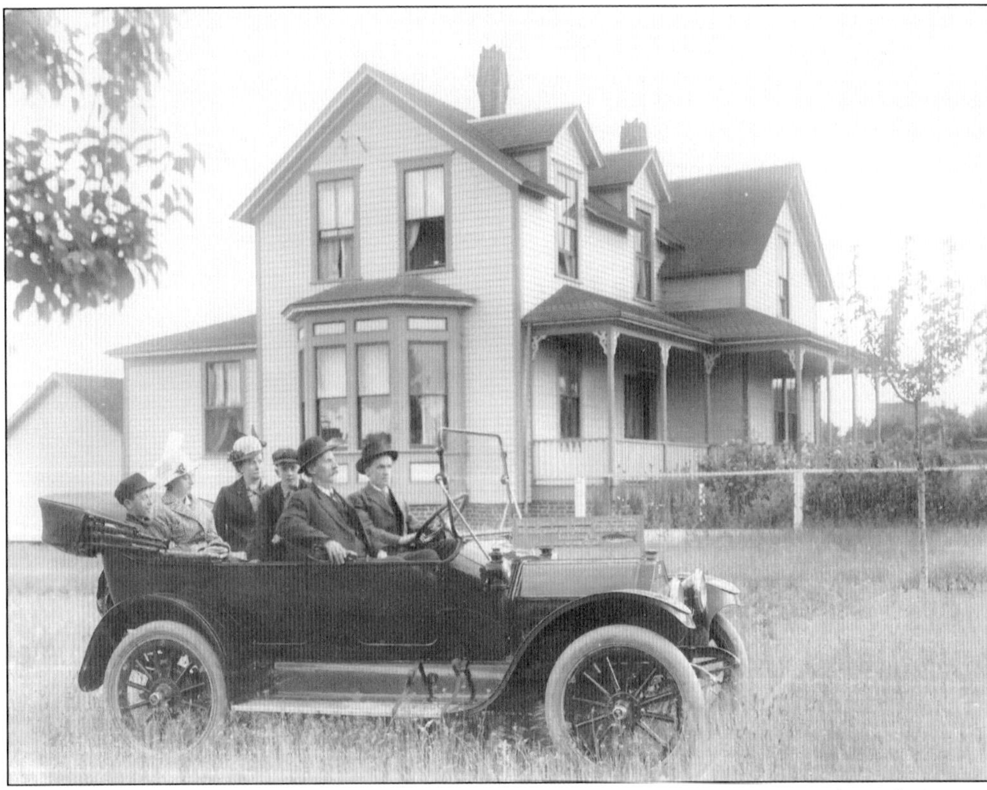

L. B. Carter rides in the front seat of a touring car next to his house at Spring Street and Argyle Avenue. During the Great Depression, Carter backed the San Juan County Bank with $30,000, enough to keep the bank afloat and save the community from disaster. He swore his nephew Cecil Carter, a bank officer, to secrecy because he did not want his children to know he had risked their inheritance.

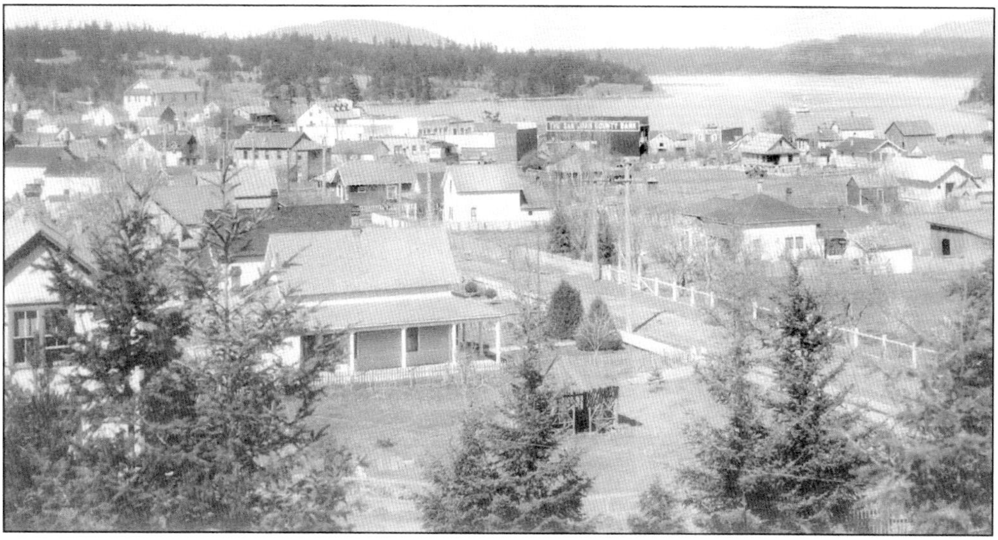

In 1890, volunteers built a wagon road from Friday Harbor to Argyle, site of the only gristmill on the island. Upon completion, a few businessmen built houses along the route in a classic frontier alignment of the high and low towns. The white, single-story house at right center (above) was the first, built by Granville B. Driggs, an entrepreneur who dabbled in retail and modest shipping, and who also grew strawberries in the field behind his house. The photograph below, taken several years later, reveals the two houses L. B. Carter built for his children next door to the Driggs place. The Peter Archambault house appears at left foreground in both photographs. Archambault is listed in the 1900 census as a "day laborer," which underscores the egalitarian nature of the neighborhood.

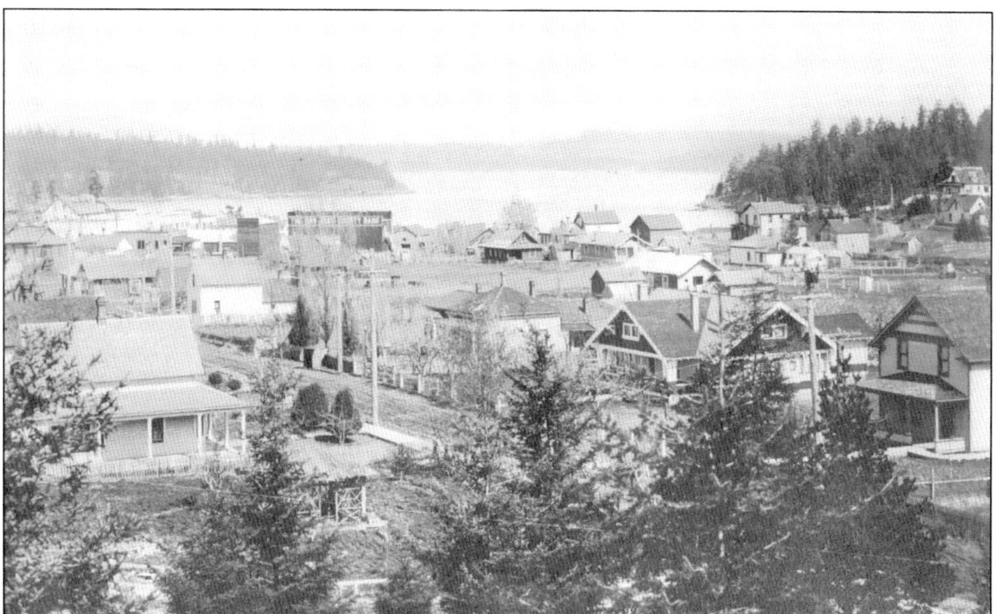

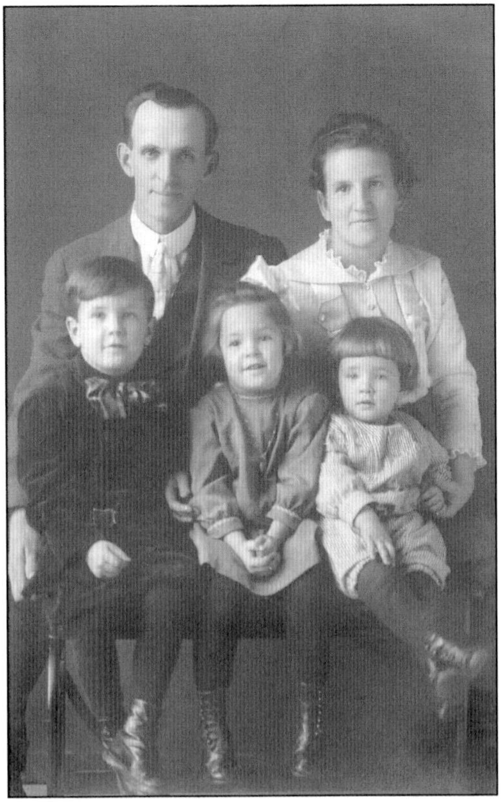

King's Market founder Lyle King sits with his family in the studio. Mrs. King is the former Agnes Wright, daughter of Dr. George Wright, and she also appears on pages 104 and 105. The children, from left to right, are Blair, Dorothy, and Mildred. The Kings divorced, and Lyle King later remarried and had two more daughters.

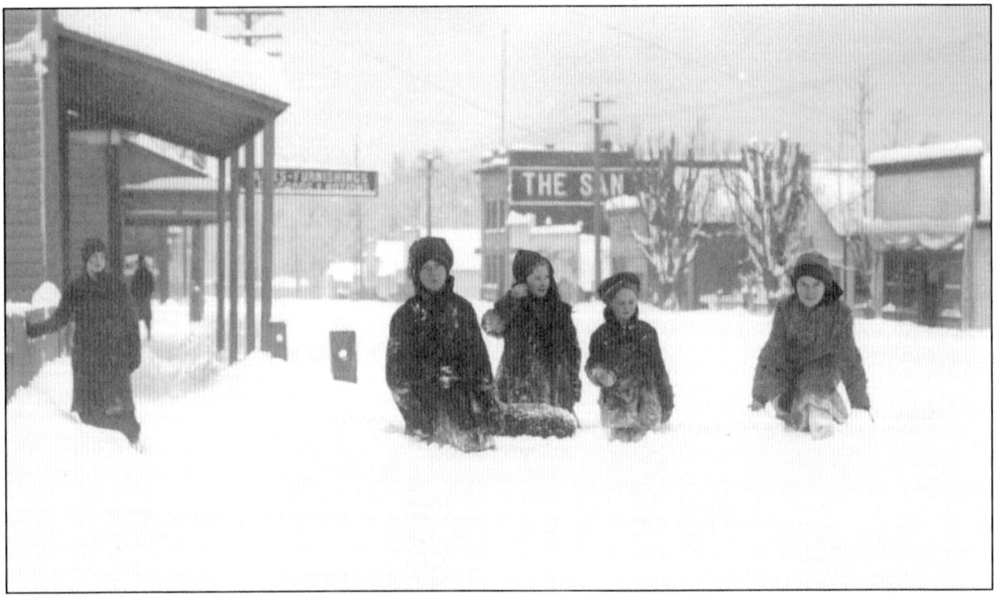


A heavy snow blanketed the island in 1909. Here children play knee-deep on Spring Street, just up from San Juan County Bank and Tony's Restaurant at far right. This was the same year as the January 11 earthquake that rattled the town when the Washington-Alaska telegraph cable snapped. Medicine bottles toppled from shelves at Dr. Wright's drugstore, and the captain of the *Rosalie* ordered the engines reversed, thinking the vessel had struck a log or rock.

Eric and Belle (McKenzie) Erickson take their ease on the porch of an island home around 1900. Erickson was a native of Finland who immigrated to the United States in 1868 and claimed his home on the island in 1872. He farmed 200 acres out of town and served several terms as the superintendent of schools.

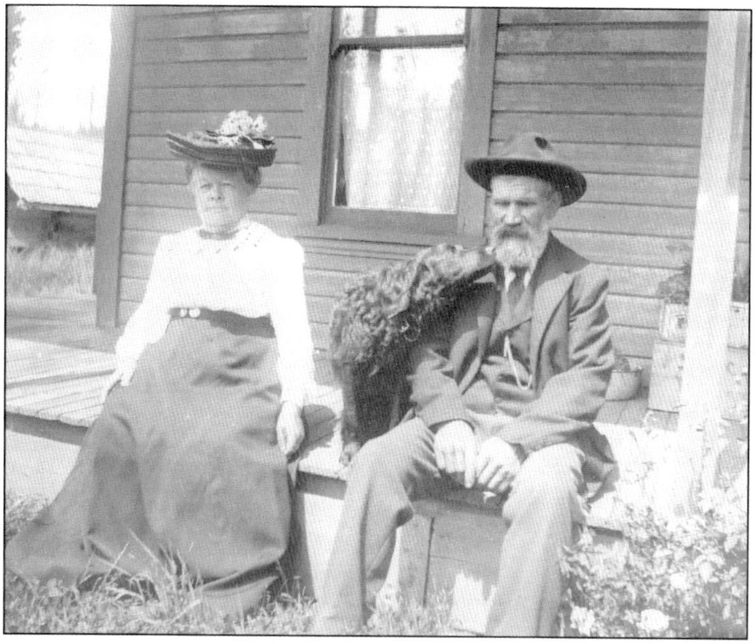

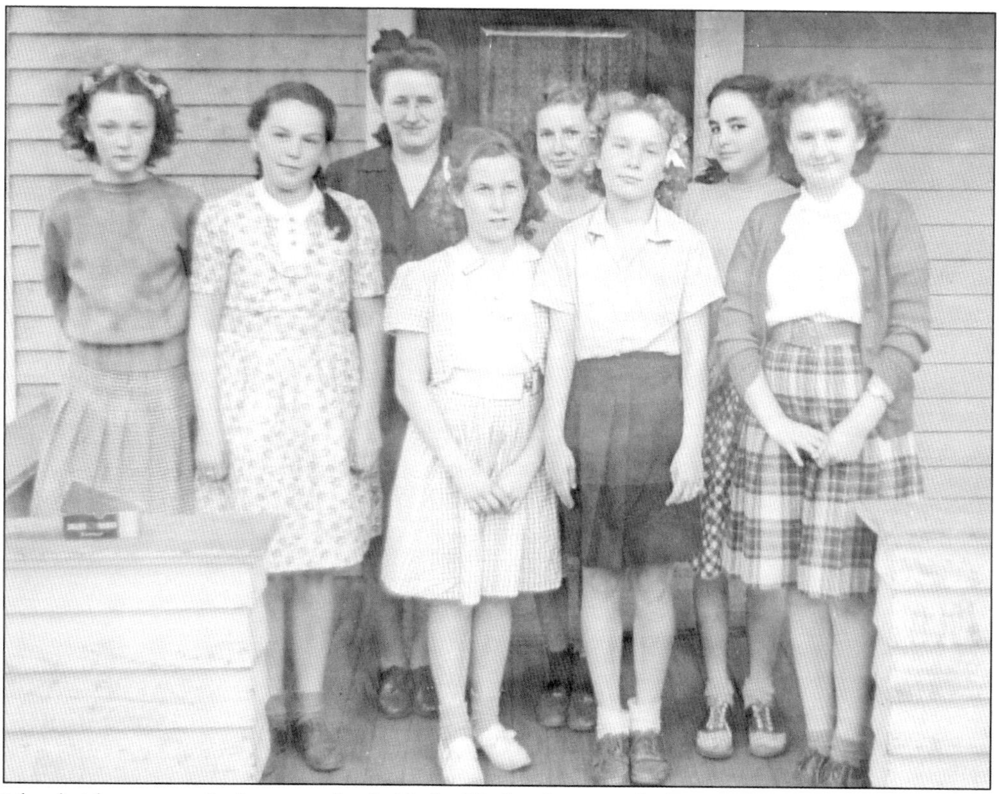

Island girls pose on the front porch of a Friday Harbor home with their teacher, Winnie Sundstrom. From left to right are Ruthie Tuck, Nancy Nash, Winnie Sundstrom, Harlene Lightheart, Mary Hale, two unidentified, and Rawleen Davis. Harlene appears to be wearing the white belt of a crossing guard.

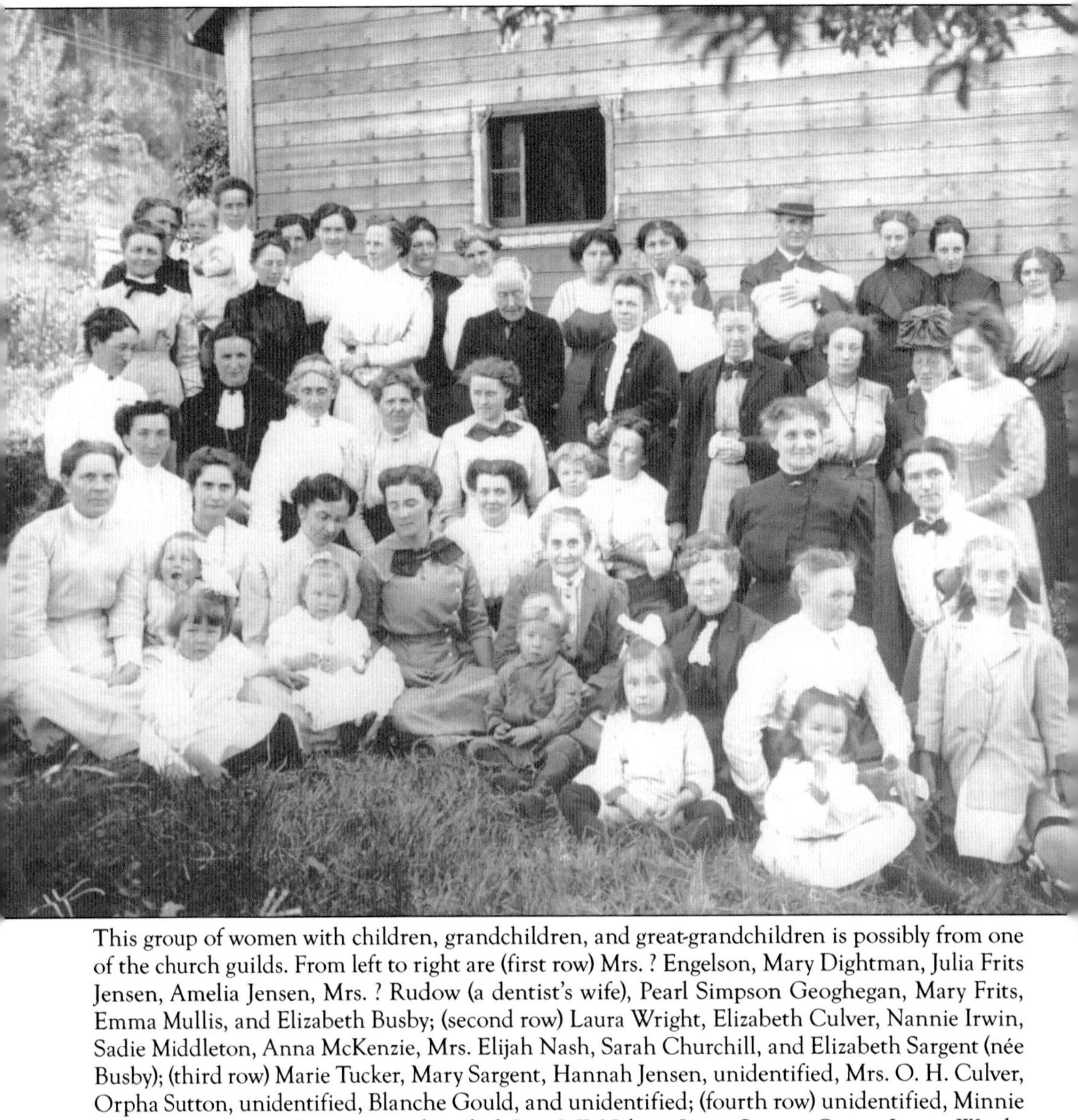

This group of women with children, grandchildren, and great-grandchildren is possibly from one of the church guilds. From left to right are (first row) Mrs. ? Engelson, Mary Dightman, Julia Frits Jensen, Amelia Jensen, Mrs. ? Rudow (a dentist's wife), Pearl Simpson Geoghegan, Mary Frits, Emma Mullis, and Elizabeth Busby; (second row) Laura Wright, Elizabeth Culver, Nannie Irwin, Sadie Middleton, Anna McKenzie, Mrs. Elijah Nash, Sarah Churchill, and Elizabeth Sargent (née Busby); (third row) Marie Tucker, Mary Sargent, Hannah Jensen, unidentified, Mrs. O. H. Culver, Orpha Sutton, unidentified, Blanche Gould, and unidentified; (fourth row) unidentified, Minnie Carter, Elizabeth Hackett, two unidentified, Rev. J. E. Nelson, Laura Sargent Carter, Louise Wright Little, and unidentified. (Jensen family.)

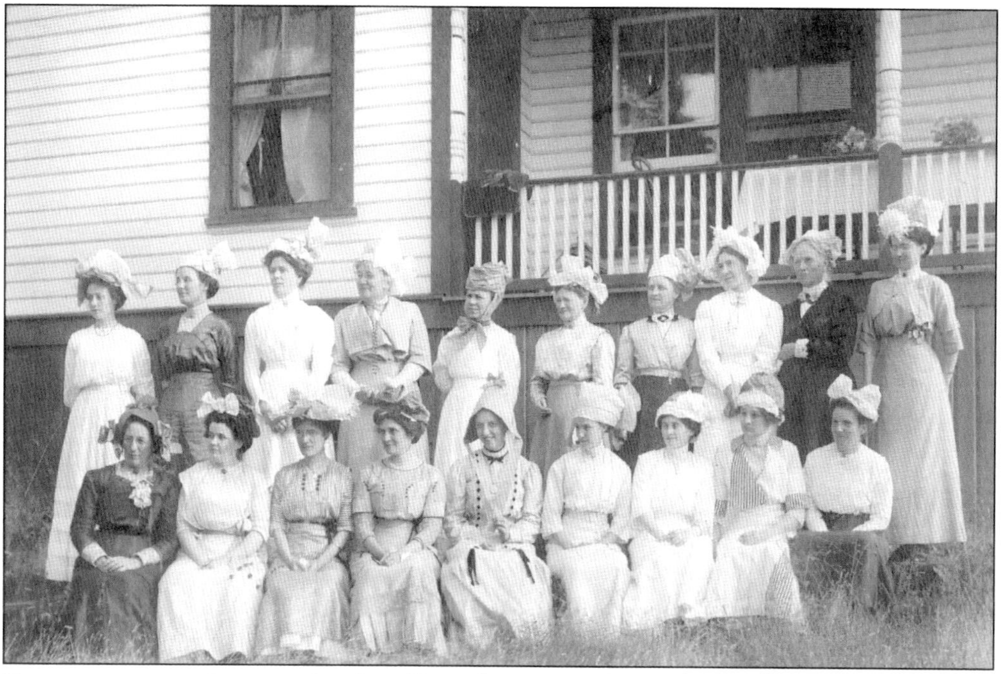

Pioneer women, perhaps wearing their Easter bonnets, gather at the Gould house around 1900. From left to right are (first row) Laura Wright, Pearl Geoghegan, Laura Perry, Clara Perry, Louise Wright, Laura Carter, Lettie Roark, Mrs. ? Rudow, and Agnes Wright; (second row) Blanche Gould, Mrs. ? Woolford, Mrs. ? Clinton, Fanny Driggs, Mrs. A. H. Culver, Emma Mullis, Mrs. C. M. Tucker, Fanny Capron, Harriet Blair, and Ada Mullis Larson.

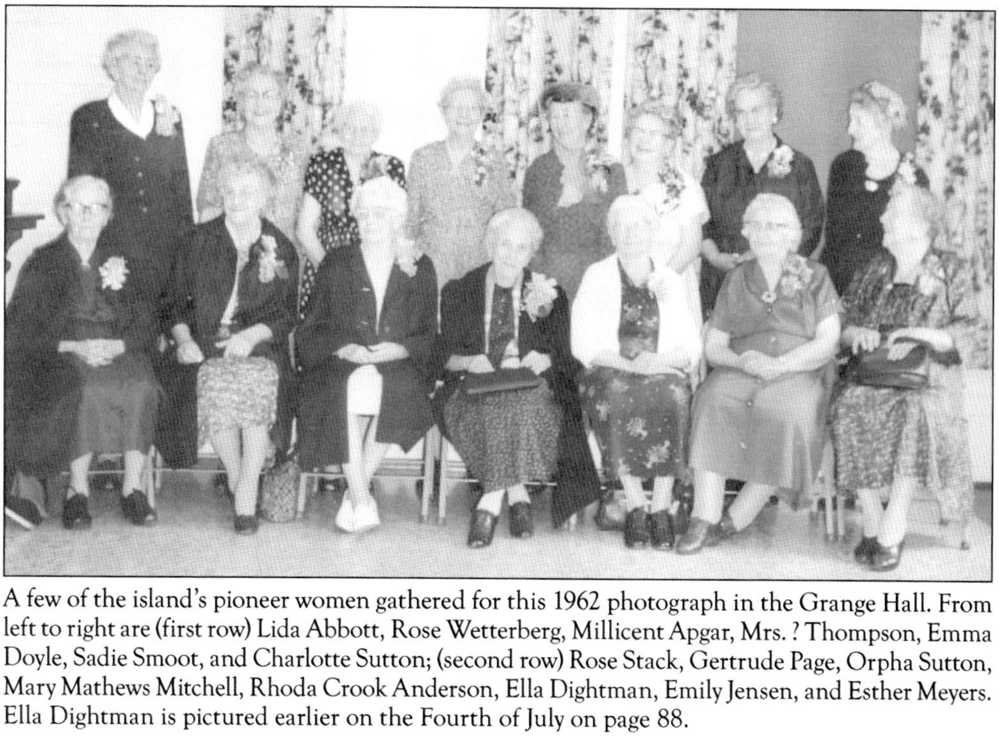

A few of the island's pioneer women gathered for this 1962 photograph in the Grange Hall. From left to right are (first row) Lida Abbott, Rose Wetterberg, Millicent Apgar, Mrs. ? Thompson, Emma Doyle, Sadie Smoot, and Charlotte Sutton; (second row) Rose Stack, Gertrude Page, Orpha Sutton, Mary Mathews Mitchell, Rhoda Crook Anderson, Ella Dightman, Emily Jensen, and Esther Meyers. Ella Dightman is pictured earlier on the Fourth of July on page 88.

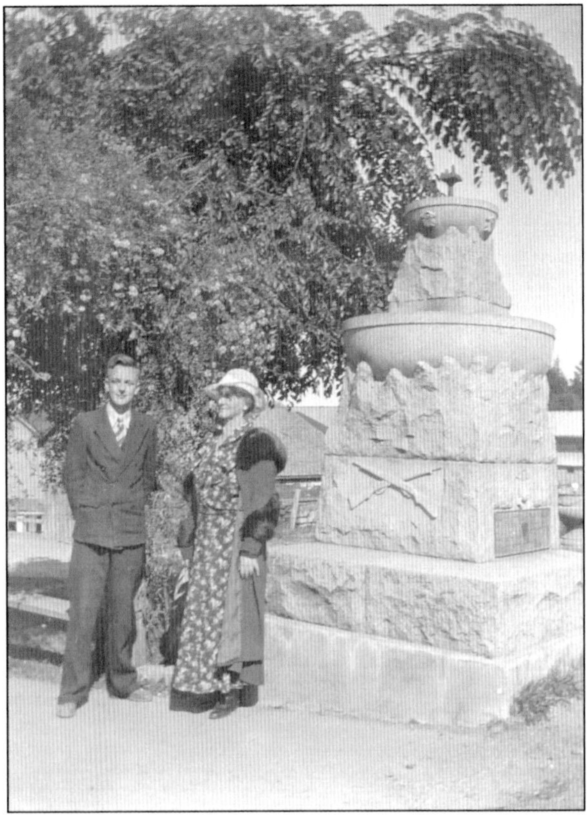

Mary Crook Davis stands next to Dr. Malcolm Heath at Memorial Park in 1950. Heath was the county's only physician for the next 20 years. During that time he delivered more than 2,500 babies (one emergency delivery in his underpants to preserve the crease in his trousers) and singlehandedly treated 11,000 patients annually. He retired in 1978.

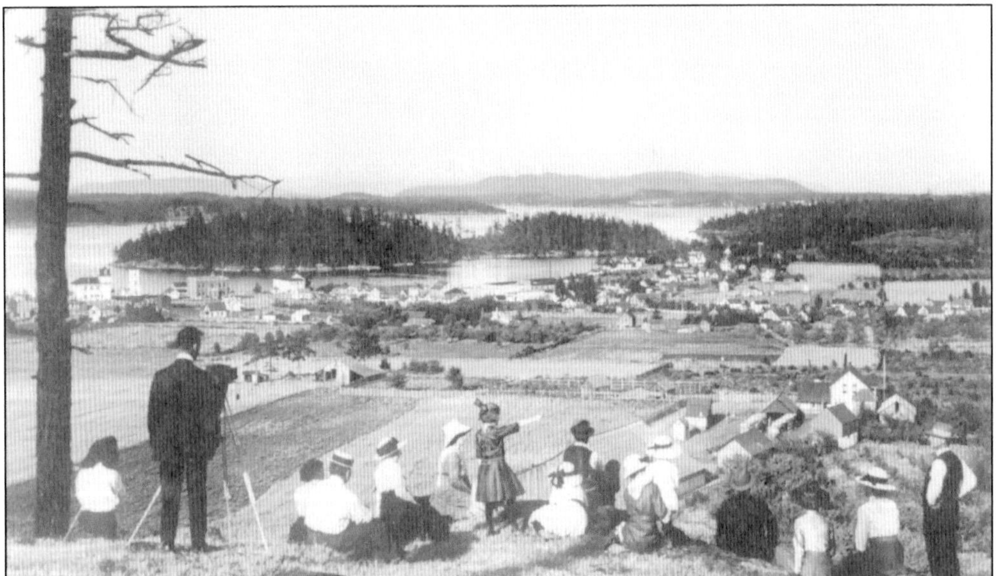

In a fitting end to this chapter, J.A. McCormick captures fellow photographer Van Johnson taking a panorama of Friday Harbor's town center and prairie lands, c. 1906–1911, from King Hill above the King Farm, now the grounds of the San Juan Historical Museum. The new courthouse is in place, but the high school has yet to be built. A perfect shot on a perfect day.

# *Eight*

# A Town in Transition

Friday Harbor is a town that would not die. This is not to say that there were not ample opportunities. With the rise of the automobile, hard-surface roads, and then interstate highways across the country, all of the island's extraction industries—from fruit to lime, canned salmon to peas—collapsed one by one as the island marched into the 20th century. Freight costs of waterborne transportation priced Friday Harbor produce out of the market, and the fishing industry sagged as well. First the fish traps were outlawed in 1934, and then the resource itself dwindled as more vessels plied the waters and shipping costs soared. It was much easier to can or freeze and ship from the mainland. During the postwar period, the canneries processed frozen fish hauled down from Alaska and once had to reprocess 10,000 cases of canned salmon when a container ship sank. By the time the cannery closed for good in 1966, it seemed that Friday Harbor was in danger of becoming an eccentric and sleepy backwater.

Fortunately, business and community leaders had been prescient enough to recognize that perhaps the greatest resource they had to exploit was the island itself. With spectacular views, rural charm, and seasonable weather, retirees, summer and weekend residents, and vacationers staked claims as early as 1906. Taking note, real estate developers began buying up property along the decaying industrial waterfront. By 1971, the Port of Friday Harbor appraised Front Street to determine market value and development of the waterfront. The primary targets were boaters and ferry travelers, whom the port hoped would extend their stays. The bottom line: "In conclusion, the most profitable use of the property would be in the new form of retail and service activities, possibly extended to motel or condominium development."

The key purchase was Sam Buck Sr.'s acquisition of the cannery and attendant lands. In the early 1970s, Buck sold the property to another developer, who razed the cannery and built condominiums and retail businesses adjoining today's ferry landing, which was installed in 1968.

A new kind of town was born.

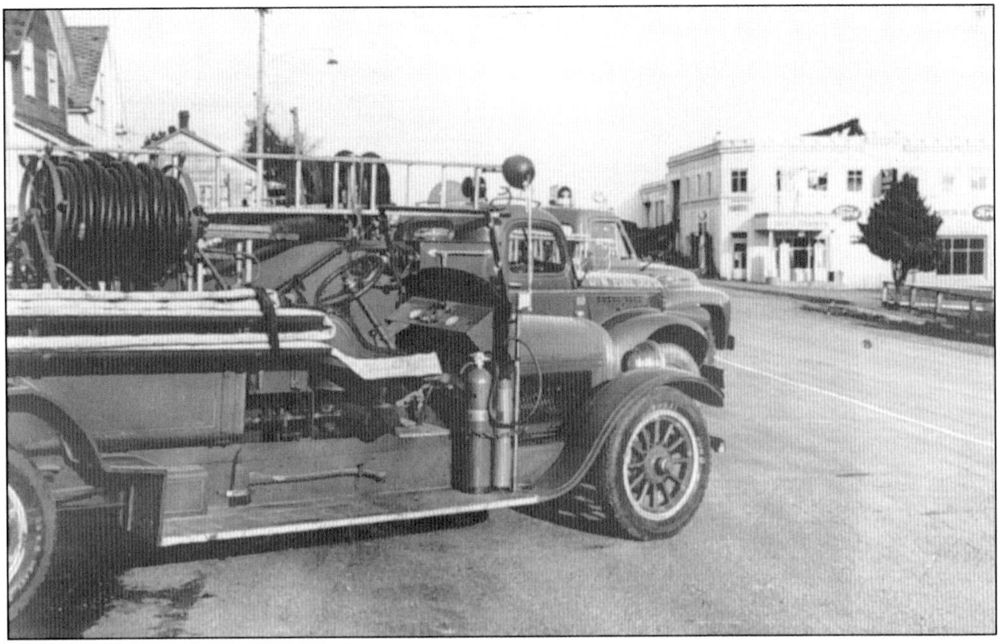

Friday Harbor Fire Department trucks point toward the Ford dealership and garage at the corner of First and West Streets. In 1906, the concrete-block building first housed an Overland and Studebaker dealership owned by Calvin Lightheart and George Franck. Franck then offered Ford Model Ts, which were built from 1908 to 1927. A sign over the garage door read "Drive slow."

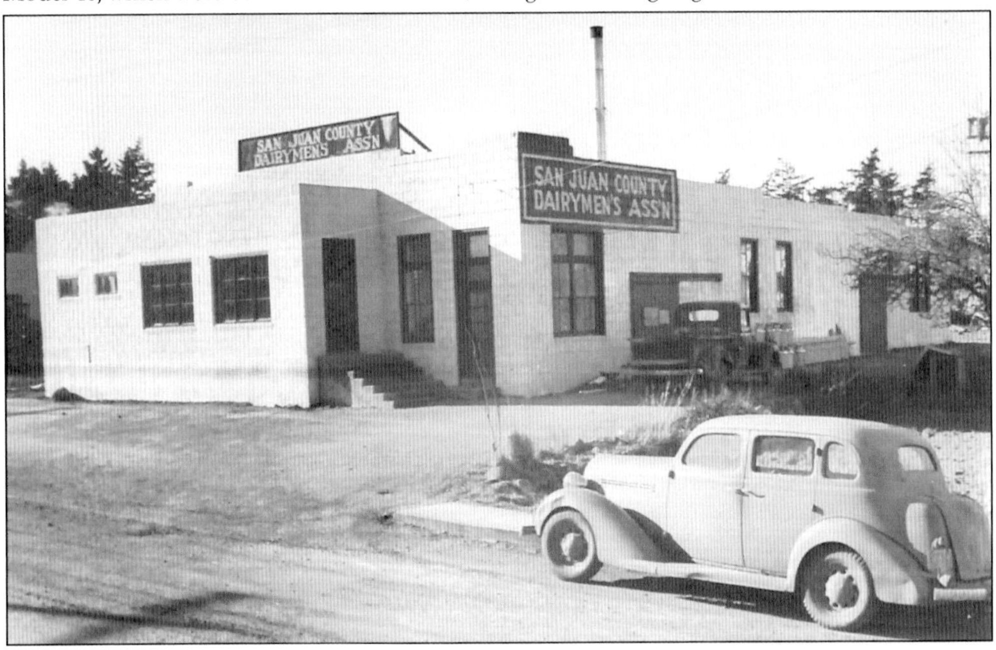


The San Juan County Dairyman's Association creamery, founded in 1904, was still a going concern in the 1930s. The creamery would dispatch trucks to dairy farms throughout the island to pick up milk and cream, then package and deliver products to front doorsteps. They also manufactured and delivered ice to the iceboxes around town. Browne Lumber occupied the building for years before it was demolished.

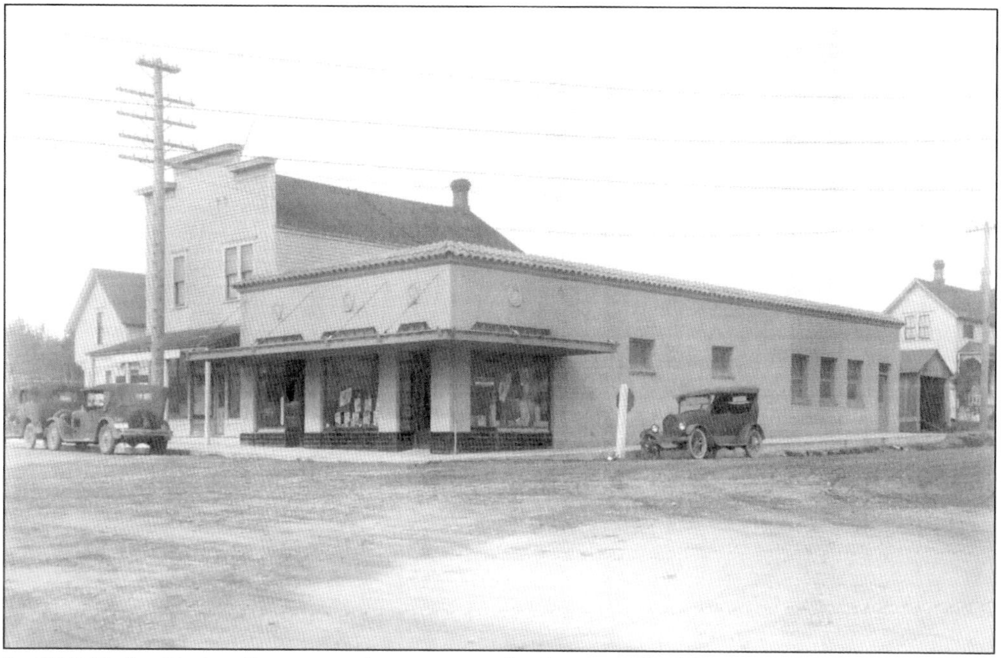

In 1929, Friday Harbor Drug moved into its new (and current) building with the Spanish-tile roof in the same location at Spring and Second Streets. The store primarily dispensed medicines but was famous for its variety. In the early years, one could find tack for the stables, corks for open containers, and veterinary medicines. A soda fountain and notions were added in later years, with the fountain closing in 1958.

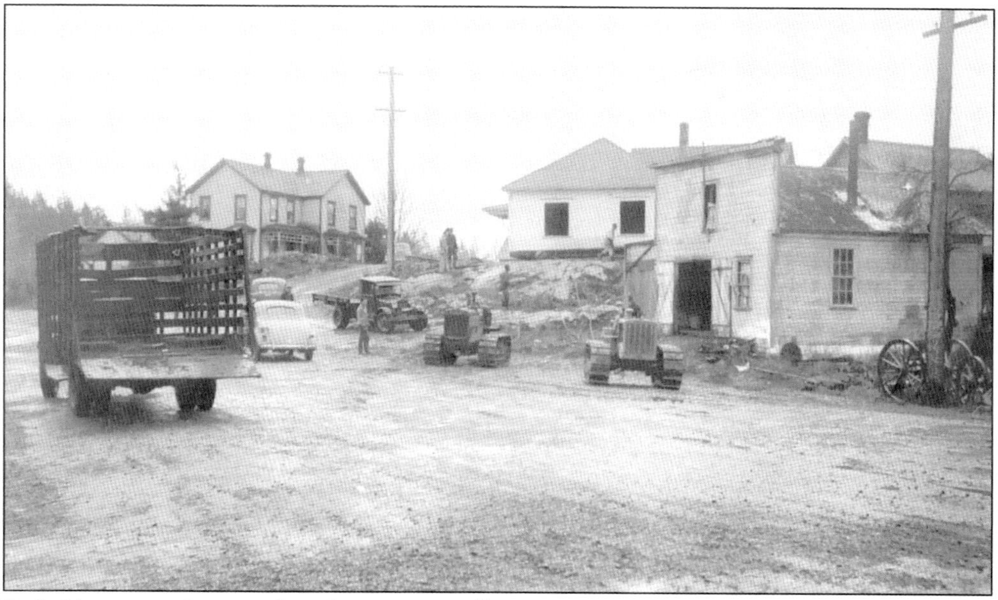

Probably no one photograph in the museum collection epitomizes transition more than this image of First Street, between Spring and A Streets, where a stable and smithy stand amid Caterpillar tractors, a Model A truck, wagon wheels, and the 1890s vintage Churchill house, since moved to Argyle Avenue. The house atop the rock (still there) was moved from Park Street to make room for the football field.

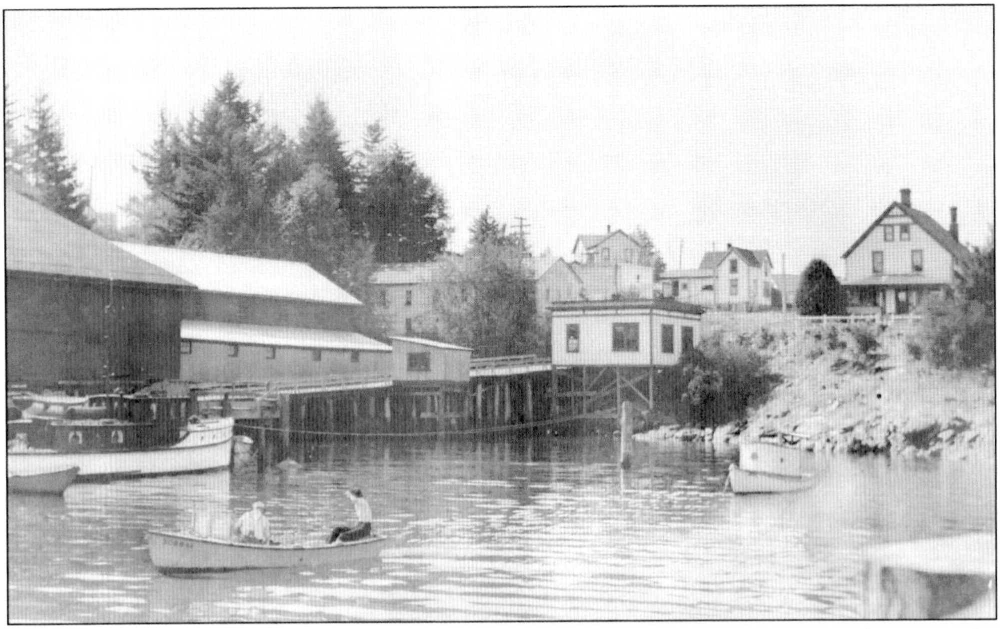

A cabin cruiser and fisherman Charlie Welch's little boat, far right, swing at anchor near the cannery dock, c. 1940s. Welch always fished with hand lines and walked to his driftwood home each evening. The cannery and net shed are left foreground, then (clockwise) the workers' dormitory, slaughterhouse, and Charles McKay's house. The small building on the dock was the cannery office and to the right was the manager's house

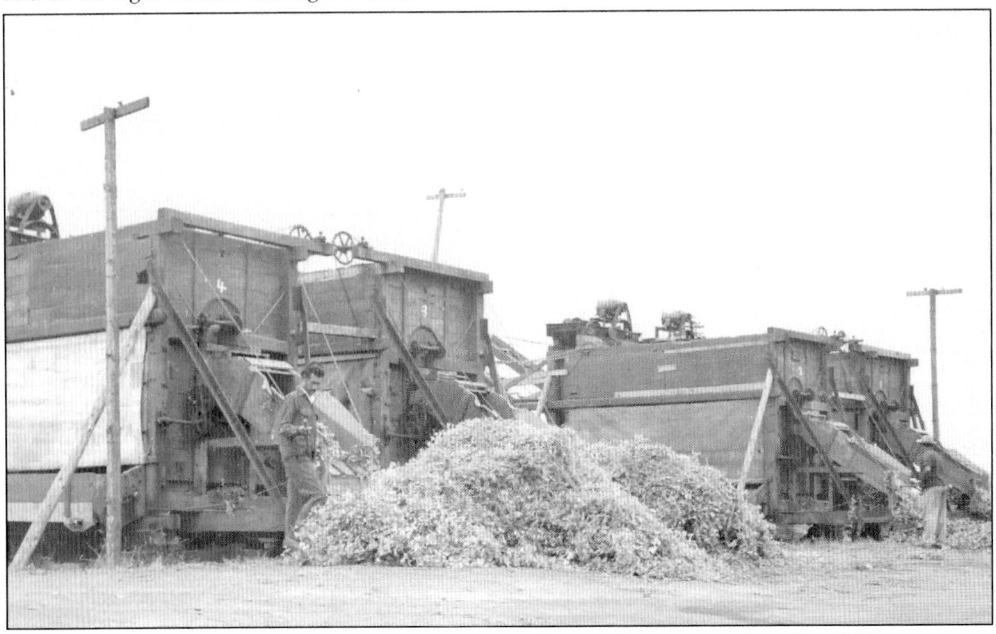

Pea-vining machines, parked at Bailer Hill and Douglas Roads, were used in the 1960s to process canned and frozen peas. This was well after thousands of cans of peas plunged to the bottom of the harbor in 1939 when the cannery floor collapsed. Island-grown peas were big business from 1923 to 1939 (when pea weevils struck), thanks to Spokane grower John M. "Pea" Henry. The cannery closed permanently in 1966.

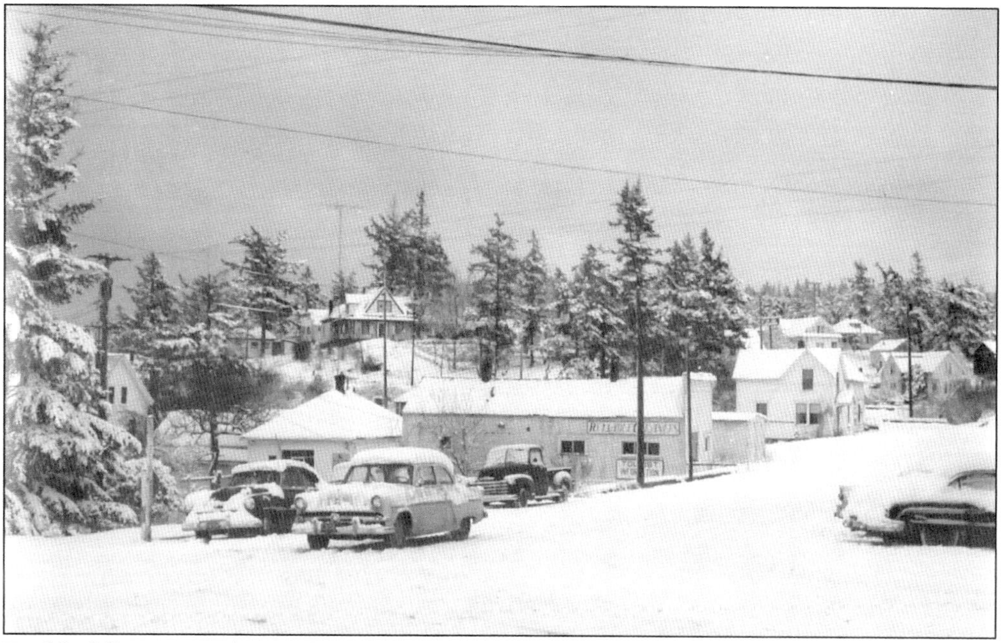

Freshly fallen snow silences the town in the 1950s. By then, a fire had wiped out most of the buildings in the block between Spring and A Streets. Charles McKay's house is the next up the road and the Gould (Geneste) house is on the hill beyond, where it still stands.

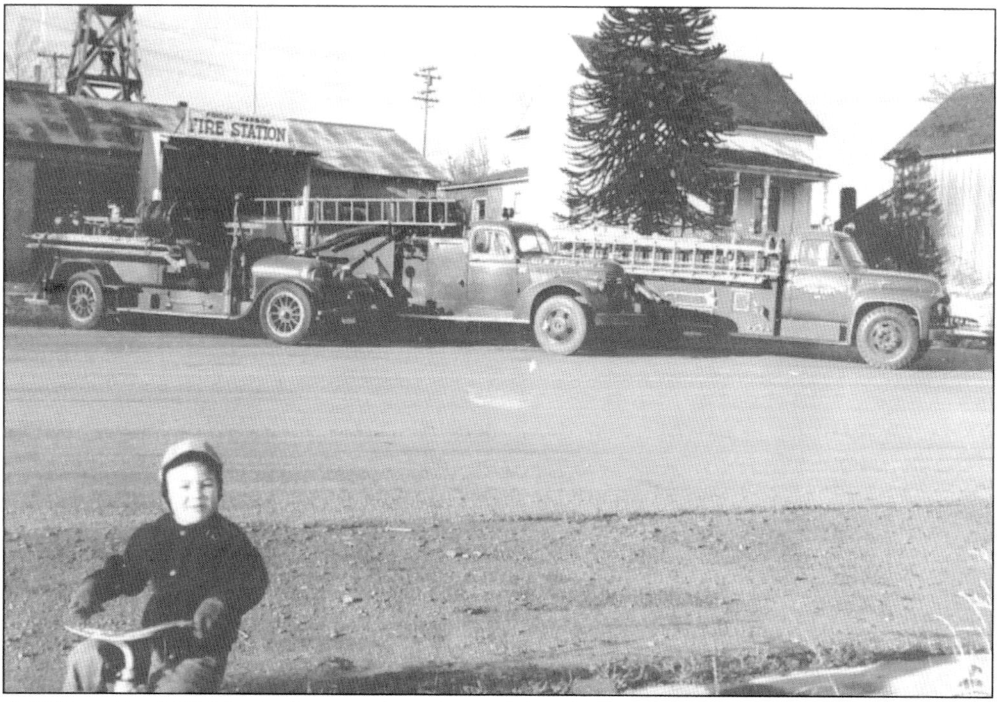


A 1953-era Brad Wold rides his tricycle in front of the old Friday Harbor Fire Station, in the same location as the current station on West Street behind King's Market. The department was founded as the Friday Harbor Hose Company in 1909 shortly after incorporation. The first chief was ice manufacturer and creamery owner Sam Bugge. It seems that, even then, islanders held multiple jobs.

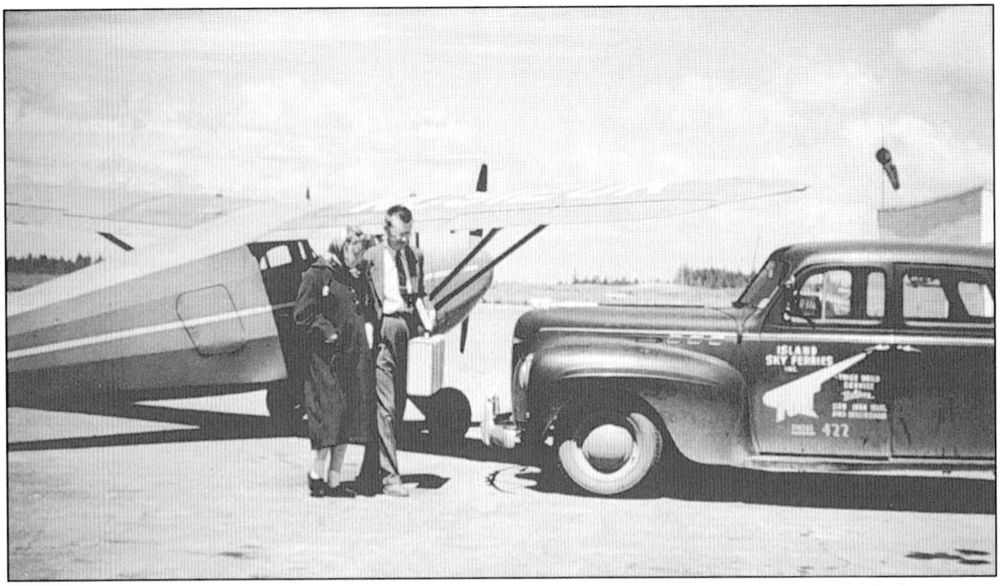


San Juan County Public Health Officer Dr. Malcolm Heath leads a patient to an Island Sky Ferries courtesy car following a flight in a Stinson Voyager, probably with owner Roy Franklin at the controls. After transiting the islands on ferries and powerboats, Heath learned to fly and bought his own airplane.

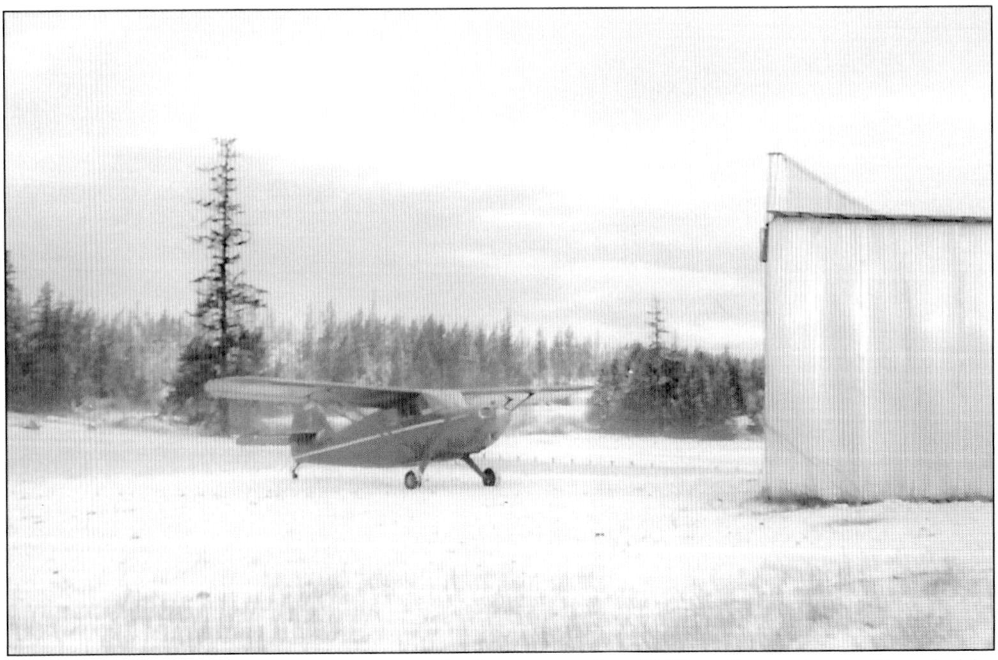

A four-place Stinson Voyager taxies toward a hangar at the old King Farm airstrip (founded by grocery store owner Lyle King) 3 miles from Friday Harbor on San Juan Valley Road. Roy Franklin came to the San Juans in 1947 to work for Island Sky Ferries owner Bob Schoen, who sold the business to Franklin in 1953.

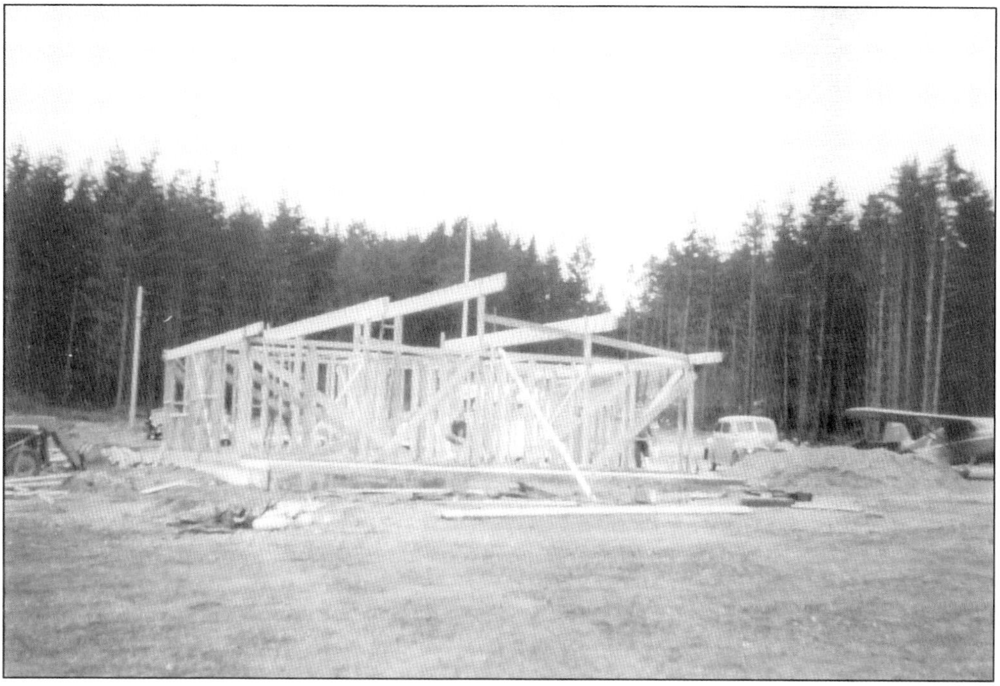

Friday Harbor Airport's first terminal gradually takes shape on land Franklin purchased to build the airport in 1953. It was another 10 years before the airport opened, as Franklin paid for excavation, materials, and labor as he went. He nearly lost the airport when an ill-fated regional partnership collapsed in 1969, but fortunately, he had deeded the land to his children. He raised $100,000 to buy back his airplanes.

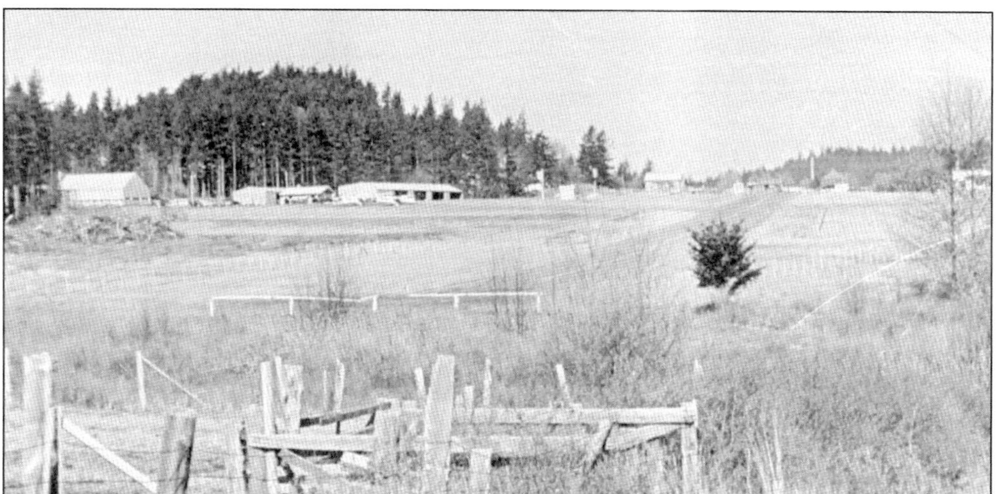

Franklin's original airport featured a 2,300-foot, north-south runway and a 1,300-foot, east-west grass strip for crosswinds, which required maneuvering around 320-foot Bald Hill, soon to be leveled as a gravel pit. The hangars, fuel dock, and terminal were at the north end of the strip. The runway was renowned for its two-percent downward slope.

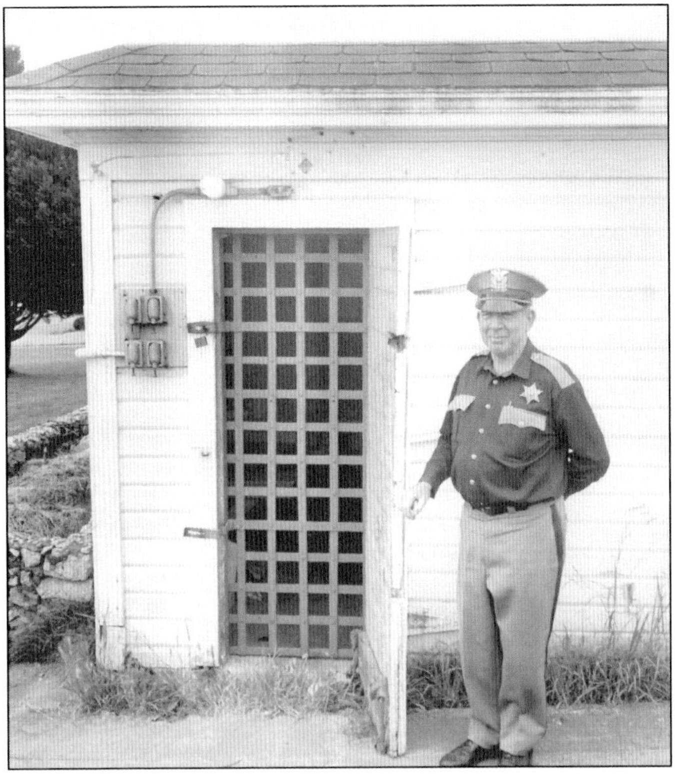

San Juan County sheriff Eric Erickson showcases the 1892 vintage county jail in July 1968. The jail, called "the worst in the state" by the *Bellingham Herald*, was somewhat of a throwback to colonial-era stocks. Located on the north side of the courthouse facing the school, a yellow light indicated that it was occupied. Anyone could stop by to have a chat—usually school kids who, for a fee, ran for candy and cigarettes. The jail's most famous inmate was schoolteacher Richard Straub, convicted of murdering a man on Blakely Island and sentenced to hang. He was executed on April 23, 1897, becoming the only person to be hung in Friday Harbor history.

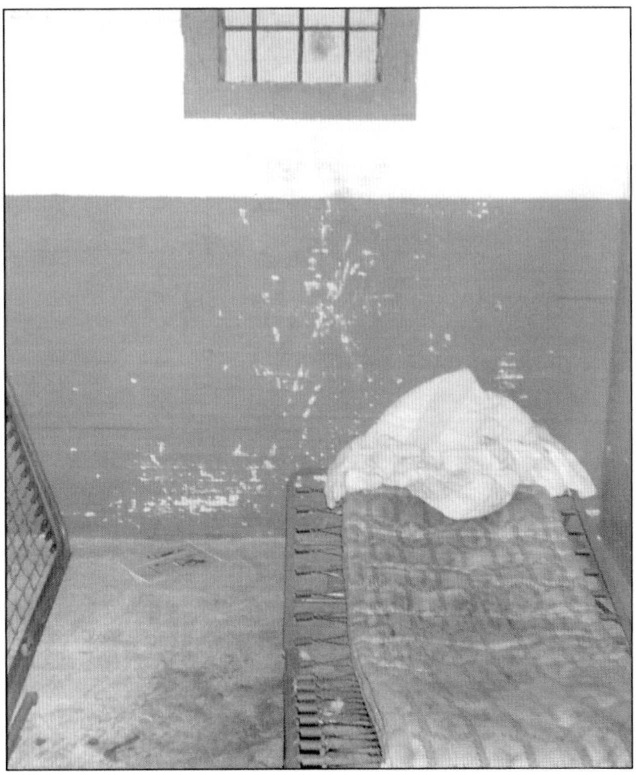

San Juan County government staff, pictured around 1955, gathers on the courthouse lawn. The three men in front, from left to right, are Orcas commissioner Howard McNally, San Juan commissioner Carl Nash, and Lopez commissioner Norman Hodgson. The empty robe on the ground symbolizes the judge who missed the photo shoot.

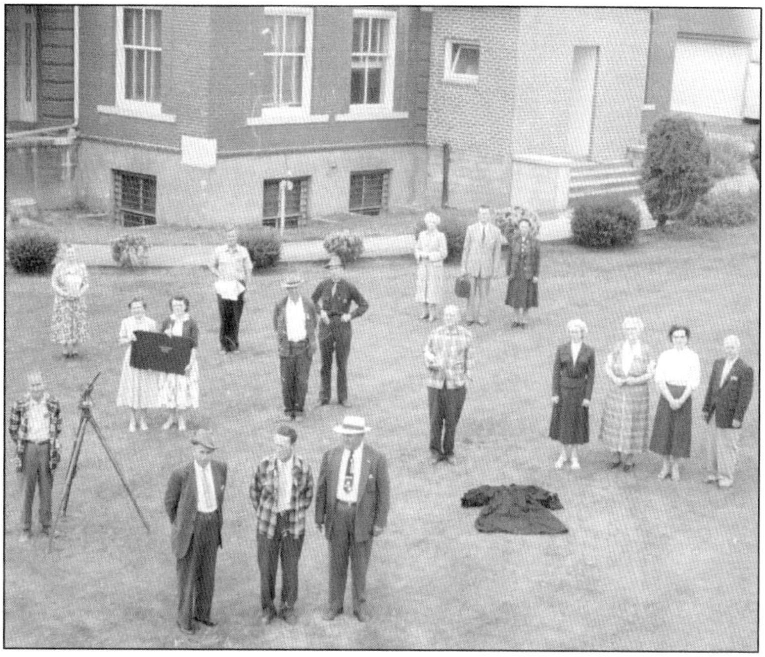

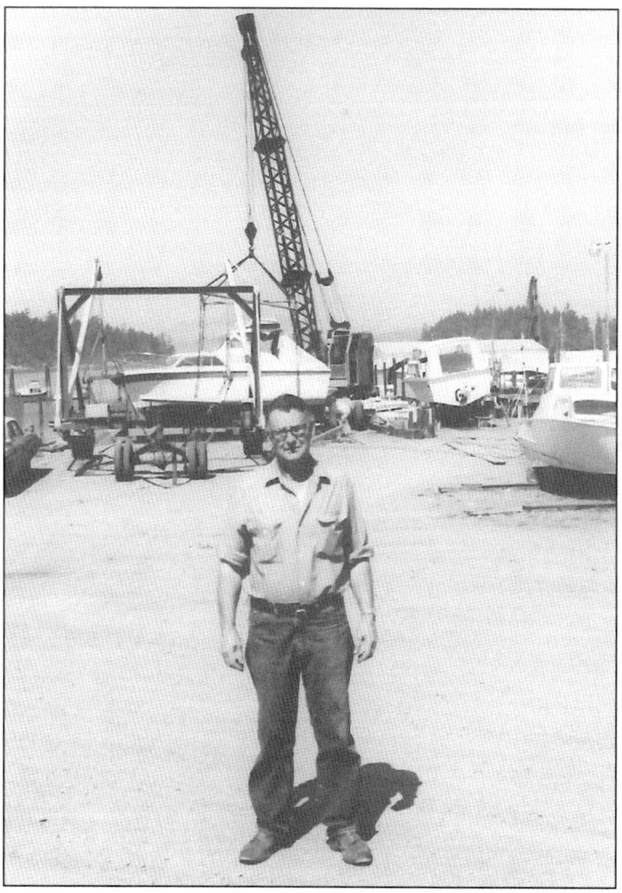

Born in 1913, Nourdine Jensen inherited ownership of the Albert Jensen & Son shipyard when his father Albert died in 1958. With the exception of his time in the U.S. Navy during World War II, Jensen, a founding port commissioner, spent his entire career in the shipyard.

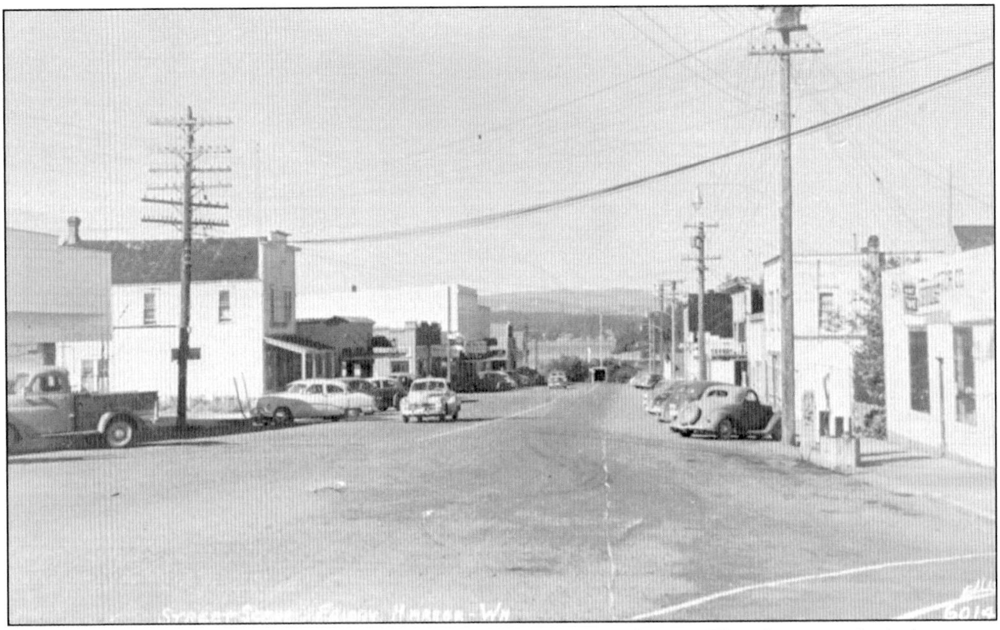

By the early 1950s, angle-in parking was the norm on Spring Street. The absence of a balcony on the original drugstore, second from right, is evidence that the 1912 vintage high school with its grand pillars was still in use. A mix of businesses occupied the block, which in 30 years would be fully encompassed by King's Market.

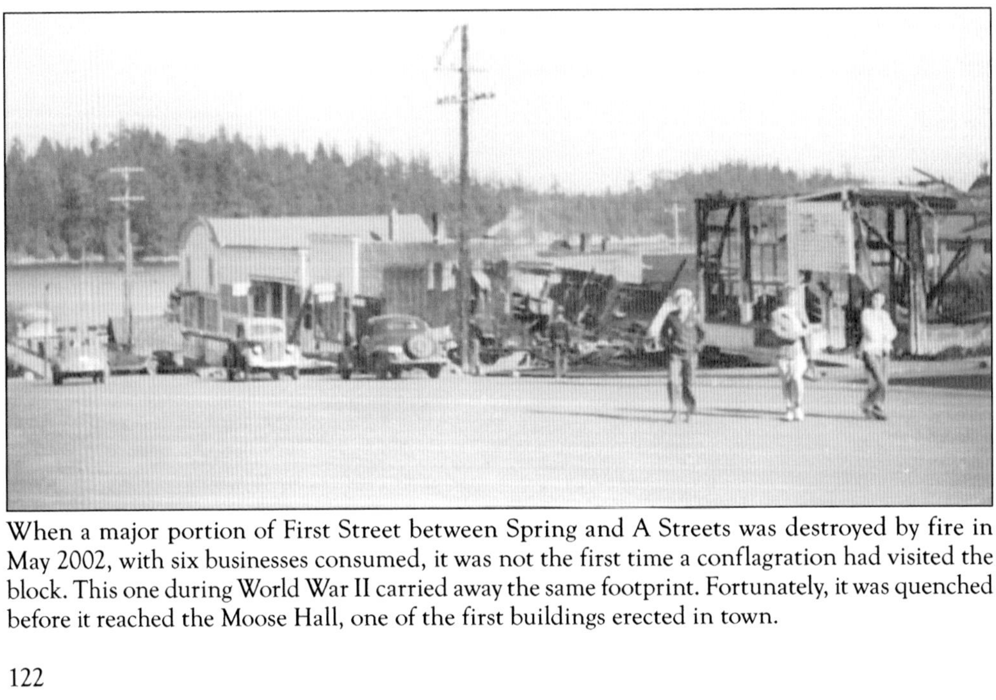

When a major portion of First Street between Spring and A Streets was destroyed by fire in May 2002, with six businesses consumed, it was not the first time a conflagration had visited the block. This one during World War II carried away the same footprint. Fortunately, it was quenched before it reached the Moose Hall, one of the first buildings erected in town.

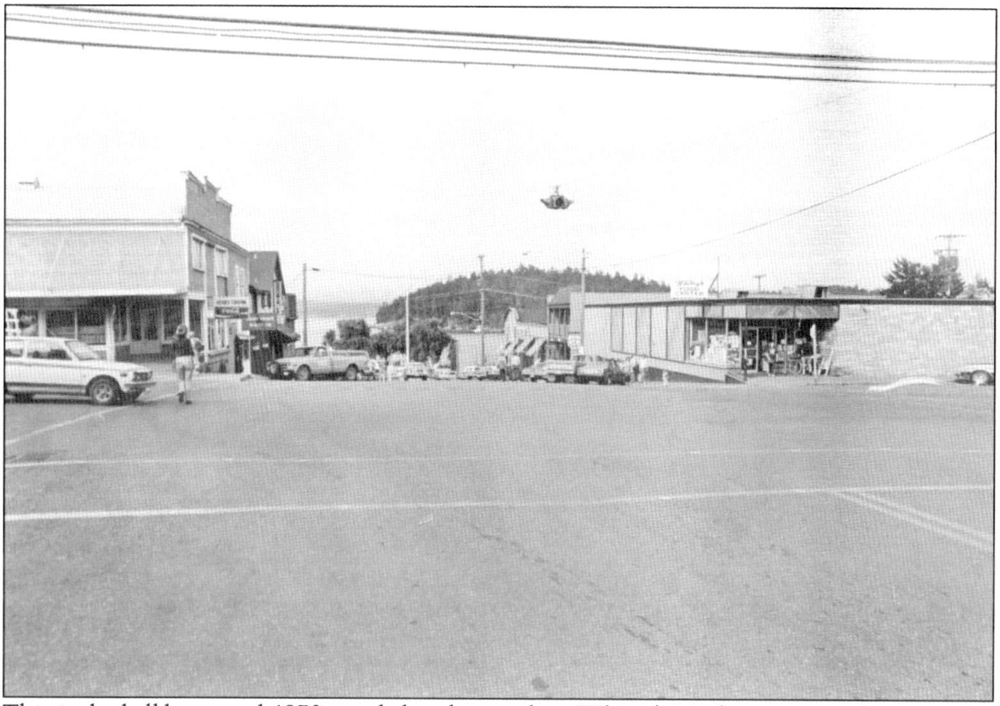

This is the bell-bottomed 1970s, and the ultra-modern Whitey's Market occupies the corner lot with what would become the China Pearl restaurant abutting the historic structures. Across the street, the old Churchill Store had become the "World Famous" Herb's Tavern, still with a recessed corner door (see page 36).

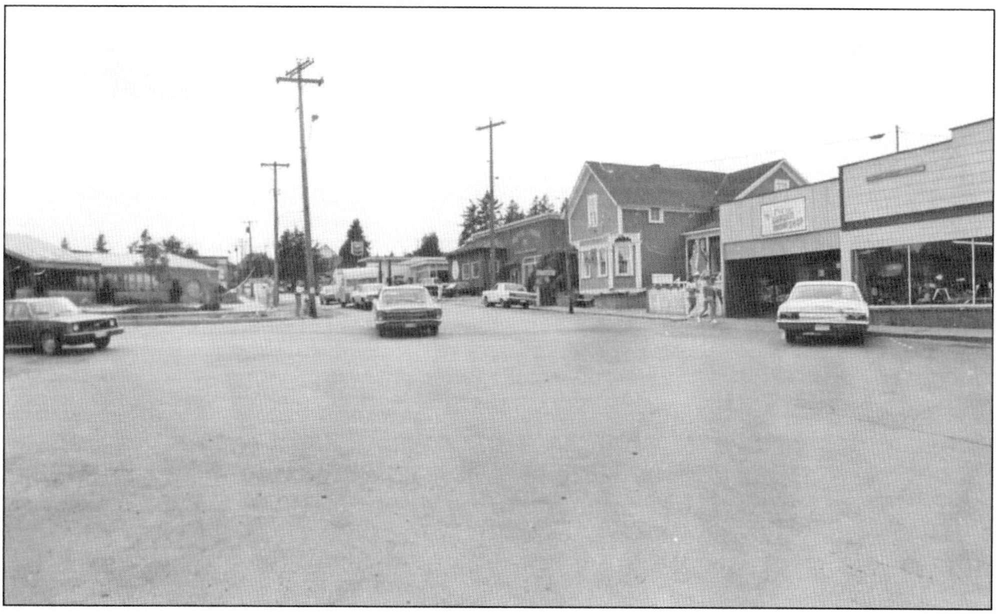

A look up Spring Street at Argyle Avenue during the same era shows what would become of the Wells Fargo Bank on the corner. A hardware store occupied the shop space at far right, the Wright house was affixed to the old creamery office, and Browne Lumber occupied the former creamery building.

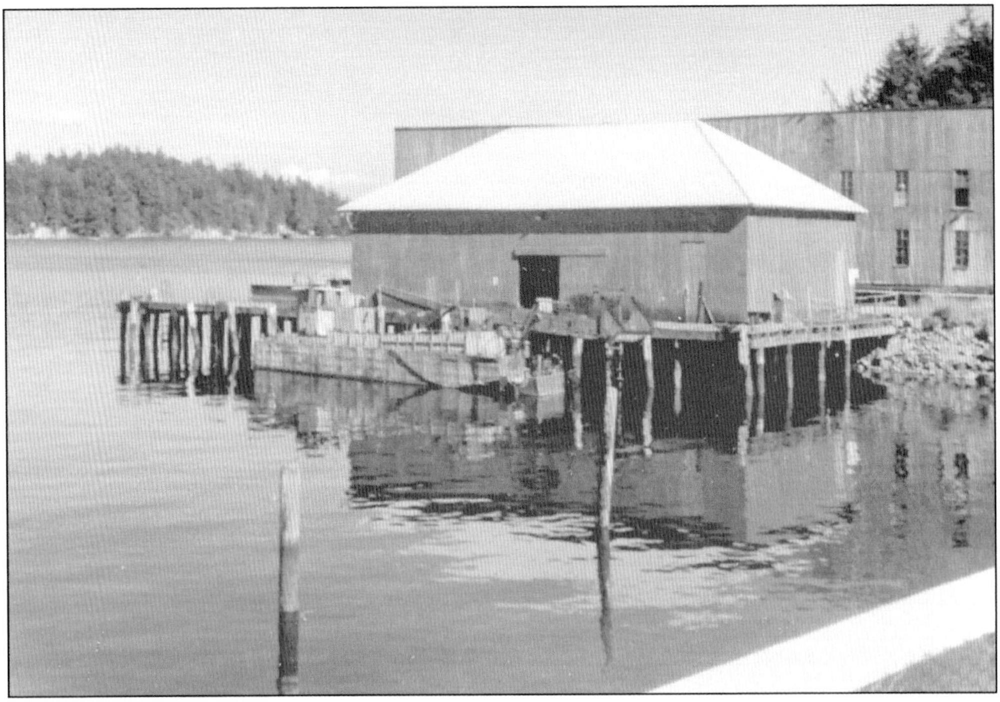

By 1970, the once-thriving cannery was nearly abandoned, save for a single vessel tied to the dock. But vacation homes were already sprouting on the Brown Island shoreline, a sign that a new economic mix was on the way. This view was taken from Sweeney's old warehouse, adjacent to today's ferry terminal.

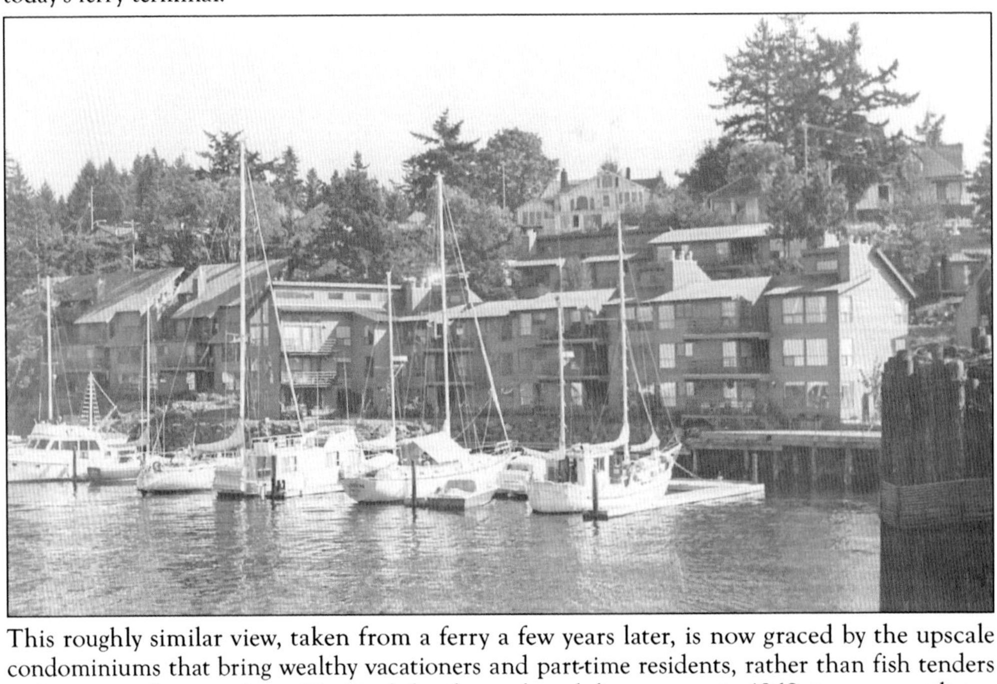

This roughly similar view, taken from a ferry a few years later, is now graced by the upscale condominiums that bring wealthy vacationers and part-time residents, rather than fish tenders and scows, to the waterfront. The Buck family purchased the property in 1968, intent on utilizing the uplands and old cannery pilings for condominiums and shops.

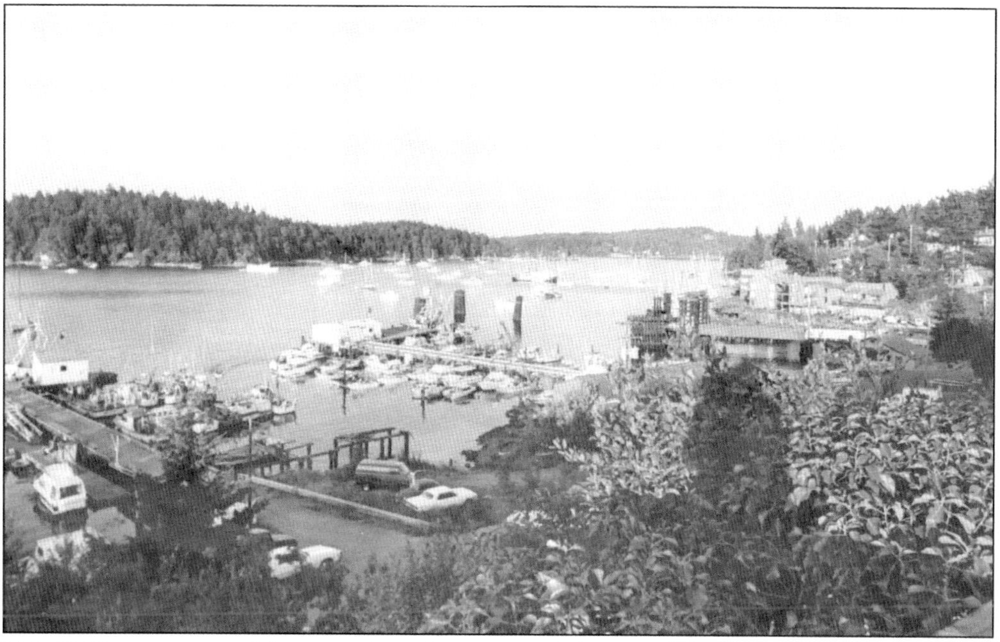

This 1970s panorama of the waterfront shows a much different bay than the image on page 70. The oil tanks are gone, and while the fishing fleet still huddles at the dock, the vast majority of the vessels in the harbor are pleasure craft. In 1972, the Port of Friday Harbor added 172 permanent slips to the marina, and by 1984, a breakwater and 500 more slips furthered the expansion.

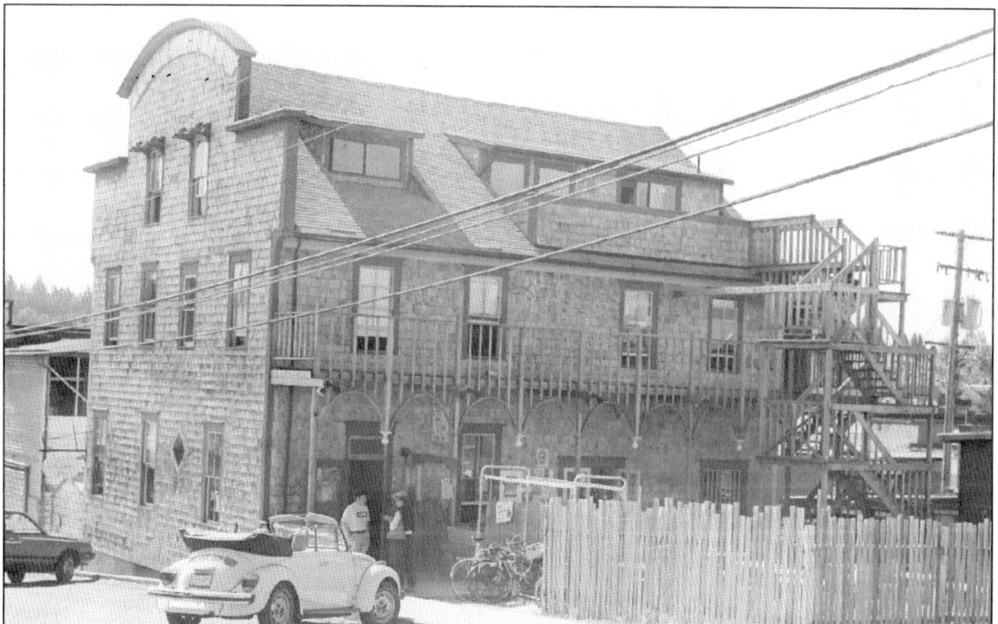

The Tourists Hotel, founded in 1891, has changed its outer skin—here in 1970s-style shake siding—about as many times as it has changed its name. Restaurants and shops have come and gone on the ground floor, but the building has remained first and foremost a place to stay the night.

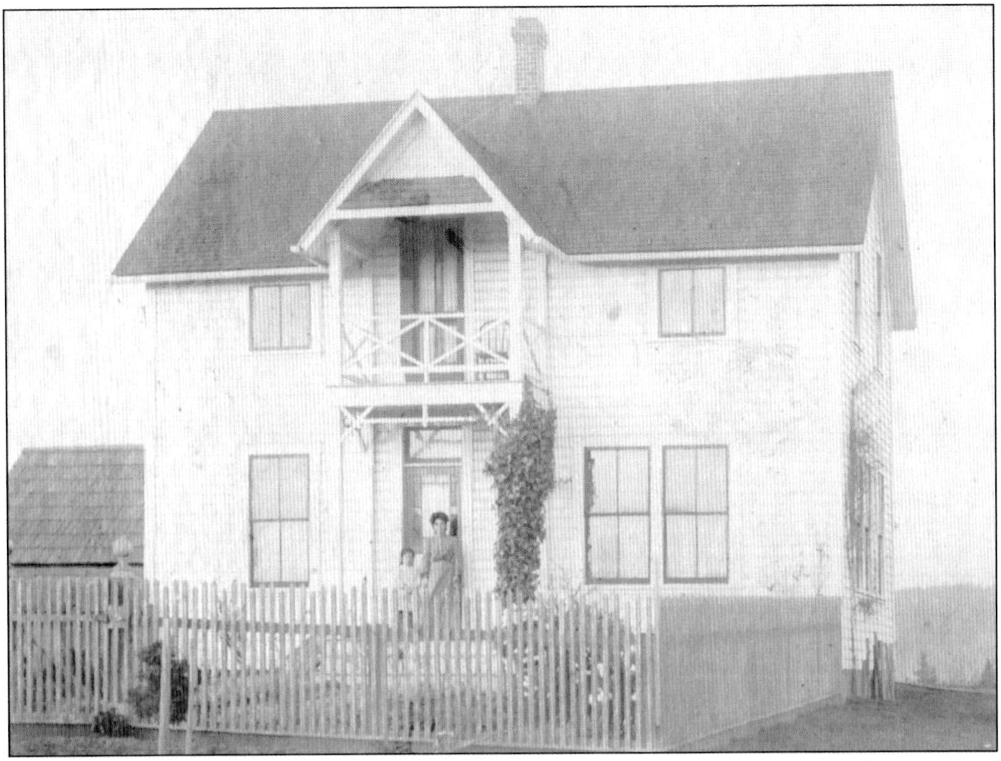

A woman, presumably Adeline Verrier King, holds hands with her daughter (probably her youngest, Alice, born in 1899) on the front porch of their home at the head of Spring Street around 1904. James King was a native of Yamhill, Oregon, and married Adeline, who was from West Sound on Orcas Island. She was only 16 when her first of six children, Evelyn, was born.

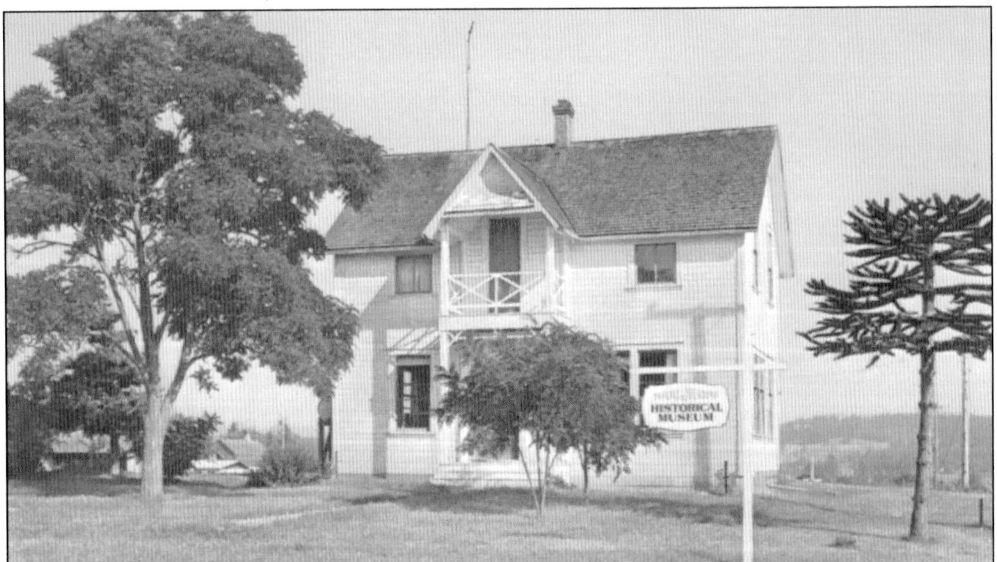


George Peacock donated the King farmhouse to the San Juan Historical Society in 1966 for use as a museum. In addition to the farmhouse, the grounds today consist of a carriage house, milk house, jail, barn, log cabin, and the Etta Lightheart Egeland Resource Center.

# BIBLIOGRAPHY

PRIMARY SOURCES

National Archives of the United States.
National Archives of the United Kingdom of Great Britain.
National Archives of Canada.
San Juan Historical Museum Archive.
Whatcom Museum of History and Art Archives.

STUDIES

Thompson, Erwin N. *Historic Resource Study: San Juan Island NHP.* Manuscript. San Juan Island National Historical Park, Friday Harbor, Washington, 1972.

Wray, Jacilee. *The Salmon Bank: An Ethnohistoric Compilation.* Port Angeles, WA: Olympic National Park/San Juan Island National Historical Park, 2003.

BOOKS

Gough, Barry M. *The Northwest Coast: British Navigation, Trade and Discoveries to 1812.* Vancouver: University of British Columbia Press, 1992.

Miller, Jerome K. *The Umbrella Guide to Friday Harbor and San Juan Island.* Friday Harbor, WA: Umbrella Books, 1988.

Newell, Gordon R. *Ships of the Inland Sea: The Story of Puget Sound Steamers.* Portland, OR: Binford and Mort, 1960.

Ramsey, Guy Reed. *Postmarked Washington: Island County, San Juan County.* Friday Harbor, WA: Lopez Island Historical Society, 1976.

Richardson, David. *Pig War Islands.* Eastsound, WA: Orcas Publishing Company, 1971.

Stein, Julie K. *Exploring Coast Salish Prehistory: The Archaeology of San Juan Island.* Seattle, WA: University of Washington Press, 2000.

Strehlou, Sandy. *Historic Friday Harbor on Foot Tour One: Historic Downtown.* Friday Harbor, WA: Town of Friday Harbor, 2006.

Van Cleve, F. H. *Friday Harbor, Then and Now.* Friday Harbor, WA: Long House Printcrafters and Publishers, 1979.

Vouri, Michael. *The Pig War: Standoff on Griffin Bay.* 3rd ed. Friday Harbor, WA: WSU Press, 2022.

———. *Outpost of Empire: The Royal Marines and the Joint Occupation of San Juan Island.* Seattle, WA: Northwest Interpretive Association/University of Washington, 2004.

———. *The Pig War.* Charleston, SC: Arcadia Publishing, 2008.

Consistent with our mission to preserve history on a local level, this book was printed in South Carolina on American-made paper and manufactured entirely in the United States. Products carrying the accredited Forest Stewardship Council (FSC) label are printed on 100 percent FSC-certified paper.

MADE IN THE USA